Human Security

Human Security

Reflections on Globalization and Intervention

MARY KALDOR

polity

First published in 2007 by Polity Press
Reprinted in 2011

Polity Press
65 Bridge Street
Cambridge CB2 1UR, UK

Polity Press
350 Main Street
Malden, MA 02148, USA

ISBN-13: 978-07456-3853-9
ISBN-13: 978-07456-3854-6 (pb)

A catalogue record for this book is available from the British Library.

Typeset in 11 on 13 pt Berling
by SNP Best-set Typesetter Ltd., Hong Kong
Printed and bound by Odyssey Press Inc., Gonic, New Hampshire

For further information on Polity, visit our website: www.polity.co.uk

Contents

Acknowledgements   vi
Abbreviations   viii

Introduction   1

1 A Decade of Humanitarian Intervention,
   1991–2000   16

2 American Power: From Compellance to
   Cosmopolitanism?   73

3 Nationalism and Globalization   101

4 Intervention in the Balkans: An Unfinished
   Learning Process   122

5 The Idea of Global Civil Society   134

6 Just War and Just Peace   154

7 Human Security   182

Notes   198
Index   216

Acknowledgements

First and foremost, I would like to thank David Held, for proposing this book and for his unfailing help and support. I would also like to thank: Sabine Selchow for her invaluable critical scrutiny and for help with references and information; Marlies Glasius for comments on the original version of the first chapter and for the ideas, which we developed together, on human security – some bits of the last chapter were originally co-written; Caroline Soper for commissioning the first version of the 'American Power' chapter and for very helpful suggestions on both 'American Power' and 'The Idea of Global Civil Society'; Montserrat Guibernau for commissioning and commenting on 'Nationalism and Globalization'; Charles Read for comments on the original version of the 'Just War' essay; Heba Raouf Ezzat for introducing me to Islamic principles of Just War; and Jo Stone for help with references and formatting and for administrative support. I am also grateful to everyone at Polity, which is an especially author-friendly publisher, particularly Emma Hutchinson, who oversaw the publication, and Ann Bone who has been my copy editor for most of the books I have written. Finally I want to thank my colleagues at the Centre for the Study of Global Governance and at LSE in general, as well as my family, for providing a stimulating and convivial environment.

The chapters in this book are revised and updated versions of essays that were originally published as book chapters or journal articles. I am grateful for permission to reproduce all or parts of the original essays from Cambridge University Press, *International Affairs*, *Nations and Nationalism*, Oxford University Press and Routledge.

Abbreviations

AU	African Union
CARE	Cooperative for American Relief Everywhere
CDD	Centre for Democracy and Development (Sierra Leone)
CIS	Commonwealth of Independent States
DDR	disarmament, demobilization and reintegration
DRC	Democratic Republic of Congo
ECOMOG	Economic Community of West African States Monitoring Group
ECOWAS	Economic Community of West African States
EU	European Union
FBI	Federal Bureau of Investigation
GDP	gross domestic product
HCA	Helsinki Citizens' Assembly
HDZ	Croatian Democratic Union
ICC	International Criminal Court
ICRC	International Committee of the Red Cross
IDPs	internally displaced persons
IMF	International Monetary Fund
INTERFET	International Force for East Timor
KLA	Kosovo Liberation Army
MEP	Member of the European Parliament

MIME-NET	Military-Industrial-Media-Entertainment Network
MSF	Medécins sans Frontières
NATO	North Atlantic Treaty Organization
NEPAD	New Partnership for Africa
NGOs	non-governmental organizations
NLA	National Liberation Army (Macedonia)
NMSP-WOT	National Military Strategic Plan for the War on Terror
OAS	Organization of American States
OAU	Organization for African Unity
OSCE	Organization for Security and Cooperation in Europe
PDD	Presidential Decision Directive
PGMs	precision guided munitions
R&D	research and development
RMA	Revolution in Military Affairs
RUF	Revolutionary United Front (Sierra Leone)
SADC	Southern African Development Community
SALT	Strategic Arms Limitation Treaty
UAVs	unmanned aerial vehicles
UNAMIR	United Nations Assistance Mission to Rwanda
UNAMSIL	United Nations Mission in Sierra Leone
UNICEF	United Nations Children's Fund
UNITAF	United Nations Unified Task Force
UNOSOM	United Nations Operation in Somalia
UNPROFOR	United Nations Protection Force
UNSCR	United Nations Security Council Resolution
WMD	weapons of mass destruction

Introduction

> War no longer exists. Confrontation, conflict and combat undoubtedly exist all round the world . . . and states still have armed forces which they use as symbols of power. None the less, war as cognitively known to most combatants, war as battle in a field between men and machinery, war as a massive deciding event in a dispute in international affairs: such war no longer exists.
>
> Rupert Smith, *The Utility of Force*

The war in Iraq can be considered an illustration of why we need a new approach to security. President Bush and his former Defense Secretary Donald Rumsfeld claimed that they were fighting a new type of war, based on the application of information and communications technology. Yet in fact the approach was rather traditional; it reproduced the methods that General Rupert Smith says we cognitively know as 'war', using conventional military forces to invade Iraq and subsequently to try to defeat the insurgents. What Rumsfeld called 'defense transformation' merely means incorporating new technologies into traditional structures and strategies.

The transformation in security goes well beyond technological change; it involves a transformation of the social relations of warfare and the character of the threats that we face. It is failure to understand this transformation of the social relations of warfare that explains why the Americans (and the British) have been dragged ever deeper into a combination of insurgency and sectarian 'confrontation, conflict and combat' that has provided a magnet for global terrorism.

This book is a compilation of essays on this theme written during the first five years of the new century. It argues for a new approach to security based on a global conversation – a public debate among civil society groups and individuals as well as states and international institutions. The chapters are a logical follow-on to my work during the 1990s on the character of 'new wars' in places like the Balkans or Africa, or what Rupert Smith calls 'wars amongst the people'.[1] In this introduction, I sketch my thinking on new and old wars, the Cold War, and on global civil society because it provides a conceptual and historical background to the chapters in this book. Then I raise some brief methodological and normative considerations and, in the last section, I outline the essays.

Background

I began to use the term 'new wars' in the middle of the 1990s when I was co-chair of the Helsinki Citizens Assembly and visited local branches in places like Bosnia-Herzegovina or Nagorno Karabakh. I realized that these conflicts were very different from my preconceptions of war, which were largely based on what I had learned both in my research and from the media about the world wars of the twentieth century. I also realized that most people, including policy-makers in key positions, shared my preconceptions and that this prevented them adopting appropriate policies. I therefore chose the term 'new wars' to show that these conflicts are very different from the 'old wars' on which our preconceptions of war are based.

By 'old wars', I mean the wars that took place in Europe from the late eighteenth century to the middle of the twentieth century – it is this idealized version of this type of war that has come to represent what we cognitively understand as war. 'Old war' is war between states fought by armed forces in uniform, where the decisive encounter was battle. 'Old wars', as Charles Tilly has convincingly argued, were linked to the rise of the modern nation-state and were state-building.[2] '[W]ar made states, and vice versa,' says Tilly.[3] In wars, states were gradually able to monopolize organized violence and to eliminate private armies, brigands, feudal levies, etc., and establish professional forces subservient to the state. Taxation and borrowing were increased, as was administrative efficiency and public services, and above all the concept of political community was forged. Imagined communities, based on the development of newspapers and novels in vernacular tongues through which people who spoke the same language came to see themselves as part of one community, were consolidated in war. Carl Schmitt talks about the concept of the political that underlies the modern state. For him, intrinsic to the concept of the political is the friend–enemy distinction, and this, he says, is linked to the 'real physical possibility of killing'.[4] The job of the state was to defend territory against others, and it was this job that gave the state its legitimacy. *Protecto ergo obligo* ('I protect therefore I am obeyed'), says Schmitt, 'is the *cogito ergo sum* of the state.'[5]

'Old wars' were fought according to certain rules, at least in theory, rules codified in the late nineteenth and early twentieth centuries in the Geneva and Hague Conventions – rules about minimizing civilian casualties, treating prisoners well and so on. Rules were critical to establishing the legitimacy of wars. There is a fine line between heroes and criminals, legitimate killing and murder.

What I call 'new wars' are just the opposite. These are wars that take place in the context of the disintegration of states (typically authoritarian states under the impact of globalization). They are fought by networks of state and non-state actors, often without uniforms, sometimes with distinctive signs, like crosses, or Ray-Ban sunglasses as in the case of the Croatian militia in Bosnia-Herzegovina. They are wars where battles are rare and where most violence is directed against civilians as a consequence of counter-insurgency tactics or ethnic cleansing. They are wars where taxation is falling and war finance consists of loot and pillage, illegal trading and other war-generated revenue. They are wars where the distinctions between combatant and non-combatant, legitimate violence and criminality are all breaking down. These are wars which exacerbate the disintegration of the state – declines in GDP, loss of tax revenue, loss of legitimacy, etc. Above all, they construct new sectarian identities (religious, ethnic or tribal) that undermine the sense of a shared political community. Indeed, this could be considered the purpose of these wars. They recreate the sense of political community along new divisive lines through the manufacture of fear and hate. They establish new friend–enemy distinctions. Moreover, these sectarian political identities are often inextricably tied to criminalized networks that provide a basis for a global shadow economy.

Unlike 'old wars', which ended with victory or defeat, 'new wars' are very difficult to end. The various warring parties have a vested interest in continuing violence for both political and economic reasons. Moreover, they tend to spread through refugees and displaced persons, criminalized networks, and the sectarian ideologies they manufacture.

Of course, these wars are not entirely 'new'. They have much in common with wars in the premodern period in Europe, and with wars outside Europe throughout the period of 'old wars'. It is even possible to identify some elements of what I have called 'new wars' within 'old wars' – for example, in the effect of the First World War on the Ottoman Empire. I emphasize the distinction because it helps our understanding of what is happening today and what we need to do about it. In much contemporary literature, the 'new wars' are described as 'civil wars'. It is widely argued that interstate wars have declined and civil wars have increased. I have resisted this terminology both because the 'new wars' involve a blurring of internal and external, and because of the policy implications of the term. Was the war in Bosnia a Yugoslav civil war or an international war? Was the war in the Democratic Republic of Congo (DRC) in which several neighbouring states were involved interstate or civil? In policy terms, the use of the word 'civil war' implies non-intervention. The notion of international intervention to protect people from large-scale human rights violations is much more contested, despite the recent approval of the concept of 'responsibility to protect'. There is a case for international intervention to defend a state against aggression in the context of interstate wars. But does it matter whether human rights violations are conducted by outsiders and therefore count as 'aggression', or by insiders and termed 'repression'? In Bosnia, did it matter whether ethnic cleansing was carried out by Bosnian Serbs or Serbs from Serbia? Moreover, the use of the term 'civil war' has meant that outside efforts, whether they count as intervention or not, have tended to focus on individual nation-states when in reality all 'new wars' spill over borders and have to be addressed in a regional context. A similar argument can be made about the term 'privatized war', which is used by some authors. It is true that new wars involve non-state armed groups, but usually with links to regular armies or the remnants of regular armies. The point is rather that, in the 'new wars', the distinction between public and private is also blurred.

'Old wars' reached their apex in the middle of the twentieth century. The application of science and technology to killing, and the increased mobilization capacities of states led to a destruction on an unimaginable scale. Some 35 million people were killed in the First World War and 70 million people in the Second World War. As many people were killed in a few weeks in Auschwitz as were killed in the tsunami, or in the entire war in Bosnia-Herzegovina. Similar numbers were killed in a single night in the bombing of Tokyo, Dresden, Hamburg, Hiroshima or Nagasaki. Moreover, half of those killed in the Second World War were civilians. Out of the experience of those wars came the centralized totalitarian state and blocs of states – the high point of state-building. When George Orwell wrote *1984*, his nightmare vision of competing totalitarian blocs, he was thinking not just of the Soviet Union but of postwar Britain. *1984* was 1948 upside down. Above all, these total wars gave rise to a new concept of the political that extended beyond the state to blocs of nations, the idea of democracy against totalitarianism or of socialism against fascism. The Cold War can be conceptualized as a way of keeping this idea of 'old war', linked to an extended notion of political community, alive. 'Old war' ways of seeing the world run very deeply in the discourses of politicians. And this, it can be argued, prevents them from seeing the reality of 'new wars'.

During the Cold War, it used to be said that Europe or even the world, enjoyed 'peace'. Quite apart from the fact that there were real wars in Hungary and Czechoslovakia and in large parts of what was called the Third World, we lived in Europe as though we were at war with millions of men under arms, with frequent exercises, spy stories, hostile propaganda and so on. And we lived with much of the anxiety and fear associated

with war as well as with the organizations – the defence indus-
tries, the centralized state – and, of course, the friend–foe distinction that defined the world in two ideological camps and
provided a mechanism for discrediting opposition. That is why
I prefer to describe the Cold War as 'imaginary war'.[6]

Throughout the period, the Cold War was seen as a mighty
ideological clash, a 'Great Contest' as Deutscher put it, between
democracy and totalitarianism, or between capitalism and
socialism.[7] And I would argue that this idea, this 'global clash',
was a way of defining political community within each bloc.
The Cold War suited both sides. The Second World War had
solved the problems of the mass unemployment and destructive economic nationalism of the 1930s in the West, and of
inefficiency and lack of legitimacy in the East. The Cold War
reproduced those solutions. In a way, both right and left col-
luded in this idea. The right described the conflict as one
between freedom and totalitarianism. The left discredited
themselves by seeing the conflict as one between capitalism and
socialism.

None of this was a result of conscious decisions by their
elites. Rather it was the outcome of their own experiences in
the Second World War, the state structures that had been
established during the period. If you analyse, for example, the
evolution of the arms race during the Cold War, it is much
better explained on each side as though they were arming
against a phantom German enemy than against each other.
Thus the Americans continued to emphasize strategic bombing;
with the advent of missiles, nuclear weapons were seen as
a continuation of long-distance bombing and placed under
Strategic Air Command. The US anticipated a conventional
Blitzkrieg across the north German plains and they envisaged
themselves rushing to the aid of the Europeans, making use of
superior know-how. Russians, on the other hand, never did
strategic bombing – on the contrary, bombing was considered
a fascist tactic. They believed that there was no alternative to
conventional ground forces. Aircraft were seen as assisting
ground forces, 'hand maidens of artillery', as Stalin called them,
so when missiles were developed they were seen as artillery and
placed under the command of the artillery academy.

Nor was there symmetry between the two sides. Large
numbers of people in the West supported the Cold War and

felt they benefited from it. But the imposition of Stalinism was a tragedy for the peoples of central Europe and, it can be argued, the Soviet hold over central Europe was sustained by the Cold War.

Throughout the period, at least on the Western side, there was always a problem of 'credibility'. If war was purely imaginary, how long would enemies and friends continue to believe in American power? Astonishing numbers of nuclear weapons were accumulated during the 1950s and 1960s – enough to destroy the world many times over. Strategy, according to von Clausewitz, is the use of military force for political ends. But what, pondered strategists like Schelling, did strategy mean if the weapons were too dangerous to be used? What if insurgents in Latin America or South East Asia were not deterred? How could force be used in a limited way? Indeed the sophisticated differentiation of different types and roles of nuclear weapons (tactical, theatre and strategic) in a context where the use of any one weapon would be devastating was, to say the least, profoundly puzzling.

My answer to this puzzle was that strategy came to be about how force might be used in an imaginary war where everyone knew the rules. The arcane Western debates about, for example, mutual assured destruction versus flexible response, have to be explained in these terms. The complex esoteric argument for acquiring nuclear weapons put forward by Richard Perle, Assistant Secretary of Defense in the Reagan administration and one of the better-known nuclear strategists, and more recently one of the neocon team around President Bush, illustrates the imaginary nature of nuclear strategy: 'I've always worried less about what would happen in an actual nuclear exchange than the effect the nuclear balance has on our willingness to take risks in local situations,' said Perle. 'It is not that I am worried about the Soviets attacking the United States with nuclear weapons confident that they will win that nuclear war. It is that I worry about an American President feeling he cannot take action in a crisis because Soviet nuclear forces are such that, if escalation took place, they are better poised than we are to move up the escalation ladder.'[8] Star Wars, the Strategic Defense Initiative, or now National Missile Defense, was supposed to protect America in the imagination so that force could be usable again.

The Global War on Terror can be understood as an attempt to reproduce the narrative of the Cold War by a generation that was schooled in the mentality of permanent imaginary war – an argument I develop in chapter 2 of this book. They believed that the United States had 'won' the Cold War because the Soviet Union was no longer able to compete with the United States in the arms race. The 'old war' recipe was therefore trundled out again after 9/11; it was intrinsic to the psychological make-up of the men around President Bush. But unlike the Cold War, the Global War on Terror has led to two real wars. In Iraq, the United States is being dragged into a real global 'new war'. Because of shortages of troops, more private contractors are drawn into the war, so it is fought by a network of state and non-state actors. Because it is so difficult to distinguish insurgents from combatants, the main victims are civilians. Because the insurgents are mainly Sunni, the war has increasingly taken on a sectarian character, constructing sectarian identities in mixed urban settings. And the war is spreading to Iraq and Afghanistan's neighbours, and to East Africa as well.

Of course, there were real wars in the Cold War period, of which the most important were Korea, Vietnam and Afghanistan. They were called 'limited' even though millions died – many more than in today's Iraq and Afghanistan – because they did not involve direct US–Soviet confrontation in Europe. But despite their 'limited' nature, both Vietnam and Afghanistan did call into question the credibility of large-scale conventional military force and began a questioning of the Cold War narrative. In the twenty years after Vietnam, a new discourse began to develop based on the coming together of the concepts of peace and human rights – the 'new peace', if you like, or better still, human security. In the period of 'old wars', peace referred to relations between states,[9] whereas law and rights referred to domestic affairs – something International Relations theorists call the 'Great Divide'.[10] The development of what has come to be called the 'human rights regime', as a result of both the development of human rights law, the Conventions and the Helsinki Agreement of 1975, and the proliferation of human rights activists concerned about human rights abuses, especially in Latin America and Eastern Europe, was key in starting to overcome the 'Great Divide'. Peace movements, which had focused on opposition to war and the arms race, began to take up human rights issues after the signing of the Helsinki Accords. I was involved in the dialogue between the West European peace movement and the opposition in Eastern Europe during the 1980s. It was through this dialogue that concepts like pan-European or global civil society or civic or human security were debated and elaborated. My version of the end of the Cold War is that the Cold War narrative, the idea of a permanent East–West dialogue, lost its hold on the imagination, especially but not only in the East.

By analysing 'new wars' in terms of social relations of warfare, we come up with a very different approach about how to deal with these types of conflict, and indeed, how to deal with terror in general. The global 'new war' that may develop as a consequence of the wars in Iraq and Afghanistan and the way they are spreading can be viewed as a way of constructing a 'clash of civilizations', and it is already perhaps contributing to the growth of extreme Islamism. The risk of terror is too serious to be hijacked by fantasies of 'old war'. In much the same way, I would argue, the Cold War and nuclear weapons prevented us from adopting a serious strategy for undermining communism; this was only possible in a détente context. The Second World War really did mark the end of 'old wars'. Wars of this type are impossible; they are simply too destructive to be fought and have become unacceptable and, indeed, illegitimate. The eight-year war between Iraq and Iran was probably the exception that proved the rule. It was immensely destructive and led to military stalemate; and, at least on the Iraqi side, far from consolidating the state, it was the beginning of state disintegration, the slide into new war.

'New wars' deliberately violate all the conventions of 'old war', as well as the new body of human rights law that has been introduced since the Second World War. The key to dealing with 'new wars' is the reconstruction of political legitimacy around the ideas about human rights and global civil society that were reinvented in the last decades of the Cold War. If 'old wars' established a notion of political legitimacy in terms of the friend–enemy distinction, in 'new wars', the friend–enemy distinction destroys political legitimacy. So political legitimacy can only be reconstructed on the basis of cosmopolitan consent and within a framework of international law. It means supporting efforts of democratization in difficult situations or using various international tools and law to support such processes. One of these tools is the use of military force, but an important theme of this book is the need to use military forces, together with civilian capabilities, in quite new ways that are more akin to law enforcement than to war-fighting.

The chapters in this book elaborate this approach. Carl Schmitt would argue that there can be no political community without enemies. And that where force is used in the name of humanity, the adversary is no longer an enemy but an outlaw, a disturber of the peace, so political community no longer exists. If he is right, the future is very grim; we can anticipate a pervasive global 'new war'. But if we believe political communities can be held together by reason rather than fear, then there is an alternative possibility, a transformation of statehood, in which states are no longer intrinsically linked to warfare and operate within a multilateral framework. And as for the argument about humanity, we could turn it on its head. If we dub the terrorists as enemies, we give them political status; indeed this may be what they are trying to achieve. Perhaps it is more appropriate to view them as outlaws, disturbers of the peace, and to use the methods of law enforcement rather than 'old war'.

Some Methodological and Normative Considerations

My starting point is the assumption that there is a real security gap in the world today. Millions of people in regions such as the Middle East or East and Central Africa or Central Asia where 'new wars' are taking place live in daily fear of violence. Moreover 'new wars' are increasingly intertwined with other global risks – the spread of disease, vulnerability to natural disasters, poverty and homelessness. Yet our security conceptions, drawn from the dominant experience of the Second World War, do not reduce that insecurity; rather they make it worse. The objective of most of the essays is to develop new proposals to address that security gap.

But this needs a new language. It is the way we currently perceive security, the 'old war' language we use, that prevents us from finding new solutions. Most of these essays analyse different positions, the arguments that are used to legitimize policy. Social science is about telling stories. Some stories can be matched with evidence better than others. There cannot be a perfect fit because the story would be as slow to tell as life itself. It would be a mirror on life rather than an abstraction that pulls out certain aspects of life that help us guide our actions.

Stories can have enormous political ramifications. In democratic societies, contenders for power use their competing stories to mobilize political support. Relatively stable societies usually have a common narrative that holds them together, a 'disciplinary technology' to use Foucault's term,[11] although even in authoritarian societies it is possible to identify alternative versions. Moments of dramatic change are moments of experimentation when rival stories gain credibility and the implications of alternative stories are tried out. Stories become dominant if they can be reproduced, if the policies justified in terms of the story lead to outcomes that can be explained by the story. There is no inevitability about which story becomes dominant. In the Second World War, there were competing visions of postwar international arrangements. Roosevelt and the New Dealers imagined a new global order, based on collective security, free trade, and the right to self-determination. Churchill and Stalin envisaged a world divided into spheres of influence. Those who took part in the European resistance dreamed of a united Europe. That the Cold War story succeeded does not mean that the others could not also have been tried out had they been able to mobilize sufficient political support.

In these chapters, I have been experimenting with different ways of describing the competing stories of the current period. The 'old war' story I sometimes describe as 'geopolitical' or 'top-down' or even 'sovereignist'. The International Relations theorists call it the 'realist' position, even though it may no longer be realistic. The American narrative was never a classic 'old war' story, though there were some like Kissinger who tried to make it so. It was always tempered by a strand of idealism – the notion that the United States is the leader of a democratic crusade. And it is this revamped American story that is promulgated by the neocons and under attack in Iraq. The nationalists and the Islamists have other stories to tell – often drawn from the experience of communism and/or

of anti-colonial movements. But their stories fit the 'old war'
narrative and can therefore reinforce the idea of the Global
War on Terror.

In describing these competing stories, I am also trying to
elaborate my own story, which has its origins in the dialogue
between the peace and human rights groups in the last years
of the Cold War. In these chapters, I also experiment with different terms. Terms like 'new wars', 'global civil society', 'cosmopolitanism' or 'human security' are all different ways in
which I have tried to draw attention to the global context, the
ways in which the difference between inside and outside have
become blurred, and our growing concern about the fate of
individual human beings and their communities, rather than
states. The adjective 'new' attached to war is not so different
from the adjective 'global' attached to civil society.[12] What is
'new' about 'new wars' has to do with globalization and this, in
turn, is related to the changed role of the state. Indeed, I am not
even sure that the word 'war' is appropriate because war does
refer to political violence between social organized groups and,
as I often stress, the 'new wars' are a mixture of war, human
rights violations and organized crime. Likewise, global civil
society is unbounded civil society; it is 'new' compared with the
bounded civil societies found in North-West Europe and North
America in an earlier period. In experimenting with terms, I am
partly wrestling with their usage in relation to the real world and
how well they fit our knowledge of what is happening in different regions, and whether they help us to ask new questions and
acquire new knowledge. And I am partly concerned about their
political resonance, how well they open up new ways of seeing
the world that could lead to better policy.

Plan of the Book

The first chapter was originally written for the first edition of
the *Global Civil Society* yearbook.[13] It described the emerging
discourse and practice of humanitarianism in the aftermath of
the Cold War. In particular, it aimed to show that civil society
had been instrumental in shaping this discourse, introducing a
new dimension into world politics. The chapter outlined the
various positions on humanitarian intervention and argued that

the practice had veered between 'sovereignist', that is to say, non-intervention, and 'just war', that it is to say, using conventional military means to avert or respond to a humanitarian catastrophe. It concluded that a new type of intervention was required based on the enforcement or implementation of human rights. This notion of human rights enforcement is very close to what I describe as a human security approach in later essays.

The next two chapters deal with the challenges to the emerging humanitarian consensus. The second chapter was written for *International Affairs* soon after 9/11.[14] It was about the nature of American power and the bizarre combination of unilateralism and idealism that characterized the Bush administration. It argued that the United States was adopting a narrative drawn from the memory of the Second World War and the Cold War, in which the United States makes use of superior conventional military forces to spread democracy. The term 'compellance' refers to the Clausewitzean notion that war is designed to compel an opponent to 'submit to our will'. Since the narrative is staged to appeal to domestic public opinion, the fact that compellance does not work any longer may not matter. A 'long war' against terror will allow the narrative to be replayed over and over again. However, in a globalized world, public opinion can be alerted to what happens elsewhere, and I make the case for an alternative cosmopolitan foreign policy, based on a combination of multilateralism and idealism.

The third chapter was written as part of a collection designed to honour Anthony Smith, the distinguished scholar of nationalism, on his retirement. It was first published in the journal *Nations and Nationalism*, which he founded.[15] It represents a critique of both the modernist argument that nations will disappear in a global era and Anthony Smith's own view that nations are enduring phenomena. I argue that the nationalist and religious militant movements that have developed during the first decade of this century are a contemporary phenomenon that has to be analysed in the context of globalization. A particular theme is the way in which the sacred nature of nationalism and religious movements, something Anthony Smith emphasized in his writings, the passion they invoke, is linked to violence. Rather than being a cause of war, such movements are the consequence of war; they provide a post hoc legitimation for killing, as well as self-sacrifice, explanations for dying. There is a parallel in this chapter with the analysis of American power; in both cases, war is considered a tool for political mobilization.

The fourth chapter deals with the themes of the previous chapters in relation to the international and European interventions in the Balkans.[16] It describes the tension between geopolitical (top-down, statist, military-backed) and humanitarian approaches to intervention in the region. It argues that the Balkans has represented a learning process in which humanitarian intervention has been tried out, and puts the case for a cosmopolitan political stance in dealing with the rise of new nationalist movements.

The last three chapters are about the construction of a new global order in the context of the profound transformations associated with globalization. They express an aspiration for a more humane set of global political arrangements, despite the reversion to sovereignty represented, on the one hand, by the Bush administration, and, on the other hand, by new nationalist and religious militant movements. The fifth chapter is a distillation of ideas contained in my book *Global Civil Society: An Answer to War*.[17] It is based on the Martin Wight memorial lecture, which was published in *International Affairs*.[18] I have added a section on the chorus of critics of the concept of global civil society and also incorporated additional material on the public sphere and on Islamic notions of civil society that I have used in my teaching. The basic argument is that despite changing meanings of civil society, there was always a common core. That common core was about a society characterized by consent or, if you like, by a social contract. Civil society is the medium through which consent is generated, or through which a social contract is discussed and negotiated. Its changing meanings reflect the changing character of political authority and the changing spaces for debate and discussion. Today, civil society is global because a social contract is being negotiated at several different overlapping layers – national, local and global.

The penultimate chapter was originally written for a conference organized by the Archbishop of Canterbury and the Catholic Bishops Conference of the United Kingdom to rethink the precepts of 'just war'. Just war theory was always directed towards the use of force by states, legitimate political authorities whose legitimacy derives from a domestic social contract. I argue that in a globalized era, where a global social contract is in the process of being debated, just war theory no longer applies since our concern is with the defence of individuals rather than states. A new approach, called human security, might draw on much of the thinking developed over the centuries by Christian, Islamic and secular scholars, but it would reject the key distinction between external war and domestic law enforcement. The only legitimate use of force would be intervention to prevent genocide, large-scale violations of human rights or 'ethnic cleansing' – crimes against humanity – but such intervention would need to be authorized at a multilateral level and would need to adopt methods akin to law enforcement and not war-fighting.

The final chapter defines human security as the new security paradigm and tries to indicate how a human security approach applies to both security and development and what this might mean in practice. It is based on a series of reports, papers and articles written for the Study Group on Europe's security capabilities, which I was asked to convene by Javier Solana.[19]

1

A Decade of Humanitarian Intervention, 1991–2000

This developing international norm in favour of intervention to protect civilians from wholesale slaughter will no doubt continue to pose profound challenges to the international community.

Any such evolution in our understanding of state sovereignty and individual sovereignty will, in some quarters, be met with distrust, scepticism, even hostility. But it is an evolution we should welcome.

Why? Because despite its limitations and imperfections, it is testimony to a humanity that cares more, not less, for the suffering in its midst, and a humanity that will do more, and not less, to end it.

It is a hopeful sign at the end of the twentieth century.

Kofi Annan, Report to the United Nations
General Assembly, 20 Sept. 1999

The progress made . . . in standing up to crimes against humanity represents more than a doctrinal qualification of the prerogatives of sovereignty. Behind the advances in international justice and the increased deployment of troops to stop atrocities lies an evolution in public morality. More than at any time in recent history, the people of the world today are unwilling to tolerate severe human rights abuses and insistent that something be done to stop them. This growing intolerance of inhumanity can hardly promise an end to the atrocities that have plagued so much of the twentieth century. Some situations will be too complex or difficult for easy outside influence. But this reinforced public morality does erect an obstacle that, at least in some cases, can prevent or stop these crimes and save lives.

Human Rights Watch[1]

It was a French idea . . . We came over the border . . . The appeal must not come from the government but from the voice of the victims . . . The right to interfere has now been written into 150 resolutions of the United Nations. Victims are now a category of international law. So we succeeded . . . This is the revolution . . . The victim, not the government, speaking in the name of the victim – for the first time . . . We are coming back to '68. We want to change the world. We want no more Auschwitz, no more Cambodia, no more Rwanda, no more Biafra.

Bernard Kouchner, founder of Médecins sans Frontières[2]

Humanitarian intervention can be defined as military intervention in a state, with or without the approval of that state, to prevent genocide, large-scale violations of human rights (including mass starvation), or grave violations of international humanitarian law (the 'laws of war'). During the 1990s there was a fundamental change in the norms governing the behaviour of states and international organizations. Throughout the Cold War and the anti-colonial period, the principle of non-intervention expressed in Article 2(4) of the United Nations Charter was the dominant norm in international affairs. Starting with the establishment of a safe haven in northern Iraq in 1991, and culminating in the NATO air strikes in Yugoslavia in 1999, the presumption that there is a right to use armed force in support of humanitarian objectives has become much more widely accepted. It is now enshrined in the 'responsibility to protect' adopted by the United Nations General Assembly in September 2005.

This evolution is demonstrated by the increase in, and the changing character of, peace-monitoring, peacekeeping, and peace-enforcement operations. At the start of the 1990s there were only eight United Nations peacekeeping operations, involving some 10,000 troops. As of the end of 2000, there were some fifteen United Nations operations involving some 38,000 military troops.[3] And a number of regional organizations were also involved in various missions concerned with conflict prevention or management. In Europe the most significant were the three NATO deployments in the former Yugoslavia (Bosnia, Kosovo and Macedonia) authorized by the

Table 1.1 *The evolution of humanitarian intervention*

	Purpose	Dates	Troops involved	Authorization	Global civil society groups	Comments
Northern Iraq Operation Provide Comfort	Provide safe haven for Kurds in northern Iraq. Establish no-fly zones in north and south of Iraq	April 1991–3	20,000 troops from US, Britain and France	United Nations Security Council Resolution (UNSCR) 688	Pressure from media and groups such as Human Rights Watch. Hesitation from humanitarian groups such as Oxfam	First safe haven; provided precedent for humanitarian intervention. Initial success but not sustained
Bosnia-Herzegovina	Safe havens, humanitarian corridors, no-fly zone, establishment of war crimes tribunals	1992–5	UNPROFOR, involving 23,000 troops	Various UN SCRs, esp. 770 (protection of humanitarian convoys) and 836 (safe areas)	Combination of NGOs, think tanks, local groups in Europe and inside Bosnia, networks	Marked an important precedent but insufficiently robust. Low point was fall of Srebrenica in July 1995

Somalia	Protect food convoys and provide secure relief centres	1992–3	UNITAF (37,000 troops led by the US) and UNOSOM II (28,000 troops)	UNSCR 794 authorized UNITAF, UNSCR 814 authorized UNOSOM II	Humanitarian NGOs mainly in favour. Save the Children and Africa Rights against	Excessive use of force, failure to disarm militia. Widely considered a debacle. American soldiers killed and bodies publicly paraded
Rwanda	Small UN force withdrawn before massacre. French-led force to protect refugees after the massacre	1994	UNAMIR I (1,500 troops) and II (5,500 troops). Main contingents: France, Canada and Belgium	UNSCR 872 authorized UNAMIR to monitor ceasefire. Request for reinforcements when massacre began, followed	NGOs and media strongly in favour of intervention. ICRC lost 13 staff members	Failure to intervene and prevent genocide despite request of UN Commander General

Table 1.1 *continued*

	Purpose	Dates	Troops involved	Authorization	Global civil society groups	Comments
				by decision to withdraw UNAMIR. UNAMIR II authorized after massacre was over		Dallaire
Haiti Operation Restore Democracy	American-led force to restore democratically elected government	Sept. 1994	Multinational force (MNF) including 21,000 US troops and 1,250 troops from the Caribbean	UNSCR 940	Apparently successful operation	Generally considered a successful intervention carried out in the US national interest. Situation subsequently deteriorated

Kosovo	NATO airstrikes against Yugoslavia	Mar.–July 1999	NATO aircraft from 13 countries flew 38,400 sorties, including 10,484 strike sorties	No UN authorization	Civil society groups involved in transnational networks' call for intervention. Demonstrations against in Greece, Italy and Serbia	Did not prevent ethnic cleansing of first Albanians and then Serbs but did enable the return of all Albanians
East Timor	Australian-led force after massive violence following referendum on independence	Sept. 1999	INTERFET (International Force for East Timor). Some 10,000 troops led by Australia	UNSCR 1264	Civil society pressure for intervention much earlier	Too late although effective
Sierra Leone	Series of interventions to restore democratic government	1994–2000	Gurkhas. Executive Outcomes, ECOMOG, UNAMSIL, British forces	UNAMSIL authorized by UNSCR 1270. ECOMOG authorized by ECOWAS	Strong civil society pressure in West Africa. International NGOs divided	Eventually led to a cease-fire

United Nations, now taken over by the European Union (EU). There were also four Russian peacekeeping operations, under the umbrella of the Commonwealth of Independent States, in Tajikistan, Transdnestr, Abkhazia and South Ossetia. In addition, the European Union had three missions, now many more, and the Organization for Security and Co-operation in Europe (OSCE) had some eleven missions, all of which involved small numbers of military personnel. In Africa, the Economic Community of West African States (ECOWAS) was heavily involved in Sierra Leone and conducted operations in Liberia and Guinea-Bissau. The Organization for African Unity (OAU), now the African Union (AU), also had three mainly civilian missions in Burundi, Comoros and the Democratic Republic of Congo.[4] Only a few of these missions can be defined under the rubric of 'humanitarian intervention'. But their number is evidence of the growing acceptance of the use of military force for humanitarian purposes during this period. Table 1.1 summarizes the most significant interventions of the decade of the 1990s in terms of the evolution of a humanitarian norm.

The changing international norms concerning humanitarian intervention can be considered an expression of an emerging global civil society. The changing norms do reflect a growing global consensus about the equality of human beings and the responsibility to prevent suffering wherever it takes place, which necessarily has to underpin a global civil society. Moreover, this consensus, in turn, is the outcome of a global public debate on these issues. It should be stressed that a growing global consensus about the need to prevent suffering does not imply a consensus about military intervention. On the contrary, the actual experience of intervention has been disappointing and in some cases shameful. The failure to intervene to prevent the genocide in Rwanda and the failure to protect the UN-declared safe haven of Srebrenica are two moments of particular opprobrium in the history of international action. Indeed, it is hard to find a single example of humanitarian intervention during the 1990s that can be unequivocally declared a success. Especially after Kosovo, the debate about whether human rights can be enforced through military means is ever more intense. Moreover, the wars in Afghanistan and Iraq, which have been justified in humanitarian terms, have further called into question the case for intervention.

This chapter is about the role that civil society actors played in bringing about the changing international norms and about the character of the public debate. The first section describes the actors who participate in the debate. The second section describes the evolution of humanitarian intervention, with particular emphasis on the role of civil society groups, up to the end of the 1990s. The third section summarizes the character of the global public debate. The final section is about developments in 2000, in particular the military intervention(s) in Sierra Leone.

Global Civil Society Actors

The actors who have put pressure on governments and on international organizations for or against humanitarian intervention can be divided into three groups. One group comprises what are normally considered the classic actors of civil society, who often claim to speak on behalf of the victims: NGOs, social movements and networks. The second group comprises those who tend to be closer to the elite and make use primarily of the power of words: think tanks and commissions. The third group consists of forms of communication, in particular the media: radio, television, print media and websites.

It should be stressed that in the debate about humanitarian intervention a key role has been played by dynamic individuals. Names like Bernard Kouchner or Fred Cuny (see box 1.1)

Box 1.1   The role of individuals: Fred Cuny and Bernard Kouchner

The lives of two individuals – one American, Fred Cuny, and one Frenchman, Bernard Kouchner – could be said to encapsulate the story of the evolution of humanitarian intervention over the last three decades.

Both were born during the Second World War. Both were influenced by the student movement of the 1960s. Cuny, who had been a Republican, became active in the civil rights movement in the late 1960s. Kouchner was involved in the French *événements* of 1968. Cuny was training to be an engineer and Kouchner was training to be a doctor.

continued

Both went to Biafra in 1969 and were involved in the airlift that was undertaken without the permission of the Nigerian government. Kouchner, who was working for the International Red Cross, was shocked by the unwillingness of the ICRC to speak out about what was happening. 'By keeping silent, we doctors were accomplices in the systematic massacre of a population.'[1] Kouchner started the International Committee against Genocide in Biafra and started to use the media to publicize what was happening. 'We were using the media before it became fashionable . . . We refused to allow sick people and doctors to be massacred in silence and submission.'[2]

Biafra, according to Cuny, was the 'mother' of all humanitarian operations. 'We still use the yardstick of Biafra to measure our performance in other disasters. It's the defining moment.'[3] Cuny was shocked by the lack of planning and the amateurishness of the relief effort. In 1970, he left Biafra convinced that the airlift was prolonging the war.

In 1971, Kouchner founded the NGO Médecins sans Frontières (MSF). The aim was the rapid deployment of doctors to disaster areas, with or without official permission, with heavy reliance on the use of the media both to secure funding and to provide immunity from hostile governments. The same year Cuny founded a company, Intertect Relief and Reconstruction, which specialized in giving technical assistance and training in disaster relief to UN and volunteer agencies. Unlike MSF, which raised money from the public, the company depended on contracts from governments and international institutions.

Both MSF and Intertect were involved in numerous disasters in the 1970s and 1980s – earthquakes, wars, floods, massacres, hurricanes – and gained their practical and political experiences from these events. Disaster areas included Nicaragua, Honduras, Peru, Sri Lanka, Sudan, Ethiopia, Cambodia, Bangladesh, Vietnam, El Salvador, and the Lebanon, among others. Both published books. In *Disasters and Development*,[4] Cuny says that it was during this period that he began to understand the connection between the military and humanitarianism. 'More than anything else, the images of those planes delivering everything from food to coal fostered acceptance of the link between armed forces and humanitarian assistance and, more importantly, acceptance of the costs involved.'[5]

Kouchner's book *Charité Business* is about the relationship between the media, NGOs, and policy-makers.[6] Indeed, it was Kouchner's emphasis on dramatic media events which led to the split in 1979, when Kouchner went on to found Médecins du Monde.

The turning point for both men was the Gulf War of 1991. Kouchner had begun to promote the concept of a *droit d'ingérence* (right of interference) in the late 1980s. In 1988 he was appointed Minister for Health and Humanitarian Action in the French government led by Michel Rocard. He was able to promote his ideas in the United Nations, and after the Gulf War pushed for the *droit d'ingérence* to help the Kurds in northern Iraq. The haven in northern Iraq did provide an important precedent in humanitarian intervention. Cuny was also there; he had convinced the US ambassador to Turkey, Morton Abramowitz, that it was possible to bring the Kurdish refugees back to their homes in a two-month period and was given an opportunity to carry our his ideas. Subsequently, through Morton Abramowitz, Cuny was able to influence policy in Washington.

Both Cuny and Kouchner advocated military intervention in Somalia, and their voices were influential in both the US and France. Cuny favoured the creation of armed relief enclaves. Both were critical of the way the intervention was carried out. Cuny thought it was inefficient from the point of view of delivering aid. Kouchner considered the intervention to have been a success, although he was critical of the American use of overwhelming force. 'There are no humanitarian catastrophes only political catastrophes . . . No! What was catastrophic was the American attitude . . . A war without prisoners, a war without dead people . . . this is just crazy.'[7]

During the Bosnian war Cuny was recruited by George Soros to provide $50 million of humanitarian assistance to Bosnia. He focused on the restoration of basic utilities in Sarajevo, building a protected water purification plant and providing access to gas for heating. Kouchner was a staunch advocate of an international air offensive and became known as the proponent of 'war to end war'.

continued

Thereafter, their careers diverged. Cuny was sent by Soros to Chechnya. After his first visit in December 1994 he said that the destruction of Grozny made Sarajevo seem like a picnic. He was convinced that he could arrange a ceasefire but he disappeared when on a trip to try to meet the Chechen leader. He was probably executed on 14 April 1995.

Kouchner was appointed UN Special Representative in Kosovo and became head of the new UN administration in Kosovo established after the NATO bombing. He left after a year and became French Minister of Health again in the government of Lionel Jospin. His record in Kosovo has been criticized but he enjoyed the full support of Kosovar Albanians. After the election of President Sarkogy in France in 2007, he was appointed French Foreign Minister.

The differences between the two men reflected their cultural backgrounds. Cuny focused on practical solutions to humanitarian crises; Kouchner focused on political solutions. Kouchner tried to develop a new language and a new ethics of humanitarianism. Cuny tried to develop new methodologies and procedures. But their differences were complementary; Kouchner's approach necessarily involved practical implementation and Cuny's search for common-sense solutions led him to politics. Both contributed in important ways, for good or for ill, to the emerging consensus about humanitarian intervention by the late 1990s.

Notes

1 Quoted in T. Allen and D. Styan, 'A Right to Interfere? Bernard Kouchner and the New Humanitarianism', *Journal of International Development* 12, no. 6 (2000): 830.
2 Quoted in ibid.
3 Quoted in William Shawcross, 'A Hero of our Time', *New York Review of Books*, 30 Nov. 1995.
4 Frederick C. Cuny, *Disasters and Development* (Oxford: Oxford University Press, 1983).
5 Quoted in T.G. Weiss, *Military–Civilian Interactions: Intervening in Humanitarian Crises* (Lanham: Rowman and Littlefield, 1999), p. 17.
6 Bernard Kouchner, *Charité Business* (Paris: Le Pré aux Clercs, 1986).
7 Quoted in Allen and Styan, 'A Right to Interfere?', p. 838.

have resonance throughout the field of humanitarianism and undoubtedly directly or indirectly influenced government action. In the US, where there has been little in the way of a grass-roots movement, individuals like George Soros, Morton Abramowitz of the Carnegie Endowment, and Aryeh Neier of Human Rights Watch and the Open Society Foundation have been very influential in the debates about various interventions. In France and in Central Europe, individual intellectuals have been heavily engaged in the debate. In France, for example, Bernard Henri Levy had a powerful impact with his film about the siege of Sarajevo; and in Central Europe many of the well-known former dissidents became deeply involved in the debate about intervention in Bosnia and later Kosovo.

As well as intellectuals, public personalities from the world of popular culture have added their voices to concerns about victims of war and/or starvation, thus helping to popularize humanitarian consciousness. Examples include Bob Geldof and Band Aid, and Bono of U2. During the siege of Sarajevo, a number of these figures travelled to Sarajevo to support secular culture.

Many of these individuals are, of course, linked to civil society organizations described below.

NGOs, social movements, networks

NGOs are professional organizations, sometimes with member-ships, and often dependent on a few donors, including govern-ments. International NGOs, that is to say, NGOs that operate across borders, tend to be based in advanced industrial coun-tries. NGOs can be both service providers – delivering humani-tarian assistance, monitoring human rights, and providing mediation services in conflicts – and advocacy groups – putting pressure on governments and international organizations. Social movements are looser organizations, often based on grass-roots groups and making use of volunteers. By and large they are campaigning groups engaged in various, often innovative, forms of protest. Because of their grass-roots nature, social move-ments tend to be locally based, although they can and do make coalitions across borders. Networks have been an increasingly significant phenomenon in the 1990s. They are loose coalitions of NGOs and social movements, often making use of the opportunities offered by the internet and providing a vehicle to transmit the voices and arguments of groups in the South and East directly, rather than indirectly through NGOs in the North.

NGOs concerned with humanitarian intervention are primarily humanitarian and human rights NGOs, although there are increasing numbers of conflict-resolution NGOs. Humanitarian NGOs were initially formed to provide relief to the victims of war, but increasingly the term has come to include the victims of all types of disasters which result in mass suffering: floods, earthquakes, and so on. These NGOs have a long history. The International Committee of the Red Cross (ICRC) was founded in 1859 by Henri Dunant after he witnessed the horrors of the Battle of Solferino. The ICRC provided the impetus for the development of humanitarian law in the late nineteenth century and subsequently. It was the ICRC that pioneered some of the principles of humanitarian action such as impartiality, neutrality, and the principle of consent: principles which presupposed a notion of 'civilized' wars and 'honourable' soldiers.[5] The wars and famines of the twentieth century and the erosion of notions of 'civilized' forms of warfare have spawned many more humanitarian NGOs. Thus, Save the Children was formed in the Second World War. Cooperative for American Relief Everywhere (CARE) was formed by twenty-two charities and trade unions in 1945 to distribute leftover American army rations to Europe; later it shifted to the distribution of American agricultural surpluses to the Third World. Oxfam was founded in 1942, and Médecins sans Frontières (MSF) in 1971 during the war in Biafra. In the 1980s and 1990s a myriad of NGOs were formed in response to increased 'complex emergencies', which included both famines and wars, greater public consciousness of suffering in faraway places, perhaps as a result of television, and the growing tendency of governments to contract out relief to NGOs. Many humanitarian NGOs are church based or linked to other religions. An increasing share of official humanitarian assistance is disbursed through NGOs, and, in parallel, NGOs are becoming increasingly dependent on government funds.

Human rights NGOs differ from humanitarian NGOs in that their concern is primarily with state repression and with violations of human rights, especially political and civil rights. Like humanitarian NGOs, human rights NGOs have a long history. The Anti-Slavery Society founded in 1839 is probably the oldest international human rights NGO still in existence.[6] The term 'human rights' is a post-Second World War invention, attributed to Eleanor Roosevelt, who objected to the 'rights of man', although the term *Menschenrechte* was always used in the Germanic languages. The official international commitment to human rights was expressed in the Universal Declaration of Human Rights (1948), the Genocide Convention (1948), and the two human rights Covenants (1976), among other treaties and declarations. As in the case of humanitarian NGOs, the 1980s and 1990s witnessed a proliferation of human rights groups and a strengthening of those that already existed. Since the wars of this period also involved massive violations of human rights, these groups necessarily became more concerned with war. The best-known international NGOs are Amnesty International and Human Rights Watch, but there are thousands of smaller groups, not only in advanced industrial countries but especially in the East and South.

Conflict-resolution NGOs are more recent. Well-known examples include International Alert and Conciliation Resources, based in Britain, and San Egidio, the Vatican group, both of which have played significant roles in mediation in recent years. San Egidio, for example, was responsible for initiating peace negotiations in Mozambique, for the Education Agreement in Kosovo in 1997 (which seemed to offer a prospect for averting war), and also for bringing together the various opposition groups in Algeria. The Carter Center in the US has also been an important player in conflict mediation. There are many less well-known groups, especially women's groups, that engage in conflict resolution at local levels. Conflict-resolution groups were established in part by peace groups seeking a new direction after the end of the Cold War, and in part by human rights and humanitarian groups who became aware of the need for a more political approach.[7]

Three types of social movement have been involved in humanitarian intervention. First of all, in the countries where wars have taken place, movements supporting intervention have developed among the potential victims. Thus, an anti-war movement developed in Bosnia calling for an international protectorate before the outbreak of war; and the Kosovar resistance movement was making similar appeals throughout the 1990s.[8]

In the countries where outside governments have been involved, civil society actors have tended not to be movements, except in the case of the former Yugoslavia. During the Bosnian war, however, a second type of movement developed, primarily in Europe. Although it had its origins in peace, human rights, and women's movements, it was a new movement in which local groups sprang up primarily to provide humanitarian assistance but also to express political positions on the Bosnian war, often with deep divisions among them. During the Kosovo war, there were mass demonstrations against the NATO bombing or against the 'double war' (NATO bombing and Serbian President Milosevic's campaign of ethnic cleansing), especially in Serbia, Greece and Italy.

A third type of movement, which has been influential both for and against intervention, is nationalist and fundamentalist. In this chapter, I do not include non-state warring parties – paramilitary groups or warlords – as part of civil society. But the warring parties are often linked to organized nationalist movements or nationalist currents of opinion. These movements intensified in the 1990s in response to globalization. In particular, diaspora groups have become increasingly significant in influencing both the character of nationalist movements and their impact on the international community. On the whole, this type of movement jealously guards the notion of sovereignty, as in Serbia, for example. But some nationalist movements favour intervention: Palestine and Kosovo are two current examples. The role of transnationally organized Islamic movements in calling for intervention in, say, Bosnia is also important.

One of the criticisms that is often made about NGOs based in the North is that, while claiming to speak on behalf of the victims, they often drown out the victims' voices. The advantage of networks is that they provide an organizational form that allows NGOs and grass-roots organizations outside war zones to link up with local groups within the war zones. Networks may be less effective at organized lobbying but they do provide a forum through which the knowledge and views of local groups can be transmitted. This was very important during the Yugoslav wars; important examples were the Helsinki Citizens' Assembly (see box 1.2) and the Verona Forum

Box 1.2   Helsinki Citizens' Assembly activities during the war in Bosnia

In the second half of the 1980s, parts of the West European peace movement developed a strategy of 'détente from below', making links with opposition groups in Central and Eastern Europe. Many of the techniques of transnational networking – providing transnational support to groups in difficult and dangerous situations, and simultaneously lobbying different governments and international institutions – were developed during this period, even before the advent of the internet.

The Helsinki Citizens' Assembly was established in 1990 to formalize this network. The goal was to integrate Europe from below, to establish a pan-European civil society. Vaclav Havel, then the new president of Czechoslovakia, spoke at the Founding Assembly which brought together over 1,000 people from all over Europe who had been involved in the dialogue, and the international secretariat was based in Prague.

The Yugoslav branch of the Helsinki Citizens' Assembly was founded in Sarajevo in May 1991. The chairperson was Zdravko Grebo, a law professor from Sarajevo, who had played a key role in the democratization process in Bosnia-Herzegovina. At that time, the slogan was 'Lets Cooperate!'. Whether Yugoslavia falls apart or stays together, civil society must remain united.

When federal troops entered Slovenia in June 1991, an emergency meeting of the HCA was organized in Belgrade to discuss how to prevent war. The meeting included several luminaries of the Cold War oppositions, including Milovan Djilas, Adam Michnik, Bronislaw Geremek and Ernest Gellner. Grebo warned that if Yugoslavia fell apart, Bosnia would fall apart and that a war in Bosnia 'would be hell'. It was agreed to press for an international protectorate for Bosnia-Herzegovina, and a series of activities were planned which laid the basis for the later wartime activism.

One of these activities was a peace caravan, which was held in September 1991. Some forty European activists travelled

continued

by bus through Slovenia, Croatia, Serbia and Bosnia, making links with local anti-war activists. The caravan culminated in Sarajevo, where a human chain of 10,000 people linked the mosque, the synagogue and the Orthodox and Catholic churches. The links made during the visit of the peace caravan were sustained, by and large, throughout the war. Another activity was Yugofax, a monitoring service written by people from the region which later became the Balkan War Report and is now the Institute for War and Peace Reporting.

As war in Bosnia-Herzegovina became imminent in the spring of 1992, it was Grebo who called on people to come into the streets and tear down the barricades being erected by Serbian, and Muslim, paramilitary groups. Indeed, the war began when Serb snipers fired at a citizens' demonstration of some 200,000 people mobilized by Grebo; it demanded the resignation of the government and the establishment of an international protectorate. Thousands more had come by bus to join the demonstration but were prevented from entering Sarajevo by roadblocks. The official international negotiators who were visiting Sarajevo that day did not have time, so they said, to meet with the demonstrators. The demonstration of 12 April 1992 was the last peace demonstration of its kind; no wonder that the Sarajevans were later to say that 'Europe ends in Sarajevo'.

During the war, HCA activities were of three kinds. First, the network of civic activists was maintained through meetings, conferences and workshops, as well as electronic communication – it was in Bosnia, that the HCA e-mail network was first established. A parallel network of municipalities was also established at that time. A particularly important event was the Citizens' and Municipal Peace Conference held in Ohrid, Macedonia, in the autumn of 1992. The network was a way of providing solidarity to the groups in the region and planning future activities.

Second, many groups collected and delivered humanitarian assistance – the Italians and the Czechs were particularly active in this respect.

Third, HCA campaigned and lobbied governments and international institutions for what in effect was a new form of humanitarian intervention. HCA pushed for an international protectorate. At Ohrid the idea of local protectorates was developed. And this was the origin of the Safe Havens campaign in early 1993, in which some 300,000 postcards calling for safe havens were sent to the negotiators and to governments.

HCA also campaigned for international administrations in Sarajevo and Mostar. And a major effort of HCA from 1994 onwards was the campaign to publicize and support the town of Tuzla, which was the only town in Bosnia-Herzegovina which had maintained a non-nationalist administration and which kept alive multicultural civic cosmopolitan values throughout the war.

A seminar held in Tuzla in September 1994 brought NGOs and municipalities to Tuzla and they pledged all kinds of support to the town. A year later, one week after the ceasefire, HCA held its Assembly in Tuzla, bringing 300 activists from abroad to Tuzla, including over seventy people from Serbia.

Undoubtedly, the HCA campaign did contribute to the international community's policy towards Bosnia-Herzegovina. But official support for humanitarian intervention was half-hearted; the safe havens were never defended effectively; there was no serious support at that time for citizens' efforts.

The Helsinki Citizens' Assembly sometimes describes itself as a family, founded on certain shared values and a commitment to mutual solidarity, which takes precedence over loyalty to governments, or to abstract principles. All the local groups are self-organized and self-financing. They gain legitimacy and visibility in their own societies from being branches of a transnational organization with access to international policy-makers. They gain strength from international contacts and meetings where they can develop and discuss their campaigns and projects and plan joint activities. HCA's networking involves a two-way learning process. By comparing experiences, and trying to understand different local situations on the basis of the knowledge of those who live in the region, HCA develops new ideas, practical analyses and strategies. Essentially, HCA is a mechanism for the transmission and processing of information from local activists to other activists and to institutions.

continued

This work has not always been easy because of the difficult circumstances in which some groups operate; local activists are often harassed and some have lost their lives in war. Several activists from Bosnia, France and Italy were killed during the war in Bosnia.

Another obstacle is the character of the organization. HCA emerged from the movements of the 1980s; it was never able to transform itself into an international NGO of the type demanded by donors. The latter tend to expect more emphasis on the transfer of skills from West to East than on the transfer of understanding from East to West, on the provision of services at a local level rather than campaigns at an international level, on offices rather than groups, and on professionalism rather than political mobilization. For all these reasons, HCA has found it difficult to sustain the expensive task of international networking. Nevertheless, this strange 'political animal' as the co-chair Bernard Dreano has described it, continues to exist. There is now a new generation who are not so bound by the movement traditions of the past and who may be better able to combine new forms of individual activism with the professionalism demanded by the global donors.

established by the Italian Green MEP Alexander Lange. There are also a number of emerging networks in Africa: the West Africa peace-building network and the Great Lakes Policy Forum. Women's groups have played a pioneering role in developing the network form of organization. Women in Black is an important example, which began out of solidarity with the Belgrade-based group Women in Black and has spread to other conflict regions. It organized weekly international vigils during the war in Bosnia and also increasingly engages in various conflict-resolution projects.[9]

Although the distinctions between humanitarian, human rights, peace and women's groups are useful in tracing the history of these civil society organizations, in practice they are becoming less and less meaningful. Today's wars involve massive violations of human rights, including atrocities against women.

In this context, peace movements may engage in solidarity actions, as do the humanitarian groups, or may find themselves increasingly taking on the human rights agenda. Women's groups become peace and human rights groups. Human rights groups are increasingly concerned with violations of international humanitarian law and war crimes as well as human rights violations. Humanitarian groups, traditionally non-political, find themselves adopting the causes of peace and justice.

Thus an important development in this period has been what is sometimes known as civil society intervention, where the presence of international civil society groups, even if unarmed, constitutes a form of protection for civilians. This was the basic idea behind Peace Brigades International, formed in 1981, which began its work in Central America and now mobilizes thousands of volunteers to accompany returning refugees, for example.[10] Many of the groups formed during the Yugoslav wars saw themselves carrying out similar missions.

Think tanks and commissions

While movements and NGOs raise public awareness, expert groups are often closer to governments and frame specific policy proposals. The growth during the 1980s and 1990s of think tanks and commissions addressing global issues is yet another sign of the emergence of global civil society. Think tanks like the International Crisis Group and the Institute for War and Peace Reporting, both established during the 1990s, have become significant purveyors of information and opinions. Older established think tanks concerned with defence and foreign affairs, which exist in almost every country, have also joined the debate. Similar to these think tanks are international commissions, both independent and under the auspices of the United Nations. The Brandt, Palme and Brundtland commissions were important in pioneering this way of using groups of prominent individuals to make policy inputs on significant global issues. In the 1990s, international commissions concerned with various aspects of humanitarian intervention proliferated. The Carnegie Endowment organized two commissions, one on 'Preventing deadly conflict' and one on the Balkans,[11] recalling the experience of an important and pioneering Carnegie Commission on the Balkans in 1913. There have been three important reports under UN auspices concerning Rwanda, Srebrenica and UN Peacekeeping.[12] After Kosovo, the Swedish government took the initiative in establishing an independent international commission to investigate the Kosovo crisis under the chairmanship of the South African judge Richard Goldstone. The Commission on Intervention and State Sovereignty under the chairmanship of Gareth Evans and Mohamed Sahnoun provided the impetus for the adoption of 'the responsibility to protect'.[13]

As Richard Goldstone has put it in the course of an interview for the BBC in February 2001, these commissions are an important device for increasing the transparency and public accountability of international institutions: they represent 'civil society judging governments'.

Media and websites

The importance of the international media in drawing attention to crises in far-off places is often stressed. Politicians often complain about the way their actions are media led. Undoubtedly, at certain moments – the famine in Ethiopia in the 1980s, the discovery of detention camps in Bosnia in 1993 by ITN and the *Guardian*, the furore about the camps in eastern Zaire in the autumn of 1994 – media attention has played an important role. But by and large the media have been a tool, an expression of a public debate rather than an actor in their own right. Undoubtedly, access to the media has been uneven and sometimes distorting; in particular, starvation and violence are more newsworthy than peace negotiations. Nevertheless, those civil society actors who have learned to use the media have been able to make their voices heard more effectively.

In the 1980s and 1990s, many NGOs and social movements deliberately fostered what the French call a *médiatique* strategy. MSF under Bernard Kouchner pioneered the *médiatique* approach. But it was also taken up by other NGOs and, in the 1990s, by social movements.

The media and the civil society groups have developed a sort of symbiotic relationship. As George Alagiah of the BBC put it:

Relief agencies depend upon us for publicity and we need them to tell us where the stories are. There's an unspoken understanding between us, a sort of code. We try not to ask the question too bluntly: 'Where are the starving babies'. And they never answer explicitly. But we get the pictures all the same.[14]

A very important development in the 1990s was the extensive use of websites. Many civil society organizations have websites, which have speeded up information gathering on these issues. Websites have also provided a way in which institutions in the war zones can have more impact on the global debate. Thus the Radio B92 website, which provided an English language digest of developments in Serbia, or the website of the independent Kosovar newspaper *Kohaditore* were crucial sources of information about developments in former Yugoslavia. Likewise, the South Asia Citizens Web has provided a local perspective on the Kashmir conflict and also a mechanism for networking within South Asia. Websites are also important sources of propaganda for nationalist and fundamentalist movements, a service often provided by more extreme groups in the diaspora.

The Evolution of Humanitarian Intervention

The idea of intervention 'to defend the rights of foreign subjects of an oppressive ruler' was advanced by Hugo Grotius in the seventeenth century.[15] But the term 'humanitarian intervention' was first used in the nineteenth century to justify interventions by European powers to protect (mainly Christian) people oppressed by the Ottoman Empire. The first instance was the intervention in Greece in 1827, which was to lead to Greek independence in 1830. This notion of humanitarian intervention clashed with the growing presumption that states had equal rights to protect their sovereignty and that interference in the affairs of other states was therefore wrong. This insistence on the importance of sovereignty and non-interference is sometimes dated back to the Treaty of Westphalia of 1648. But actually it is a more recent idea, which gained intellectual credentials in the middle of the eighteenth century in the writings of Christian von Wolff and Emerich de Vattel, but became widely accepted only in the twentieth century with the independence of many former colonies and the spread of communism. Newly independent and/or communist countries regarded the doctrine of non-intervention as an important defence against what they saw as the 'constant and endemic intervention' of great powers.[16]

During the Cold War period, the principle of non-intervention was widely considered to take priority over humanitarian considerations. After 1945, the United Nations Charter strengthened the rules restricting the rights of states to use force. At the same time a body of law developed in the various human rights declarations and conventions which forbade states to ill-treat individuals, including their own nationals. In practice, the former overrode the latter up until the end of the 1980s.[17]

There were many interventions during this period, especially by the two superpowers, but these were justified in Cold War terms as interventions against communism or capitalism and usually legitimized on the grounds that outside powers were 'invited' to intervene (Vietnam, Czechoslovakia or Afghanistan). As Nicholas Wheeler shows, there were also interventions which could be described as humanitarian, notably the Indian intervention in Bangladesh in 1971, the Vietnamese intervention in Cambodia in December 1977 which led to the fall of the Khmer Rouge, and the Tanzanian intervention in Uganda which led to the overthrow of Idi Amin in April 1979. But none of these interventions was justified in humanitarian terms.[18]

The debates in the United Nations Security Council during this period, described by Wheeler, show the strength of the non-intervention norm. Thus in the debate over Vietnam's intervention in Cambodia, the French ambassador Leprette said: 'The notion that because a regime is detestable foreign intervention is justified and forcible overthrow is legitimate is extremely dangerous. That could ultimately jeopardise the very maintenance of international law and order and make the continued existence of various regimes dependent on the judgement of their neighbours'.[19] Similar arguments were put forward by other members of the Security Council. As late as 1986, the prominent international theorist, Hedley Bull, argued:

The growing moral conviction that human rights should have a place in relations among states has been deeply corrosive of the rule of non-intervention, which once drew strength from the general acceptance that states alone have rights in international law.[20]

What were the factors that led to such a dramatic change in international norms in the late 1980s and 1990s? One was the spread of 'new' or 'postmodern' wars, especially in Africa and Eastern Europe. These are wars that have evolved out of the guerrilla and counter-insurgency wars of an earlier period. They are often called 'civil' or 'internal' wars, although they involve an array of global actors. They are wars in which direct fighting between the contestants is rare and most violence is directed against civilians. Indeed, techniques such as population displacement, and various atrocities which directly violate both the laws of war and human rights are central to the strategies of these wars. They are also wars in which the manipulation of food supply, loot and pillage, and the control of valuable commodities are built into the functioning of a war economy. Not only did these wars increase in number during this period but there was also a big increase in civilian suffering, as measured by the ratio of military to civilian casualties and by the explosion of refugees and internally displaced persons.[21]

A second factor was the growth of humanitarian NGOs. The war in Nigeria in 1967–70 was a turning point for the humanitarian NGOs. It was the moment when the ICRC abandoned its insistence on neutrality and on operating within the framework of consent. The ICRC was conscious that its insistence on neutrality had prevented it from publicly protesting about what it knew to be happening to the Jews in the Second World War, and there were fears of genocide in Biafra. Thus the ICRC, together with more recent humanitarian NGOs influenced by the student movements of the 1960s and the interrogations about the Second World War, decided to organize an airlift to Biafra without the consent of the Nigerian authorities.

For many of the newer NGOs, Biafra was the defining moment. Subsequently many of the groups formed or shaped by that experience went on to respond to crises in various parts of the world: earthquakes, floods, famines and war. In 1984, the famine in Ethiopia sparked a debate about humanitarianism and political action. Groups like Band Aid had helped to stimulate a media-orchestrated response to the famine. But other groups argued that the famine was being created deliberately as an instrument of war by Mengistu, the Ethiopian leader, and that the humanitarian agencies were keeping Mengistu in power. MSF, which took this position, was thrown out of Ethiopia at this time. During this period, the NGOs increasingly began to operate without consent, as had happened earlier in Biafra. Indeed, in Ethiopia a split developed among those NGOs that worked in non-governmental areas and those that cooperated with the government. Only the ICRC was allowed to work openly with both sides, although Save the Children managed to do so informally.

By the mid-1980s this new type of war had become increasingly important. In Mozambique and Afghanistan, official agencies increasingly began to see the advantage of NGOs as a form of non-governmental intervention and a way of working in war zones without permission. In several places, 'corridors of tranquillity' or 'humanitarian corridors' were established to provide relief. Operation LifeLine in Sudan was another particularly important episode where many of these techniques were developed, particularly through UNICEF and its programmes for the immunization of children. It was then that 'clamours for more muscular support' began to be raised.[22]

This was the period that Bernard Kouchner, together with his colleague, the lawyer Mario Bettani, launched the idea of a *devoir d'ingérence* (duty to interfere), which later became a *droit d'ingérence* (right/law of interference). Kouchner became French Minister of Humanitarian Action in 1988, and in the same year the United Nations General Assembly passed Resolution 43/131, which put these arrangements on a more formal footing. The resolution reaffirmed the sovereignty of states but recognized that the 'international community makes an important contribution to the sustenance and protection' of victims in emergency situations. Failure to provide humanitarian assistance 'constitutes a threat to life and human dignity'. The resolution stressed the 'important contribution' of 'intergovernmental and non-governmental organisations working with strictly humanitarian motives'. Subsequently, General Assembly Resolution 45/100 praised the Secretary-General for continuing consultations on the establishment of 'humanitarian corridors'.[23]

A third factor in the changing international climate was the growth of human rights groups. Particularly important were the emergence of pro-democracy and human rights movements in the Third World and Eastern Europe. In part, this was a consequence of the exhaustion of post-colonial and communist projects: the loss of appeal of earlier emancipatory ideas. And it part it has to be understood in the context of growing global interconnectedness and the possibility of obtaining support and making links across borders, which provided a way of opening up closed societies. In Europe and North America, the movements which evolved after the 1960s spawned human rights groups sometimes in dispute with the traditional left. In the United States, it was the coup in Chile and the growth of human rights groups in Latin America during the 1970s and 1980s that led to the emergence of transnational human rights networks.[24] In France, the debate about *tiermondisme* led many French intellectuals to attack the simplicities of those traditional left groups who had unquestioningly supported liberation movements in the Third World, and to place increasing emphasis on democratic freedoms and human rights; the group Libertés sans Frontières was an expression of this line of thought. In the rest of Europe, the mass peace movement of the 1980s stimulated a debate about human rights and the relationship of peace to justice. Some parts of the peace movement made links with Eastern human rights groups and pioneered the concept of 'détente from below' and the idea of a new form of civil society intervention in support of human rights; they argued that the threat of nuclear weapons had prevented interference in support of human rights. Other parts of the peace movement insisted on non-interference, arguing that the danger of nuclear war was the overriding concern and that support for human rights could contribute to Cold War rhetoric.

The 1989 revolutions gave further impetus to the human rights movements. The discourse of civil society was the discourse of the movements which toppled the communist regimes. To this was added the language of transnationalism and global responsibility that came out of the cross-border links made in the 1980s. Moreover, the revolutions seemed to discredit traditional left thinking, which was associated with notions of non-interference and of collectivism that were supposed to take priority over individual rights.

The final factor was, of course, the post-Cold War global context. The end of the Cold War provided an opportunity, for the first time, for concerted international action. It also allowed the 'new wars' to become more visible and a new global discourse about humanitarianism and human rights to supplant the tired Cold War rhetoric.

The Gulf War of 1991 provided the first opportunity to display the new international consensus. The war, of course, was not a humanitarian intervention; it was a response to the invasion of Kuwait by Iraq, and once Kuwait had been liberated a ceasefire was declared. Indeed, the war is probably better described as an American attempt to assert its newfound unchallenged global hegemony: this was the essence of President Bush's 'new world order'.

In the aftermath of the war, however, there were uprisings by Kurds in the north and Shi'ites in the south in the expectation that Saddam Hussein would be overthrown. The uprisings were brutally suppressed. This was the moment for Kouchner and the French government to push for a *droit d'ingérence*. Public sympathy for the plight of the Kurds also propelled other governments, particularly in Britain and the United States, into action. The consequence was United Nations Security Council Resolution 688, which established a safe haven in northern Iraq for the Kurds. The resolution did not actually mandate the use of troops; nevertheless Operation Provide Comfort involved the deployment of over 20,000 troops to protect the safe haven. At the time, only the French were pushing for a *droit d'ingérence*. The resolution was couched in terms of the threat to 'international peace and security' posed by refugees and by the situation in the area. The term 'haven' was used in preference to 'enclaves' at the insistence of the British ambassador, Sir David Hannay, on the grounds that 'enclaves' suggested a redrawing of boundaries. Nevertheless, the resolution did create a precedent in that it demanded that Iraq 'immediately end this repression' and 'ensure that the human and political rights of all Iraqi citizens are respected'.

Although public pressure and media exposure of what was happening in northern Iraq were important in propelling forward the proposal for a safe haven, it is interesting to note that, at the time, there were doubts among UN officials as well as NGOs operating in northern Iraq, who feared alienating the Iraqi government. According to an Oxfam staff member in the region: 'The feeling is that we can't jeopardise the good work we already have going by getting into a conflict with the Iraqi government up here . . . It's the sort of thing we ought to be doing but it would violate Oxfam's line at the moment.'[25] The relative success of the safe haven, at least initially, was to change attitudes among many NGOs.

The international troops were withdrawn in 1993 and replaced by a small UN guard and a 'residual' force based in Turkey. The Kurds were able to re-establish a measure of autonomy (which they had enjoyed years earlier) but they remained vulnerable to Iraqi raids. The no-fly zone did not prevent the ethnic cleansing of Shi'ites in the south.

But the safe haven in northern Iraq did turn out to be a precedent. The genie was out of the bottle. As Adam Roberts points out, the proclamation of humanitarian interests has an inevitable 'ratchet effect'.

> It is inherently difficult for major powers to proclaim humanitarian principles and policies in relation to a conflict, and then do nothing to protect the victims and/or punish their tormentors when atrocities occur. Thus an initial humanitarian involvement can lead to a more military one – a process involving awkward changes of direction. Further, it is inherently difficult to preach humanitarianism in one crisis and then not to do so in the next, however unpromising the situation and however slim the interests of outside powers.[26]

The war in Bosnia

After Iraq came the disintegration of Yugoslavia and the wars in Slovenia, Croatia and Bosnia-Herzegovina. It was the war in Bosnia, which lasted from April 1992 to October 1995, which was to generate the most heated public debate about humanitarian intervention. There were many other wars in the world, and many other tragedies just as terrible as in Bosnia, as the United Nations Secretary-General, Boutros Boutros Ghali, was to point out when he visited Sarajevo in 1992. But it was the war in Bosnia and the plight of Sarajevo that captured global attention.

In Europe a mass movement developed in the wake of the war. Hundreds of groups sprang up both to collect and distribute aid and to increase awareness and make protests. In Italy, for example, the Italian Consortium for Solidarity was established in 1993 to link civil society groups and organizations. From Italy alone more than 15,000 volunteers travelled to the war zones and some 2200 convoys were organized. But throughout Europe similar mobilizations took place, including the new democratic countries of Central Europe. In the Czech Republic, for example, the People in Need Foundation (*Clovek v Tisni*) ran a television campaign and even persuaded army officers to donate part of their salaries. A particularly interesting group was Workers' Aid for Tuzla, which later became International Workers' Aid. This group was started by British miners who had received support from the town of Tuzla during the 1984 miners' strike and wanted to repay their debt. Those who drove convoys or established local offices in war zones did risk their lives and a number of volunteers from several European countries were killed.

As well as collecting aid, local groups organized novel forms of protest to draw attention to the plight of Sarajevo, especially in France. In Nantes, the main square was renamed Sarajevo Square. In Strasbourg, a checkpoint was set up on one of the main bridges, arbitrarily stopping people from crossing. And in Grenoble, the sound of shelling and sirens was reproduced throughout the town at 2 am to give the local inhabitants the feeling of what it was like to be in Sarajevo. In Britain, a group of well-known personalities presented bottles of dirty water to the Prime Minister's residence and to Members of Parliament to show what the people in Sarajevo were being forced to drink.

A remarkable feature of the movement was the role played by local municipalities, a development of the nuclear-free zone idea of the 1980s. Many municipalities were twinned with municipalities in the former Yugoslavia and others introduced twinning arrangements during the war. Thus Norwich was twinned with Novi Sad and, at the height of the war, Tuzla decided to twin with Bologna. These twinning arrangements provided a mechanism for the provision of humanitarian assistance and for various other kinds of support. Particularly in Germany, the Netherlands and Scandinavia, municipalities became an important source of relief and political support. The Council of Europe built on these initiatives to introduce the concept of local democracy embassies, established in Tuzla and in eastern Slavonia.

As well as grass-roots groups, intellectuals and cultural figures (artists, writers, actors) played an important role in the movement. In France, prominent intellectuals became the 'voice' of the movement. In the United States, where there were fewer grass-roots movements, and in Europe, elite campaigning groups were established, such as Action Council for Peace in the Balkans, which were to be very influential. There were also cultural festivals aimed at drawing attention to Sarajevo's secular culture; and a number of writers, film-makers and people from the world of theatre travelled to Sarajevo.

Unlike the peace movement of the 1980s, the movement against the war in Bosnia was rather fragmented. There were some Europe-wide networks, for example the Helsinki Citizens' Assembly, but these could by no means claim to speak for the movement as a whole. Indeed, in political terms the movement was deeply divided and these divisions generated a debate about Bosnia that constituted a social learning process. Although there was an implicit consensus about the role of civil society in providing solidarity and a sort of unarmed protection, there were big differences about what governments and international organizations should be doing and these differences tended to reflect different analyses of the character of the war.

Public pressure led to a series of interventions by the international community: the protection of aid convoys and the establishment of humanitarian corridors, safe havens, a no-fly zone, a tribunal for war crimes committed in the former Yugoslavia, and international administrations for Sarajevo and Mostar. In retrospect, the latter two innovations were to have considerable significance. The Hague tribunals created a momentum for an international criminal court; and the demand for the arrest of war criminals raised the issue of international law enforcement. Likewise, the establishment of international administrations paved the way for the protectorates in Bosnia and Kosovo. Again, the problem of public security in both these cases led to further demands for some form of international policing.

But despite these innovations and despite the continuing negotiation process, the war continued for three and a half years. It was brought to an end through the Dayton Agreement, which some attribute to the NATO air strikes at the end of the war and others to the fact that ethnic cleansing was virtually complete and the Serbs and Croats had, more or less, succeeded in carving out ethnically pure territories. The humanitarian innovations are widely considered to have been a failure. Despite the presence of troops, the Serbs and Croats were still able to dictate the terms of aid delivery. The safe havens of Srebrenica and Zepa fell towards the end of the war. In particular, the massacre of 8000 men and boys in Srebrenica was, at least for the international community, the most humiliating moment of the war.

The failure is attributed to the inadequacy of the mandate and the provision of insufficient troops. Nevertheless, there were successes that suggest the failures had more to do with the difficulty of adapting traditional military concepts than with insufficient resources. Both the British and the Danish demonstrated on occasion that more 'robust' peacekeeping could be effective, even though they were reprimanded by the UN command for their actions. In Zepa, Ukrainian troops refused to hand over local people to the Serbs and in the end were able to negotiate their safe passage.

From Somalia to Kosovo

The war in Bosnia is the context in which to understand the decision of President George Bush Sr to intervene in Somalia. The Bush administration was under pressure to make a stronger commitment to Bosnia and to give substance to the notion of a 'new world order'. It believed that Somalia was an easier case than Bosnia and that intervention in Somalia would relieve the pressure to step up intervention in Bosnia. According to Lawrence Eagleburger, then Secretary of State:

> The fact of the matter is that a thousand people are starving to death every day and that is not going to get better if we don't do something about it, and it is an area where we can affect events. There are other parts of the world where things are equally tragic, but where the cost of trying to change things would be monumental. In my view, Bosnia is one of those.[27]

After the fall of the long-time Somalian dictator, Mohammed Siad Barre, a 'new war' developed in which clan-based warlords established control over territory through displacement and atrocities inflicted by groups of fighters known as *mooryan*, often under the influence of the drug Qat. Between November 1991 and March 1992, some 50,000 people died and 1.5 million became refugees or internally displaced persons (IDPs): some 29 per cent of the pre-war population. Humanitarian NGOs were calling for intervention and drawing the media's attention to the suffering in Somalia. CARE was particularly influential and held regular meetings with the Bush administration. Fred Cuny was calling for armed protection of relief enclaves. The ICRC hired armed guards for the first time in its history. The European Commission was calling for UN convoys as early as August under the influence of European NGOs. A large advertisement in a Dutch newspaper calling for intervention was signed by several European NGOs, including Oxfam. According to Eurostep, an organization representing some twenty European NGOs, there is 'general agreement among many European NGOs that it was not sufficient to send aid without a certain level of military protection to stop piracy'.[28]

A few NGOs opposed the intervention. These included Save the Children, particularly its director, Mark Bowden, and a group of individuals, including Alex de Waal and Rakkiya Omaar, who broke away from Human Rights Watch because they opposed the intervention and formed Africa Rights. They believed that the negotiations carried out by the UN envoy Mohamed Sahnoun were bearing fruit, that the immediate needs for food supply had already been solved, and that a US-led intervention could be the harbinger of a new form of imperialism.[29]

United Nations Security Council Resolution 794, which was passed unanimously on 2 December 1992, was widely considered to break new ground. Even though the resolution mentions, as in 688, the threat to 'international peace and security', it was the first resolution to authorize the use of force, under Chapter VII of the UN Charter, to relieve human suffering. Many states that had opposed 688, particularly in Africa, supported 794. For Kouchner, it was a triumph: 'a fantastic step forward, a new legal base for the international Droit d'Ingérence'.

The headline in *Liberation* the next day was: 'L'humanitaire s'en va t'en guerre'.[30]

The Somali intervention turned out, however, to be a debacle, as a few groups had predicted. The American-led Unified Task Force (UNITAF) succeeded at first in protecting aid convoys and providing secure relief centres, but failed to disarm the militias, disappointing most local Somalis. In May UNITAF was replaced by UNOSOM II (United Nations Operation in Somalia), with an even stronger mandate. However, attacks on Pakistani troops led the American commander Admiral Howe to engage in warfare against the clan faction responsible, led by General Aideed. Despite the use of what many considered to be excessive force, the Americans failed to capture Aideed. On the contrary, Somali militia succeeded in shooting down two American helicopters, killing eighteen American soldiers and wounding seventy-five. The bodies of the American soldiers were paraded publicly in front of international television cameras. Shortly thereafter the Clinton administration took the decision to withdraw from Somalia.

The debacle in Somalia led to the decision to issue Presidential Decision Directive (PDD) 25 in May 1994, which one author has described as a 'Somali corollary to the Vietnam syndrome'.[31] PDD 25 strictly limited American participation in future peacekeeping operations. It was invoked as pressure mounted from NGOs and the media to intervene to stop the horrifying genocide of Tutsis and tolerant Hutus that was taking place in April, May and June 1994 in Rwanda. Between 500,000 and 1 million people were killed in a hundred days. The massacre was orchestrated by the government and the army, and carried out by local officials and government-organized paramilitary groups using machetes and mobilized through 'hate radio', Radio Milles Collines.

There was at the time a small UN force of 1,500 troops, United Nations Assistance Mission to Rwanda (UNAMIR). Despite warnings from the local commander General Dallaire and proposals to seize weapons and create safe havens, the Security Council took the decision to prepare for withdrawal and to scale down the UN force. Later, when it was clear that Dallaire's warnings should have been taken seriously, the Secretary-General proposed an intervention force of 5500; several African forces were prepared to take part but they needed American logistical support, which was not forthcoming. Indeed, the Clinton administration actively mobilized against those governments, NGOs and media who wanted to describe what was happening in Rwanda as 'genocide' for fear that this would oblige it to act under the 1948 Genocide Convention.[32]

At the end of August 1994, a French intervention force was dispatched. But by this time the genocide was over and the Rwandan Patriotic Front had succeeded in part in overthrowing the extremists. The French intervention was suspect because of French support for the previous regime; and all it was able to achieve was to provide safe havens for fleeing Hutus, many of whom were former militiamen engaged in the genocide.

The tragedy and disgrace of Rwanda had a powerful impact on the humanitarian NGOs and on public opinion. The ICRC lost thirteen staff: it was the moment of change of heart towards humanitarian intervention. All the same, the immediate aftermath of the tragedy seems to have led to excessive enthusiasm for interventions; many humanitarian NGOs called for intervention to protect the refugee camps of eastern Zaire, which were run by former Hutu militiamen. Before a Canadian intervention force could be mobilized, however, the camps were overrun by Zairian rebels, and the refugees returned to Rwanda. It was a low point for the humanitarian NGOs. As Mark Bowden of Save the Children, one of the few NGOs to oppose intervention, put it, 'Agencies are competing for dwindling resources, competing for contracts and position and profile in the media. Philosophically, we are bankrupt. "Go and feed them" is always our response'.[33] Only the human rights NGOs took a different tack, calling for the militia to be brought before a war crimes tribunal.

Interestingly enough, at the very moment that Rwanda was being debated the Americans, with UN authorization, undertook a classic humanitarian intervention in Haiti. Operation Restore Democracy was launched in July 1994 to overthrow a brutal military dictatorship that had displaced the democratically elected government. In Clinton's words, the purpose was 'to protect our interests, to stop the brutal atrocities that threaten Haitians, to secure our borders and to preserve stability and democracy on our continent'.[34] Many NGOs were doubtful about intervention by the United States, the dominant power in the region. But it did restore democracy, at least temporarily.

During this period, there were also significant regional interventions – ECOWAS Monitoring and Observation Group (ECOMOG) in Liberia, the Commonwealth of Independent States (mainly Russia) in Tajikistan – although it would probably be misleading, especially in the Russian case, to describe them as humanitarian. An important part of the story is, of course, the wars in Chechnya in 1994–6 and since 1998. Despite the fact that these wars involved widespread violations of human rights, outside involvement was minimal even from the hardiest NGOs: it was here that Fred Cuny met his end. The fact that there was no consideration of humanitarian intervention there has been cited by opponents of intervention as evidence of its selective character. Although NGOs and movements like Soldiers' Mothers and Memorial, and the well-known human rights leader Sergei Kovalev, did try to mobilize international support, none of these groups or individuals advocated international military intervention. The war against the Kurds in Turkey is also often cited as a case of double standards, since even international condemnation is rare.

The case of Kosovo was different. The crisis had been developing throughout the 1990s. From 1991, NGOs and commentators were warning of a likely war in Kosovo. After Milosevic, the Serbian president, removed the autonomy of Kosovo and imposed a form of apartheid on the province, the Kosovar Albanians organized a non-violent resistance movement, including the establishment of parallel institutions, especially in health and education. They called for international intervention and the establishment of an international protectorate. A turning point was the Dayton Agreement, from which the issue of Kosovo was deliberately excluded. Many Kosovars, exhausted by the parallel system, concluded that non-violence was an ineffective strategy for calling international attention to their plight. In 1997 the Kosovo Liberation Army first made its appearance, with the deliberate strategy of using violence to provoke international intervention.[35]

As the conflict intensified in the spring of 1998, Western leaders began to make strong statements about the necessity for action in Kosovo. 'We are not going to stand by and watch the Serb authorities do in Kosovo what they can no longer get away with in Bosnia,' said the US Secretary of State, Madeleine Albright, in March. Similar pronouncements were made by the UN Secretary-General, NATO's Secretary-General and various foreign and defence ministers. However, the method chosen to prevent war was diplomacy backed by the threat of air strikes. American leaders had drawn the (probably wrong) conclusion from Bosnia that the Dayton Agreement succeeded because of air strikes. Many groups inside Kosovo and elsewhere in Europe were calling for the deployment of ground troops to protect civilians from the ethnic cleansing that had already begun. But the Americans were unwilling to commit ground troops until a very late stage in the negotiations. When diplomacy failed, a campaign of air strikes was undertaken. At the same time, ethnic cleansing was dramatically accelerated; over a million Kosovar Albanians, the majority of the population, were expelled from the province, and some 10,000 people were killed. Eventually, Milosevic capitulated; an international protectorate was established in Kosovo and the refugees returned. Bernard Kouchner was chosen to head the UN Mission.

The war over Kosovo deeply divided civil society. Some groups felt the intervention was justified. Some favoured military intervention but criticized the form of intervention: the use of air strikes instead of ground troops, which could have directly protected people. Human Rights Watch, in particular, drew attention to the ways in which NATO bombings may have violated international humanitarian law.[36] For many human rights groups Kosovo was a troubling moment. Many sympathized with the plight of the Kosovars but at the same time found bombing repugnant and an inappropriate way to enforce human rights. This was especially true in Eastern Europe, where bombing has always been regarded as much more unacceptable than in the West. Yet, at the same time, East European human rights groups were uneasy about criticizing the air strikes, both because of sympathy with the Kosovars and because of the legacies of the Cold War. Dimitrina Petrova writes that:

> Human rights defenders feared that whatever they say immediately places them in one of two camps – for or against NATO. And if one is against NATO, one is enemy to democracy, etc. The black and white scheme prevailed and nuances were only

possible if they were about details. Political correctness dictated unholy alliances.[37]

Even an organization like Human Rights Watch was torn by the NATO bombing between those who were strongly in favour and those who felt that bombing had accelerated ethnic cleansing.[38]

Others argued more strongly that 'military humanism', the phrase coined by Noam Chomsky, had become the new justification for American imperialism and the American military industrial complex following the demise of the Soviet threat.[39] This was the predominant view among groups which viewed themselves as peace activists, for example at the Hague Peace Conference, attended by some 8000 activists from all over the world, which took place in May during the bombing. As mentioned above, there were mass demonstrations against the bombing, or against the 'double war', in several countries.

The final intervention of the 1990s was in East Timor. The intervention in East Timor was simply too late, as many civil society groups had earlier foreseen. In reaching agreement with the Indonesian government to hold a referendum on independence in East Timor, the United Nations made the tragic mistake of leaving the Indonesian government to provide security. Subsequently, Western powers may have been too preoccupied with Kosovo as army-supported violence against the population intensified in the spring and summer of 1999. When the East Timorese voted overwhelmingly for independence, militia groups supported by the Indonesian army went on an organized rampage, killing and displacing people from their homes. It was not until the Indonesian government agreed to a United Nations military presence that an Australian-led force was able to restore order, although by then much of the damage had been done. In terms of the evolution of norms of humanitarian intervention, the courageous behaviour of the non-military United Nations mission in East Timor deserves mention. They refused to be evacuated from their headquarters in Dili until local staff, family members and also Timorese who had sought refuge in the UN compound were evacuated with them. This was a notable contrast to the OSCE monitoring mission in Kosovo, which withdrew before the NATO bombing, leaving their local staff behind to be killed.

Part of the story of the 1990s is the way in which political leaders consistently learned the wrong lessons from each intervention, which then contributed to the failures of the next intervention, rather as generals tend to fight the previous war. In particular, international policy seems to have swung from inaction or inadequate action to overwhelming force, especially the use of air strikes, and back again. It seems to have been very difficult to chart a middle course. The safe haven in Iraq was initially successful but was not sustained. The intervention in Bosnia was too weak and it was (probably) wrongly concluded that air strikes had been a crucial factor in the success of the final agreement. The intervention in Somalia was supposed to compensate for the weaknesses of the mandate in Bosnia; however, the US-led force emphasized the use of overwhelming force at the expense of politics. The Somali debacle resulted in the non-intervention in Rwanda, which was probably the most serious failure of the whole period. The need to restore credibility and act forcefully led to the NATO air attacks against Yugoslavia. And the intervention in East Timor was too late.

What can be concluded from this sorry story? Is the notion of humanitarian intervention inherently flawed? Is there no middle ground between inaction and overwhelming force? Or is it still possible to adapt thinking and institutions to fit the new reality? These are the questions that confront the civil society actors concerned with this issue.

The Global Public Debate

As this story indicates, civil society actors took different positions in different conflicts, and opinions evolved throughout the period. Four broad strands of opinion can be identified, although there are overlaps and nuances that are not necessarily captured by these categories. Table 1.2 summarizes the different positions and the actors.

Sovereignist (rejectionist)

Sovereignist is a French term which describes those people or groups who oppose humanitarian intervention either because they support the principle of non-intervention or because they

Table 1.2 *The debate about humanitarian intervention*

Position	Arguments	Civil society	Bosnia	Somalia	Kosovo	Sierra Leone
Sovereignist	Believe in non-interference. Wars for national interest only	Individual politicians, especially on right. Traditional left and nationalist groups	War was a civil war. Should not risk lives of nationals for others in civil war. Should not jeopardize principle of non-intervention	Intervention was human rights imperialism. Should not risk lives for others in civil war	Air strikes were NATO imperialism. Should not prioritize Kosovo over relations with Russia	Intervention is imperialism
Just war	War is justified for humanitarian purposes. Morality is more important than legality	Rhetoric of centre politicians and prominent intellectuals. Civil society groups among victims of large-scale human rights abuses	War was an international war of aggression by Serbia (and Croatia) against Bosnia. Support for Bosnian government including lifting arms embargo and air strikes against Serb positions	Favoured overwhelming force against warring clans, particularly Aideed	Supported air strikes against Yugoslavia	Support for unilateral interventions – Executive Outcomes, ECOMOG, and Britain

Humanitarian peace	Governments cannot be trusted. Humanitarian intervention is a cover for imperialism. Should be civil society intervention	Many humanitarian and peace groups. Human rights groups divided	Opposed military intervention. Favoured negotiation both at governmental level and at grass roots	Opposed military intervention. Supported efforts of UN negotiator, Mohamed Sahnoun, to involve civil society in talks	Against 'double war' – both NATO bombing and Milosevic war against Kosovar Albanians. Supported stronger OSCE presence	Distrust of all military forces. Interventions too one-sided. Favour civil society reconciliation
Human rights enforcement	Civil society needs framework of law. Humanitarian intervention is not war but international law enforcement. Must involve direct protection of civilians and arrest of war criminals	International human rights groups, espe. in Europe and North America. Also some think tanks and commissions	Pressed for safe havens and international criminal tribunal. Wanted more robust military role on the ground in support of these objectives	Favoured military intervention aimed at disarming militias and providing security on the ground, not just delivering aid	Favoured ground intervention to protect Kosovar Albanians based on more robust OSCE presence	Favour more robust UN presence. Greater efforts to protect civilians, arrest criminals and implement disarmament and demobilization

believe that intervention should be carried out only in the national interest. The former are known in the international relations literature as 'pluralists' who believe in a rule-governed society of states in which an important rule is the principle of non-intervention. The principle is considered important because it promotes stability and inhibits powerful states from imposing their hegemony on weak states.[40] The latter are known as 'realists' in the International Relations literature; they believe in a Hobbesian world characterized by international anarchy where states have to act according to the dictates of survival. With the collapse of communism and the spread of democracy in Africa and Latin America, the number of sovereignists is declining. However, they are still to be found among elites in the Third World and the East, particularly in authoritarian states, and on the Western right.

Among intervening countries, an important version of the realist argument is the nationalist argument that nationals are privileged over foreigners. The job of states is to protect their own nationals and not others. Thus, for example, Samuel Huntington wrote in 1992 that 'it is morally unjustifiable and politically indefensible that members of the armed forces should be killed to prevent Somalis from fighting one another'.[41] Similar views were expressed during the Bosnian war, especially among those who understood the war as an endless continuation of ancient rivalries. Richard Goldstone, for example, describes meeting Edward Heath just after being appointed Chief Prosecutor for the Yugoslav and Rwanda tribunals:

> 'Why did you accept such a ridiculous job?' Heath asked me in a friendly tone. I told him that I thought prosecuting war criminals was important, especially given the magnitude of the crimes committed in Bosnia. Heath replied to the effect that if people wished to murder one another, as long as they did not do so in his country, it was not his concern and should not be the concern of the British government. At the time, his opinion startled me. Little did I realise that he was candidly stating what many leading politicians in major Western countries were saying privately – and what many of them believe.[42]

Among Third World and East European nationalist movements, intervention is viewed as imperialism. In Serbia and Iraq, nationalist demonstrations, undoubtedly orchestrated by the governments, were held to oppose Western intervention. Serbian opposition to sanctions and later to the bombing during the Kosovo war seems to have strengthened nationalist feelings and helps to explain the nationalist character of the post-Milosevic regime.

The imperialist argument is also shared by radical anti-globalization groups. These groups oppose the spread of global capitalism and see the state as defending the poor. For them, Chomsky's theory of 'military humanism' is an expression of a view of the United States and NATO as the military arm of global capitalism. They point to the selective character of inter-vention and suggest that so-called humanitarian intervention is undertaken only in places where it suits Western interests and not elsewhere. These groups bring together remnants of the traditional left and a new generation which has not experienced the traumas of communism. Of course, it needs to be stressed that these groups overlap with the humanitarian peace position (see below); they may not be against all forms of intervention.

Just war (supporters)

The most well-known proponent of the just war position is the British Prime Minister Tony Blair, who famously proclaimed that the NATO air strikes over Kosovo represented the first 'war for human rights': 'This is a just war, based not on territo-rial ambitions but values.'[43] The just war position differs from the human rights enforcement position (see below) in that it combines national and humanitarian assumptions. War is between two sides, and the goal of war is to defeat an enemy with minimum casualties on one's own side. Typically, the just war proponents favour air strikes and the use of overwhelming force, although they also favour precision bombing to minimize 'collateral damage', that is, civilian casualties.

Just war proponents tend to place more emphasis on moral-ity and military necessity than on legality. If the cause is just, they favour unilateral intervention, that is to say, intervention without UN Security Council authorization. (According to the UN Charter, all forms of force, except self-defence, are prohib-ited unless authorized by the Security Council.) Although they would insist that wars should be fought according to the 'laws of war', military necessity is considered to override the laws of war in some instances. Moreover, they privilege the lives of nationals. Thus the lives of foreign civilians are sometimes risked in order to save the lives of soldiers.

The Blair position is supported by many intellectuals who took a similar stance during the Bosnian war, especially in France, the United States and Central Europe. They argued that the war in Bosnia was international, initiated by Serbian (and Croatian) aggression against the Bosnian state; they lobbied for military intervention and tended to favour air strikes and lifting the arms embargo on Bosnia to allow for self-defence as a way of minimizing outside casualties. These groups are often the descendants of the Cold War human rights community. Kouchner belongs to this strand of opinion, as do some American intellectuals like Aryeh Neier. In the debate about the Iraq war, the so-called liberal internationalists joined the American neoconservatives in supporting the war.

Another important group that supports the just war position are the direct representatives of the victims. Civil society groups in Kosovo, Rwanda, Haiti or East Timor supported intervention of any kind; it did not matter how or by whom the intervention was carried out nor whether it was approved by the UN Security Council. They wanted protection. The Kosovars, of course, favoured ground troops but they were grateful for the air strikes. In Iraq, the Kurdish political parties supported Western intervention, although opinion in the rest of Iraq was more mixed; the invasion was described as 'liberation/occupation'.

Humanitarian peace (alternatives)

The third strand of opinion is to be found among some humanitarian organizations and among peace groups. These groups share some of the scepticism of the sovereignists. They distrust US-led interventions because they fear a new form of Western imperialism; defending human rights becomes a new 'colonizing enterprise'. They do not believe that governments, whose job is to protect the 'national interest', can act for 'noble purposes'. In addition, some of these groups are pacifist and believe that it is a fundamental contradiction to suppose that human rights can be defended by military means. Where they differ from the sovereignists is in their insistence on civil society intervention. Human rights protection, the delivery of relief, and conflict prevention and resolution, according to this view, are the job of civil society, not governments.

This debate about humanitarian peace versus just war was an important reason for the split in MSF in 1979. Kouchner and his supporters, known as the *légitimiste* tendency, took the view that NGOs lacked the capacity to meet serious humanitarian needs. Their role was symbolic: to draw attention to the plight of victims, to mobilize the media, and to influence governments. The other group, known as the *indépendantiste* tendency, argued that morality should not be confused with politics and that only NGOs were capable of genuinely humanitarian action.[44] As François Jean of MSF put it: 'We were against this principle [of humanitarian intervention] because we felt that it was mainly the right for a strong state to intervene in a weak state . . . we questioned the purity of any state undertaking so-called humanitarian intervention.'[45]

A similar position is taken by peace groups, especially those that took on humanitarian roles, and conflict resolution groups. Groups in Germany and Italy often argued that the Bosnian war was a civil war between different nationalist groups; they opposed any form of military intervention and favoured negotiations both at a political level and at the level of civil society. Many of these groups mobilized humanitarian assistance and undertook local mediation projects. Indeed, the practice of civil society intervention in conflicts greatly increased in the 1990s, not only in the former Yugoslavia but in other regions as well, especially the Transcaucasus and the Middle East. An important aspect of this civil society activity is the links that are made with local groups and the knowledge that is gained about the local situation. The argument is that civil society is better equipped than governments to undertake the actions at the level of society that are needed in the new types of wars.[46]

Human rights enforcement (reformers)

The fourth strand of opinion is to be found among parts of the peace movement, especially those which took up human rights issues like the Helsinki Citizens' Assembly, and large parts of the human rights movement. It distinguishes humanitarian intervention from war. Humanitarian intervention is a method of enforcing international law with respect to human rights and the laws of war where the state has collapsed or where the state itself violates the law. Law enforcement is different from war. It involves minimizing casualties on all sides, direct protection of the victims, and the arrest of war criminals. It scrupulously respects human rights and humanitarian law in implementing its mission. It is more like policing than war, although it may require more robust action than domestic policing. It involves impartiality in the sense that all civilians, whatever their views or ethnic background, need to be protected and, likewise, all war criminals need to be opposed whatever side they are on. But this is not the same as neutrality – a position implied by the sovereignists and the humanitarian peace groups – since one side is almost always more responsible for human rights abuses than the other. The war in Kosovo, justifiable or not, cannot be classified as a humanitarian intervention since it was a war between NATO and Yugoslavia rather than a direct intervention to protect Kosovar Albanians on the ground.

For the human rights enforcement position, legality is very important since the very concept of humanitarian intervention is based on the idea of strengthening international law. In effect, humanitarian intervention is understood as filling the enforcement gap in international law. Those who support this position would accept that, at present, there is a gap on occasion between morality and legality, since the Security Council is dominated by the great powers who can veto humanitarian intervention for reasons of self-interest. They would favour a strengthening of international law to close that gap. A thoughtful expression of this view has been elaborated by the president of the Sierra Leone Bar Association in comparing the legality of the NATO intervention in Kosovo and the ECOMOG intervention in Sierra Leone:

> Regardless of the legality, missions such as NATO's and ECO-MOG's will become the norm rather the exception. The United Nations made a mortal mistake in Rwanda, when it sat back and watched genocide occur. This must never happen again . . . Increasingly, the question will not simply be whether it is legal but whether it is moral. These moral and ethical questions will

increasingly force the international community to accept this exception and formulate better laws to avoid these catastrophes and better protect human rights.[47]

Those who favour human rights enforcement share the views of the humanitarian peace groups about the important role of civil society. But they take the view that civil society, while playing a crucial role in correcting the abuses of the state, can exist only in the framework of the rule of law. This lesson was rudely learned at the outbreak of the Bosnian war, when, in the euphoric aftermath of the 1989 revolutions, it was hoped that citizens could prevent war through mass public action. In the months leading up to the war there were demonstrations and campaigns throughout Bosnia. But the war began when snipers fired on a mass demonstration in Sarajevo, demanding the establishment of an international protectorate. In wars, civil society is the first victim, and the longer the wars continue the more civil society is destroyed.

Humanitarian intervention cannot resolve conflicts. But it can create a secure environment in which civil society can be strengthened and peaceful solutions found. It was this strand of opinion, mainly to be found in Western Europe and inside Bosnia, that in the case of the Bosnian war favoured a new kind of military intervention aimed directly at protecting civilians and creating space for political alternatives. Hence, it was this group that, together with some of the humanitarian NGOs, called for an international protectorate for Bosnia, and later for safe havens, for local protectorates especially in Sarajevo and Mostar, for opening Tuzla airport, and for lifting the siege of Sarajevo. Likewise, it was this group that favoured ground intervention in Kosovo. This position is close to the more muscular versions of human security[48] and the 'responsibility to protect'.

The version of humanitarian intervention favoured by the human rights enforcers occupies the middle ground between inaction (favoured by sovereignist and humanitarian peace proponents) and overwhelming force (favoured by just war proponents). So far, no international military operation easily fits this description of humanitarian intervention. Does this mean that the human rights enforcement position is utopian? Will either the just war position or the humanitarian peace position bring us closer to coping with 'new wars'? It is certainly true that neither the legal system nor the structure and training of military forces is yet adapted to humanitarian intervention. But those who insist on human rights enforcement would argue that this has to be done. The humanitarian peace approach, they would say, can do no more than alleviate suffering. The just war position can have the opposite effect from that intended by engaging in forms of violence that are not so very different from those they are supposed to prevent; there is no such thing as a civilized war any longer, if there ever was.

Intervention in 2000: The Case of Sierra Leone

The war in Sierra Leone began on 23 March 1991, when the Revolutionary United Front (RUF) led by Foday Saybana Sankoh invaded Sierra Leone with a group of dissident Sierra Leoneans, Liberians and mercenaries.[49] The rebels, the RUF, were led by a group of radical student leaders trained in Libya and backed by Charles Taylor of Liberia. According to one view, they were angry about the corrupt character of the patrimonial state and their exclusion from power.[50] They mobilized poor, unemployed, rural young people through a combination of fear, material inducements and the offer of adventure. The methods of the rebels were particularly brutal: the practice of amputation in the areas they conquered is legendary.[51] Some argue that whatever the original motivations of the rebels, the conflict increasingly became a war about 'pillage not politics' and about control of the lucrative diamond trade. The rebels were under the control of Charles Taylor and the war enabled him to gain access to the diamond fields. Diamonds have always played a central role in Sierra Leonean politics, involving a murky mixture of the various warring factions in Lebanon, Israeli 'investors' and American and Russian crime families, not to mention the Antwerp diamond traders. As Smillie, Gberie and Hazleton put it: 'The point of the war may not actually have been to win it but to engage in profitable crime under the cover of warfare.'[52]

Since the war began, around 75,000 people have died and around half the population of 4.5 million has been displaced. All sides recruited children; often they were given drugs, particularly cocaine and marijuana. Terrible atrocities have been committed, including 'amputation of limbs, ears and lips with machetes, decapitation, branding, and the gang rape of women and children.'[53] The first outside intervention occurred in 1993, when Gurkha Security Group, a private security company mainly made up of Nepalese Gurkhas, was hired by the government; it was forced to withdraw after suffering heavy casualties, including the murder of its American commander, Robert Mackenzie. Then in 1995 the private South African company Executive Outcome repelled an RUF attack on Freetown. Indeed, throughout the period a number of private security companies have been present in Sierra Leone.

In 1996, as a result of pressure from civil society, elections were held and were won by Ahmad Tejan Kabbah of the Sierra Leone People's Party; this was followed by the Abidjan peace agreement. However, the following year Kabbah was overthrown in a coup by parts of the Sierra Leonean army led by Major Johnny Paul Koroma. He formed the Armed Forces Revolutionary Council (AFRC) and invited the RUF to join it. Then in February 1998 the AFRC, in turn, was overthrown by the Nigerian-led West African force ECOMOG. Despite a brutal attack on Freetown by the rebels in January 1999, the return of Kabbah paved the way for a peace agreement signed in July 1999. The agreement included a blanket amnesty, as well as important positions in government for the rebels. As the then American ambassador, John Hirsch, put it, 'For the democratic forces, the Lomé negotiations were a bitter and painful reversal from the international ostracism of the RUF almost two years earlier.'[54] The agreement was criticized by Mary Robinson, the UN High Commissioner for Human Rights, and several international NGOs, primarily for the blanket amnesty. In a letter to the UN Security Council dated 19 May 2000, Human Rights Watch requested the setting up of an International Criminal Tribunal for Sierra Leone, as well as confirmation of Mary Robinson's position that the agreement cannot apply to 'crimes of genocide, crimes against humanity, war crimes and other serious violations of international humanitarian law'.

In October 1999 the UN Security Council authorized the establishment of the United Nations Mission in Sierra Leone (UNAMSIL), which replaced the UN Observer Mission set up in 1998. At that time, up to 6,000 troops were authorized. UNAMSIL's mission was to assist the implementation of the agreement and it included an explicit mandate, under Chapter VII of the UN Charter, to 'protect' civilians under 'imminent threat of physical violence'. In February 2000, UNAMSIL's troops were increased to 11,100 and its mandate further extended to include the provision of security at key locations in and near Freetown and at all disarmament sites. Despite the mandate, UNAMSIL was very slow to implement the disarmament and demobilization provisions of the agreement and was considered insufficiently robust in protecting civilians. In May, the RUF attacked UN personnel; a number of troops were killed and some 500 taken hostage.

At this point, the British sent to Sierra Leone some 700 troops, who were well trained and well equipped and given a robust mandate; they helped to protect the capital and to create the conditions for the release of the hostages. The UN troops were also increased to 13,000. In August, eleven British soldiers were also captured by the rebels. Five were released and the remaining six were rescued in September. In the process, the notorious West Side Boys, one of the most brutal rebel groups, were rounded up. British troops later withdrew, but additional reinforcements were announced in October; emphasis was placed on training the army and the police. The Indian and Jordanian contingents also withdrew after the Indian commander, Major-General Vijay Jetley, wrote a secret memorandum to the Security Council accusing Nigerian officials, including the UN special representative and the UNAMSIL deputy commander, of colluding with the rebels. A new ceasefire agreement was signed in November 2000.

Other measures taken by the United Nations included further strengthening of UNAMSIL, the imposition of an arms embargo and a diamond embargo on Liberia (from where rebel diamonds are exported), the introduction of diamond certification, a more robust DDR (disarmament, demobilization and reintegration) programme, the extension of state authority beyond the capital, Freetown, and the establishment of a war crimes tribunal.

The role of civil society

Since 1994 and 1995 a number of civil society peace initiatives have been taken. Most of these initiatives were local but they would not have been possible, at least not on the same scale, without international support. This included support from international donors, like the US and the UK, diaspora groups, international NGOs present in Sierra Leone, and West African networks, particularly links with Nigerian civil society.

In 1996 a coalition of groups including trade unions, journalists, paramount chiefs and well-known academics began to press for elections. Particularly important was the women's movement. Women's groups had always been active in Sierra Leone, in the churches, local communities or Descendants groups (that is, descendants from original slave settlers). These groups were active all over the country and had an enormous mobilizing potential.[55] But it was not until 1994 that they came together to establish the Women's Forum, in order to prepare for the United Nations Women's Conference in Beijing, with international support. This was the moment they became aware of their potential, and some of the women argued for a more political stance, and in particular the need for women to play a role in securing peace; as a result, the Sierra Leonean women's peace movement was formed. It was felt that women were able to play a more active role because they were less threatening to the military government and therefore had more room to act. The first peace demonstration was held in January 1995. It was

> a joyous carnival affair led by a then little-known paediatrician, Fattima Boie-Kamara ... Female professionals, previously known for standing aloof from the concerns of ordinary people, danced through Freetown, linking arms with female soldiers, petty traders, and student nurses, singing choruses. The message of the demonstrators was simple and compelling: 'Try peace to end this senseless war.'[56]

Previous peace groups had been considered rebel sympathizers or 'fifth columnist'. The emergence of a mass women's movement made peace a respectable option. The demand for democratization was seen as a condition for ending the war, and women played a key role in the National Consultative Conference that was held in August 1995 and prepared the way for elections. In the event, there was disappointment that the first peace agreement and the Kabbah government, in practice, excluded women.

After the coup, some 200,000 people left Sierra Leone, many of them civil society activists. Branches of the Women's Forum were established in London and in Conakry, Guinea. Nevertheless, civil society groups were to play an active role in the Lomé Agreement. In addition to the women's movement, new groups were important, like the Inter-religious Council, established in 1997, and the Campaign for Good Governance led by Zainab Bangura. A Nigerian NGO, the Centre for Democracy and Development (CDD), organized a Round Table in parallel with the formal negotiations. According to Zainab Bangura:

> To my mind, more was achieved in the two-day meeting than during the entire process of negotiation. The round-table brought together two extreme positions and unveiled the arrogance of the rebels and the defiance of civil society. The two forces clashed and accepted for the first time that they would have to deal with each other. It was a reality that was needed to cement any agreement that would come out. Both parties were confronted with what was going to happen after the signing of an agreement and the problems to be confronted in the process of peace consolidation. It also helped to bring into the open the bitterness of the war that had caused so much destruction both in terms of human life and property. The RUF needed to see and feel the bitterness of Sierra Leonean society against them to bring them down from the Ivory Tower they had created for themselves at Lomé.[57]

Civil society representatives were appointed to the various commissions responsible for the implementation of Lomé. The capture of UN equipment and peacekeepers was a bitter disappointment. As Zainab Bangura put it: 'When civil society groups realised that true peace was still an illusion, despite all efforts and sacrifices, they became very angry.' The consequence was a massive demonstration in Freetown, demanding the release of the peacekeepers. Some 30,000 people moved towards the house of Foday Sankoh, where his bodyguards opened fire and killed seventeen people. Sankoh ran away, but a few days later he was captured and arrested.

The public debate about intervention

All four global civil society positions can be identified in relation to the debate about intervention in Sierra Leone.

The *sovereignist* position is rather limited, put forward primarily by President Charles Taylor of Liberia and President Blaise Campaore of Burkina Faso. Both are authoritarian leaders supporting the rebels and engaged in the illegal diamond trade.

The dominant opinion among civil society groups inside Sierra Leone lies somewhere between *just war* and *human rights enforcement*. Civil society groups inside Sierra Leone were strongly supportive of effective outside intervention, whether or not it was authorized by the United Nations. Thus they supported Executive Outcomes, ECOMOG, the latest British intervention and, despite initial disappointment, they generally support UNAMSIL as well. When the British arrived, the main reaction of Sierra Leonean civil society, according to Kyode Fayeme of CDD, was 'thank god'.[58] The failure of the two peace agreements had left civil society activists disillusioned with the possibility of a negotiated peace, while the weakness and corruption of the government underlined the necessity for outside intervention. In an e-mail communication of 24 January 2001, Zainab Bangura explained:

> The only language the RUF understands is violence. For there to be peace, the military capability of the RUF has to be reduced. This can be only done by force. This is a fact that every Sierra Leonean with the exception of the government understands. And the only people who have ever successfully subdued the RUF are the Executive Outcomes and the ECOMOG. This is why Sierra Leoneans have very fond memories of the two forces and always want them to stay ... On the issue of neo-colonialism over 90 per cent of Sierra Leoneans believe and know that our predicament is due to mismanagement, corruption, and bad governance. The people responsible are still running the country. So there is big disdain, hatred and bitterness for the ruling class. Most people would like to see the bulk of the institutions of government run by expatriates. This tells you how despondent they are with their own people.

In other words, civil society groups inside Sierra Leone want order restored and see the rebels as the main problem. Of course, they would prefer an intervention that minimizes casualties and prioritizes the protection of civilians, just as the Kosovar Albanians would have preferred ground intervention to air strikes, but they prefer any kind of intervention to none.

Outside Sierra Leone, views are more mixed. Ambrose Ganda, who runs the influential website Focus on Sierra Leone,[59] puts forward an argument that is closer to the *humanitarian peace* position. Ganda argues that the intervention is too one-sided; basically it is propping up a corrupt government – a 'bunch of discredited, crooked and obnoxious politicians'. In theory, it should be possible to have a genuine humanitarian intervention that is non-partisan and even-handed and under UN auspices. However, in practice it is difficult to conceive of genuinely disinterested outside intervention. The UN is dominated by the great powers, which have little interest in Africa; moreover, the mainly Nigerian UN peacekeepers at present in Sierra Leone, according to Ganda, are interested only in diamonds. Ganda thinks that the British ought to have put their forces under UN command and to have helped to enhance the legitimacy and effectiveness of the UN forces. Instead, they are retraining an army which had earlier been involved in coups and repression. What is needed, according to Ganda, is grassroots reconciliation on a broad scale and not elections, since 'politicians prey on the prejudices and fears of the electorate to retain or gain power'.

A similar view is expressed by Christopher Clapham, an Africanist at the University of Lancaster. According to Clapham, the Lomé Agreement of 1999

> ostensibly established a coalition between an ineffectual elected government and a ruthless armed opposition with a record of reneging on agreements. It is open to the UN to send real fighting forces into situations like Sierra Leone, to kill or be killed, if the states concerned would allow it. That would be a very hazardous enterprise and unlikely to lead to the reconstruction of Sierra Leone. But at least the UN would have some idea of what it was supposed to be doing. Peacekeeping in recent conflicts is a farce, fuelled by wishful thinking. We'd be better off without it . . . No matter how tragic the loss of life, and how appalling the abuse of rights, the UN and its leading states must recognise the limitations on their capacities and come to terms

with a world they cannot control. They must resist the temptation to send peacekeepers into situations where they add to the number of victims of the UN's naivety and over-ambition.[60]

Clapham argues that both intervention and efforts at negotiation have failed. The only alternative is a massive internal civil society effort at reconciliation.[61]

The final position, *human rights enforcement*, can be found among international and Nigerian NGOs. Throughout 2000, human rights groups like Human Rights Watch, Amnesty International, and Friends of Sierra Leone (a group made up of former Peace Corps volunteers in Sierra Leone) were lobbying for a more forceful UN presence. They pressed for more robust protection of civilians, for the prosecution of war crimes, and for the control of diamonds. They favoured a regional approach towards negotiation. Friends of Sierra Leone[62] organized a US congressional hearing in September for child amputees. The British NGO Global Witness was also important in promoting a diamond certification process.

Nigeria dominates ECOMOG, and Nigerian NGOs faced real dilemmas about its role. The Nigerian dictator, General Abacha, was using ECOMOG to serve his own ambition of becoming a regional hegemon. This was costing some $1 million a day. Moreover, by using humanitarian arguments he was able to shore up his own position. At the same time, there was much sympathy for the plight of the Sierra Leoneans. As Kyode Fayeme of CDD put it, 'The internal project of dislodging the military from power conflicted with the pan-African ideal of helping Africans in need which all Africans imbibe from birth.'[63] A public debate after the death of Abacha and the transition to democracy led to the withdrawal of ECOMOG and the establishment of UNAMSIL, to which the Nigerians were the main contributors.

Thus the human rights enforcement position basically entails the view that outsiders do need to provide security in Sierra Leone if the project of civil society reconciliation is to be achieved. In the aftermath of the interventions of 2000, the war was finally ended. There has been a serious DDR programme, as well as other measures designed to bring security and reconciliation. Nevertheless, many of the conditions that led to war still persist, especially the exclusion of poor young people, a weak and corrupt government and regional instability. Civil society is weaker than before the war because so many activists were killed or left the country.

Conclusion

What is striking about the decade of the 1990s was the emergence of what might be called a global humanitarian regime. It involves changing norms: a growing consensus about respect for human rights, a strengthening of international law (the International Criminal Court, international protectorates, land mines convention, universal jurisdiction for grave human rights violations, and so on), a growing readiness by governments to commit resources (money and troops) to humanitarian purposes, and above all a significant growth of global civil society groups who focus on the issue of humanitarian intervention in various ways.

The role of global civil society has been crucial in underpinning this global humanitarian regime. During the 1990s, international NGOs, think tanks and commissions concerned with conflict prevention, management and resolution proliferated. Many of these groups were actively engaged on the ground in conflict zones. Equally, if not more, important was the emergence of local grass-roots groups, as in Bosnia and Sierra Leone, which have seen the advantage of making transnational links or developing networks as a way of protecting local civic space, as a source of technical and financial assistance, and as a way of transmitting local knowledge, proposals and ideas to global decision-makers. Global civil society has provided a direct form of protection for civilians in conflict zones, with or without the support of outside governments, and has generated a global public debate about whether, when and how humanitarian intervention should be undertaken.

Of the four positions outlined in this chapter, three (just war, humanitarian peace, and human rights enforcement) favour humanitarian intervention, although they differ about what this means. For the just war position it can mean war; for the humanitarian peace position it means civil society intervention; and for the human rights enforcement position it means a combination of civil society intervention and a new form of international policing. Few of the conflicts of the 1990s have been resolved. Indeed, one of the characteristics of 'new wars' is that pre-conflict and post-conflict phases increasingly resemble each other. Agreements stabilize the violence but tend not to provide solutions. Moreover, the 'new wars' have a tendency to spread through criminal networks, refugees, and the virus of exclusivist ideologies. The risk is that the just war and humanitarian peace positions could end up prolonging these wars, perhaps indefinitely. Air strikes and overwhelming force tend to reinforce particularist views of the world and can contribute to polarization and destabilization while giving the impression of action. Humanitarian peace may alleviate hunger and even sometimes protect people, but, by being ineffective, too even-handed, and sometimes vulnerable, there is a risk of discrediting the non-violent civil society position.

For human rights enforcement, the third option, to work, there needs to be a much more substantial commitment than displayed hitherto: a commitment that goes beyond rhetoric. In part it is a commitment to resources. Humanitarian intervention perhaps needs to be reconceptualized as international presence in conflict-prone areas, a presence that represents a continuum from civil society actors to international agencies up to and including international peacekeeping troops on a much larger scale than seen so far. In part it means a change in outlook, especially the training, equipment, principles and tactics of peacekeeping troops. But above all it involves a genuine belief in the equality of all human beings; and this entails a readiness to risk the lives of peacekeeping troops to save the lives of others where this is necessary. It should be stressed that I am not talking about full-scale war, and the risks are therefore less than in a conventional ground war; nevertheless, they exist. Neither the just war position nor the humanitarian peace position is ready to risk soldiers' lives. The former privileges the lives of soldiers; the latter is willing to risk the lives of human rights activists but opposes the use of soldiers. Even in the most well-ordered societies, police take risks to maintain the security of ordinary citizens. The human rights enforcement position would require the same sort of commitment at an international level.

The trend towards global humanitarianism is, of course, reversible. The fourth position – the rejectionist sovereignist position – seemed to be a minority view during the 1990s. However, since 2000, the new Bush administration in the US is much closer to a sovereignist position than the previous administration; and the spread of nationalist and fundamentalist political movements shows no sign of abating. The War on Terror in places like Iraq and Afghanistan has exacerbated 'new war' tendencies and reduced humanitarian space. An equally plausible scenario is one in which global civil society finds itself increasingly embattled both on the ground in conflict zones and in the global debate.

2
American Power: From Compellance to Cosmopolitanism?

'American democracy requires the repression of democracy in the rest of the world.' So spoke an Asian human rights activist in a democracy seminar in Krakow. I pondered this sentence when I read it in an op-ed article last summer.[1] On the face of it, it seemed so paradoxical. After all, America is the 'Crusader State'; a state based on an idea rather than a national identity, and that idea is democracy. Moreover, it is a state committed not only to preserving the idea within America but extending it to the rest of the world.[2] And yet, when I thought about it, the sentence did express what appears to the rest of the world to be the introverted nature of current American foreign policy. Seen from the outside, the war on terrorism seems to be less about defeating terrorism than a performance staged to meet the requirements of American democracy. What matters is the appearance, the spectacle, not what happens on the ground except in so far as what happens on the ground seeps through into the performance.

In all the discussions, especially in Europe, about the new American empire, this aspect seems to be missing – the difference between appearance and reality, the mimetic character of American foreign policy. When Robert Kagan talks about American power and European weakness, or when the former French foreign minister Hubert Védrine refers to *hyperpuissance*, they assume that billions of dollars spent on defence, or numbers of weapons or men under arms, can be translated into power.[3] Power means the ability to influence others, to control events elsewhere, to impose our will on others, what Thomas Schelling called 'compellance'.[4] But, in practice, American power is much less effective than is generally assumed, at least on its own. If America were truly an empire, surely it would be able to extend democracy to other regions, to impose its system on the rest of the world? The United States has the capability to be immensely destructive, but much less capability to do 'compellance'. From the point of view of American policy-makers, however, this may not matter. The policy they pursue may be rational in terms of American domestic concerns, in attempting to dominate the American political landscape, in winning or nearly winning elections.

My main argument is that there is a mismatch between American domestic concerns, how the world is perceived inside America, and the reality in the rest of the world. Or to put it another way, American political culture and institutions were shaped by the experiences of the Second World War and the Cold War. The ideology of that period continues to exert a powerful influence on American perceptions and American foreign policy, and yet it is badly suited to the changed world which we inhabit. The American foreign policy-makers continue to stage a drama drawn from the past, even though the enemies and the technologies have changed. And they will continue to do so, as long as this performance satisfies the American public, whatever the consequences for the rest of the world – unless reality begins to hit home, as it did briefly (and intensely) on September 11.

In developing the argument, I start by describing what has changed, why traditional approaches no longer work; in particular I emphasize the changed meaning of sovereignty in the context of globalization and the changed functions of military force primarily as a consequence of increased destructiveness. I then set out four different policy approaches to the current conjecture based on different assumptions about the meaning of sovereignty and the nature of military power, and I argue that America's ability to do 'compellance' can only be restored within a multilateral framework, underpinned by humanitarian norms. In the final section, I speculate on the ways in which reality might impinge on American policy-makers; in particular, the ways in which the need, at the least, to contain terrorism might propel a changed agenda.

The Changing Global Context

A decade ago, a number of scholars were predicting American decline. The United States, as the world hegemon, was becoming overstretched in the same way that led earlier empires to decline under the burden of military power. Just as Britain was overtaken by the United States in the mid-twentieth century, so, it was predicted, Japan and Western Europe would lead in the next phase of capitalism.[5] Yet today no one talks about the decline of America. Rather, the predominant debate both in scholarly and political circles concerns unipolarity and whether this is conducive to stability or whether is it dangerous. So what happened in between? Was it just the collapse of the Soviet empire, the only challenger to the United States? Or is there some deeper explanation?

It is worth revisiting the arguments of those who predicted America's decline because of their arguments about the relationship between phases of capitalism and security frameworks.[6] They argued that different phases of capitalist growth were ushered in by war, which determined the shape of the regulatory framework. Thus the Napoleonic wars led to the first phase of industrialization, underpinned by the Concert of Europe and later the inter-imperial order, together with Britain's financial hegemony. Then came two world wars and a new phase of industrialization, characterized by mass production and mass consumption and known as Fordism. Global economic growth based on the Fordist model was underpinned by the Cold War order and the hegemonic role of the United States in the non-communist world.

What was happening in the 1970s and 1980s was the decline of Fordism; the saturation of the markets for cars; the rising oil price; the boredom of workers with the routines of mass production. Declining international competitiveness and the growing cost of overseas defence and foreign economic and military assistance led many people to conclude that the American era was coming to an end. Japan and Western Europe, it was argued, less burdened by military spending and other overseas commitments, would take the lead in the new phase of capitalist technology, based on information technology.

In fact, the favourable environment generated in the 1990s in the United States as a consequence of deregulation and the investment boom has given America the leading edge in the so-called new economy. But it would be wrong to conclude that this explains the new role of the United States. I believe that we are still in a transition phase and that the outcome of the 'war on terror' will determine the future regulatory framework of the new economy. The situation at the beginning of the twenty-first century can be compared with the early 1930s. In Kindleberger's classic book on the Depression, he argued that the huge productivity increases resulting from the introduction of mass production were not matched by changes in the structure of demand, and he explained this mismatch in terms of the continued dominance of Britain and the pound sterling.[7] It was not until after the Second World War that a global institutional framework was established for the 'golden age' of Fordist economic growth. (It was not necessarily the best institutional framework, but it worked.) Today, as in the 1920s, dramatic increases in productivity brought about by computers and by new communication technologies have not been matched by corresponding shifts in the pattern of global demand. As in the 1920s, the boom of the 1990s, it can be argued, was a false boom brought about by overexpectation, by excitement about the promise of the new technology.[8]

The problem today is how to construct the institutional framework that can guarantee the spread of the new economy, and that can lead to a new golden age. Unlike the 1930s, this is not about whether hegemony passes from the Unites States to another state or groups of states; rather it is about the character of the new institutional framework. As long as American foreign policy-making remains embedded in the Cold War framework, it can be argued, this will provide a constraint on future economic development and the decline thesis could still turn out to be true. In other words, the old Cold War model of hegemony is declining and, at this moment, we face a choice about the appropriate model for the future. America will continue to be dominant in any future model because of its size and wealth but differently from in the past. In particular, this new phase of capitalist development has certain important differences in comparison with Fordism, and any new institutional framework would have to take these differences into account.

The changed meaning of sovereignty

The first difference has to do with the changed meaning of sovereignty. Fordism was associated with big government, with high levels of welfare and military spending, and with the growth of the public sector. The Cold War framework allowed for the liberalization of international trade and capital and for a great extension of state intervention at home. The new economy is associated with globalization, by which I mean the increasing interconnectedness of economies, polities and societies, and with the withdrawal of the state from a range of activities as a consequence of liberalization and privatization. Interconnectedness, as those who write about globalization point out, is an uneven process involving homogeneity and diversity, integration and fragmentation, as well as decentralization and individuation.[9]

I agree with those who argue that globalization does not mean the demise of the state but rather its transformation. However, the direction of transformation is as yet unclear. The factors which shape that transformation include:

- The difficulty of sustaining closed societies or spheres of influence. In a sense the 1989 revolutions can be explained in these terms. The Soviet Union could not maintain control over Central Europe in the face of the growing interpenetration of societies as a consequence of increases in travel and communication. Both liberalization of trade and the increasingly transnational character of civil society make it difficult for traditional authoritarian leaders to insulate their societies from the rest of the world. This is why there are only a handful of apparently stable authoritarian regimes in the world today.
- The growing importance of new layers of political institutions – global, regional and local. The growing interconnectedness of political institutions – the growth of treaties and international agreements – and the growing

complexity of decision-making in the new economy have greatly increased the number of political decision points. These new institutions are in the process of generating new overlapping and sometimes contradictory loyalties – multiple 'communities of fate', as David Held puts it.[10]

• Growing awareness of and growing resistance to the influence of events that take place far away. With the advent of the so-called new media, new imagined communities are displacing traditional patriotism. On the one hand, an emerging human consciousness has provided a basis for the new human rights regime and the popular reactions to massive human rights violations or to genocide. On the other hand, the construction of transnational networks has stimulated new or revived ethnic and religious identities that cross boundaries.

Essentially, these factors imply a move away from absolute control of territory and from geopolitics, that is to say, the control of foreign territory in the national interest. Sovereignty is increasingly conditional – dependent on both domestic consent and international respect. In traditional authoritarian states, the impact of globalization may result in state 'failure' or 'weakness'. In other states, it may mean greater insertion within a multilateral framework of global governance. Both the notion of humanitarian intervention, the idea that humanitarian concerns override the norm of non-intervention that gained ground during the 1990s, and 'new wars' based on identity politics, which aim to establish new absolutist exclusive statelets, can be viewed as differing responses to the current global conjuncture.

The changed functions of military forces

The second difference has to do with the decline of military power; that is to say the declining ability of states to use military force for 'compellance'. The growing destructiveness of all weapons means that superior military technology rarely confers a decisive advantage in conflicts between armed opponents. Moreover, it is not just weapons of mass destruction that can inflict mass destruction; the attacks of September 11 were equivalent to a small nuclear weapon. Nowadays, it is extremely difficult to control territory militarily and to win an outright military victory.

This proposition, I believe, was already becoming true at the end of the Second World War. Schelling's argument about 'compellance' derived from the advent of nuclear weapons; the question he asked was whether military force loses its utility in a world of mutual vulnerability, where nuclear weapons can inflict mass destruction. Nuclear weapons, it can be argued, became emblematic of the destructive nature of war. The allies did win a decisive victory in the Second World War, but only after 70 million people had died. The success of deterrence in the post-war period, it can be argued, was less due to nuclear weapons per se than to the unthinkability of another war on the scale of the Second World War. Indeed, the Soviet Union did not have a separate concept for deterrence; rather their concepts of *ustrashenie* (intimidation) or *sderzhivanie* (restraining or holding back) referred to the possibility of war in general.[11] It can be argued that these concepts, both deterrence and the Soviet equivalents, were ways of keeping alive the memory of what happened in the Second World War.

In the Second World War, platforms (particularly tanks and aircraft, but also submarines), using internal combustion engines and fuelled by oil, broke through the stalemate of the First World War, where the use of artillery and machine guns on both sides had prevented any territorial advances. In contrast to the First, the Second World War was a war of offence and of manoeuvre. With developments in information technology and, indeed, improvements in the destructiveness and accuracy of all types of weapons, including small arms, artillery and missiles, however, the platforms that were typical of the Fordist era have become increasingly vulnerable as well. The Iran–Iraq war of the 1980s was much more like the First than the Second World War.

It is argued that the one area where superior military technology conveys an advantage is in the air. The Americans do have the capacity to destroy or evade all known air defences. Through the use of precision guided munitions (PGMs) and unmanned aerial vehicles (UAVs), they can destroy targets from a long distance away with a high degree of accuracy, as we have seen in all recent wars fought by the United States.

But this is not the same as controlling territory or achieving outright military victory. In the Gulf War, the United States and its allies did succeed in liberating Kuwait with a massive deployment of force; if undertaken today, it would occupy some 80 per cent of American military manpower.[12] In Yugoslavia, the air attacks could not prevent the acceleration of ethnic cleansing in Kosovo; as Wesley Clark, then Supreme Allied Commander Europe, put it at the time, 'air power alone cannot stop paramilitary murder on the ground'.[13] One of the problems was that it was very difficult to lure Serb forces into the open where they could be attacked from the air, as was done in the Gulf War. In the end, Milosevic capitulated, Kosovo was liberated and the refugees returned home, but the experience left a legacy of hatred within Kosovo and undoubtedly contributed to the persistence of embittered anti-Western nationalism in Serbia today.[14] In the case of Afghanistan, the American effort succeeded in toppling the Taliban, with the help of the Northern Alliance and, at a crucial moment, some of the Pashtun warlords. In the critical battle for Mazar-i-Sharif, Taliban forces were stranded in the open, and altogether in the course of the war, thousands of Taliban troops were killed from the air. But the war effort did not succeed in capturing Osama Bin Laden and many Al Qaeda leaders and it has not succeeded in stabilizing Afghanistan.

Military commentators suggest that reluctance to use troops on the ground is a consequence of the risk averseness of American leaders. In the case of Afghanistan, in particular, it is argued that had more American troops been committed to the battle for Tora Bora (December 2002) or later to Operation Anaconda (an operation in March 2002 in the Shah-e-Kot valley where Al Qaeda operatives were hiding), Osama Bin Laden would not have got away, even though many more Americans might have died.[15] But it is not at all clear whether ground forces could be any more effective. Ground superiority is much harder to achieve than air superiority. Would the Americans have been more efficient than the Afghan fighters in Tora Bora? The Russians and the Israelis, for example, are not casualty averse. The Russians were losing two to three Russian soldiers a day in Chechnya but there is still sporadic violence. They have been immensely destructive; Grozny is reduced to rubble; there has been massive population displacement. But they have not brought stability to the region. Unlike the Russians, the Israelis are better trained, equipped and paid and claim to be operating within the laws of war and trying to avoid civilian casualties. Yet they cannot defeat the intifada and stabilize Palestine. In the war in Lebanon in the summer of 2006, air strikes failed to achieve any of the Israeli goals. The captured Israeli soldiers, the ostensible *casus belli*, have not, at the time of writing, been released. Although Israel claimed to be destroying Hezbollah infrastructure, Hezbollah was still able to fire a volley of rockets into northern Israel when a ceasefire was agreed.

The war in Iraq validates these points. With the help of accurately targeted air power, the Coalition forces were able to topple the Iraqi regime at a speed unprecedented in history. The United States had a huge information advantage; it was able to process information received both from satellite pictures and from reports from the ground so that, at any one moment, the wireless internet system could show the deployment of troops with enemy forces in red and friendly forces in blue. Known as Force XXI Battle Command, Brigade and Below, it was installed on nearly every vehicle. This allowed red forces to be directly destroyed from the air; no one knows the extent of the military casualties – those that were not killed took off their uniforms and ran away. But toppling the regime is not the same as occupying the country, as has become painfully apparent. To some extent, the problem can be attributed to inadequate troop levels and unwillingness to risk casualties.[16] But as in Chechnya, Palestine and Afghanistan, the spread of accurate and destructive light weapons has allowed for much more effective unconventional warfare and has resulted in daily attacks against American forces, Iraqis who collaborate with the Americans forces and also foreign diplomats. It has also allowed the insurgency to transmogrify into a sectarian 'new war'. It has also greatly complicated reconstruction efforts, undermining the promise of oil revenues, and greatly increasing the cost of occupation – both financial and in terms of casualties. As of September 2006, nearly 3,000 American soldiers had been killed; only a sixth of these died during the invasion.

To argue that military compellance is nowadays very difficult against an armed opponent is not to say that military forces have no rational functions. Rather, the classic function of capturing territory militarily reached its end point in the Fordist era. First of all, military forces can be used against civilian populations. This is the typical strategy of what I call 'new wars', where a combination of state and non-state actors try to gain political control over territory by killing or expelling dissenters or those of a different religion or ethnicity. In general, these are wars fought in the name of exclusive identities – religion or ethnicity. The goal is to sow 'fear and hatred' so that the local population supports the project of an exclusive ethnic or religious state. Battles between armed opponents are very rare; almost all violence is inflicted on civilians. Terrorist attacks on symbolic targets like the centre of global capitalism (the World Trade Center towers) or a place of secular entertainment (the Sari nightclub) have similar goals – they spread fear and insecurity, they polarize society, and they convey a dramatic message about modernity.

Secondly, military forces still represent a symbol of the nation, especially among current and former superpowers like the United States, Russia or Britain. Modern state-building was so bound up with war and the development of modern military forces that our idea of stateness is inextricably linked to military rituals, uniforms, and even war. Hence the deployment of military forces serves important domestic political functions, helping to instil a sense of pride and loyalty, and underscoring domestic cohesion. It is commonplace, nowadays, to argue that some military adventure, for example current Russian threats against Georgia, are best explained in terms of forthcoming elections. Just as Bush has widespread support for the war on terror, so Putin used the second Chechen war to gain power.

Thirdly, there is a role for military forces in containment, especially in 'new wars'. It may not be possible to win outright victory, but the implication of equal destructiveness is that the advantage passes to the defender. Thus it is possible to envisage defensive non-escalatory military operations designed to defend civilians where the new warriors threaten them. These operations cannot win or even stop wars, but they can reduce fear and insecurity and create a breathing space where political solutions can be discussed. Essentially, this was, for all its flaws and mistakes, the British strategy in Northern Ireland, and also, more recently, in Sierra Leone. Techniques like safe havens and humanitarian corridors, pioneered in Bosnia but not effectively carried out, could be conceived as part of a strategy of containment. To be effective, such a strategy does require risking casualties and this is one reason why the strategy failed in Bosnia, and indeed in Somalia. But it does not require the same level of risk as, for example, in the case of offensive war. At present, such risks are borne by human rights activists and journalists, but rarely soldiers. Thus, in Afghanistan, more foreign journalists were killed than Americans in combat (although more Americans were killed if you include those killed by friendly fire).

Alternative Visions of American Power

Assumptions about sovereignty and about military power are the axes which define different visions of America's role in the world. The distinction between idealists and realists can be explained in terms of conceptions of sovereignty. The realists hold to a traditional conception of sovereignty. For them, international relations consist of sovereign units each pursuing their individual self-interest; what happens inside these sovereign units is irrelevant. The job of the state is to protect the state from external enemies; tyrants only matter if they are also potential aggressors. The idealists, on the other hand, hold that sovereignty is conditional and that there are values and norms, for example human rights, which override the claims to sovereignty.

The distinction I make between unilateralists and multilateralists applies primarily to the use of military forces. Unilateralists share a belief in the efficacy of military power. By and large, those who favour multilateral approaches start from the assumption that relations among states can no longer be settled by military force. It is possible to be unilateralist in the military field and multilateralist as regards the economy. Unilateralists tend to favour a liberal world economy, especially free trade and capital movements, but they reserve the right to behave unilaterally sometimes, as, for example, in the case of steel tariffs.

In what follows, I describe four different visions of America's role in the world based on different assumptions about sovereignty and military power, as shown in table 2.1.

Table 2.1 *Different visions of America's role in the world*

	Idealist	Realist
Unilateralist	Spectacle war	Neo-realists and anti-imperialists
Multilateralist	Cosmopolitans	Cooperative security

Spectacle War

The first vision is that of the Bush administration, which I call 'spectacle war'.[17] By 'spectacle war' I mean the kind of long-distance high-technology air war described in the previous section. I call this type of war a 'spectacle' to emphasize its imaginary nature from the point of Americans. These wars do not risk American casualties and, indeed, do not even require additional taxes; American citizens merely have to watch the war on television and applaud. James Der Derian uses the term 'virtuous war' in order to combine both the virtual character of the war and the notion of virtue, the idea that the war is being fought in a noble cause;[18] 'Virtuous war relies on virtual simulation, media manipulation, global surveillance and net-worked warfare to deter and if need be to destroy potential enemies. It draws on just war doctrine (when possible) and holy war doctrine (when necessary).'[19]

The origins of 'spectacle war' can be traced back to the Cold War framework. During the Cold War, deterrence had a similar imaginary form.[20] Throughout the period of the Cold War, both sides behaved as though they were at war, with military build-ups, technological competition, espionage and counter-espionage, war games and exercises. This activity was an important way to remind people of the Second World War and, on the American side, to sustain a belief in the American mission to defend the world against evil through the use of superior technology. Technological developments responded to what planners imagined the Soviet Union might acquire – the so-called worst case scenario. This introverted planning, as I have argued above and elsewhere, meant that American and Soviet technological change was better explained as though they were both arming against a phantom German military machine that continued to evolve in the planners' imaginations, than against each other.[21] As I outlined in the Introduction above, air power was always central to the American conception of deterrence and this derived from the wartime experience of strategic bombing. Intercontinental missiles developed in the 1950s and 1960s were envisaged as an extension of strategic air power. The Russians never had a separate air arm and did not engage in strategic bombing in the Second World War; instead, they regarded missiles as an extension of artillery.

The advent of information technologies generated a debate about the future direction of military strategy in the 1970s and 1980s. The so-called military reform school argued that the platforms of the Fordist era were now as vulnerable as people were in the First World War because of the use of precision guided munitions (PGMs), and that the advantage had shifted to the defence. High attrition rates in the Vietnam and Middle East wars as a result of the use of hand-held missiles seemed to confirm that argument. The advocates of traditional American strategy argued that the offensive manoeuvres of the Second World War were even more important since the use of area destruction munitions could swamp defensive forces, and missiles and unmanned aerial vehicles (now known as UAVs) could replace vulnerable manned aircraft. The consequence was the AirLand Battle strategy of the 1980s, with its centrepiece, 'deep strike', to be carried out by the then new Tomahawk cruise missiles, at that time armed with nuclear warheads.

During the 1990s, this thinking was taken a stage further with the Revolution in Military Affairs (RMA). For RMA enthusiasts, the advent of information technology is as important as the discoveries of the stirrup or the internal combustion engine were in revolutionizing warfare. RMA is spectacle war; it is war carried out at long distance using computers and new communications technologies. The cruise missile, in particular, is the 'paradigmatic' weapon of the RMA.[22] After the end of the Cold War, US military spending declined by one-third, but this mainly affected personnel. Military research and development (R&D) declined by much less than military spending as a whole, and this allowed for the development both of follow-ons to traditional Cold War platforms and the new technologies associated with the RMA. An important aspect of the new technologies is the improvement in virtual war gaming, which further underscores the imaginary nature of spectacle war. Increasingly, the US Defense Department has recruited Hollywood producers to help invent future worst-case scenarios, giving rise to what James Der Derian describes as MIME-NET, the military-industrial-media-entertainment network.[23] One of the most quoted remarks of the Iraq war was that of General William Wallace, Commander of the army's V Corps, in charge of all US army units in Iraq, that 'the enemy we're fighting is a bit different from the one we war-gamed against'.[24]

For the Bush administration, the term 'defence transformation' has come to supplant RMA as the new jargon. As one enthusiast for defence transformation has put it:

> However jerky the transmission belt, the qualities of the modern American economy – its adventurousness, spontaneity and willingness to share information – eventually reach the American military. Just as the teenager who grew up tinkering with automobile engines helped to make the motorized armies of World War II work, so do the sergeants accustomed to playing video games, surfing web pages, and creating spreadsheets make the information-age military of today effective.[25]

Donald Rumsfeld claims that defence transformation 'is about more than building new high-tech weapons – although that is certainly part of it. It is also about new ways of thinking and new ways of fighting'.[26]

Yet it is hard to escape the conclusion that information technology is being grafted on to traditional assumptions about the ways in which military forces should be used, and to traditional institutional defence structures. The methods have not changed much since the Second World War.[27] They involve a combination of aerial bombardment at long distance and rapid offensive manoeuvres, despite the changed names every decade – AirLand Battle, Revolution in Military Affairs, and now Defence Transformation. The very use of video gaming feeds in the assumptions of the gamers who have been schooled in the Cold War framework. September 11 allowed President Bush to ask for a big increase in defence spending. Defence spending had already begun to increase again in 1998 as the new expensive systems developed during the 1990s came to fruition. During his election campaign, Bush had suggested that it might be possible to skip a generation of weapons systems to save money and focus on the cutting edge technologies like PGMs and UAVs (both of which were in short supply in Afghanistan). In fact the 2003 budget was sufficient to accommodate everything – the F22 fighter, for example, which replaced the F15, which already enjoyed air superiority over any known enemy.[28] The expensive programme for National Missile Defence was also to go ahead. It was unlikely to work but the point was rather to underscore the vision of American defence; to provide the appearance of defence against incoming missiles and, therefore, a psychological insurance for unilateral military action.

'Spectacle war' is also linked to a powerful moral crusade. There was always an idealist strain in American Cold War thinking. Bush's Axis of Evil echoes Ronald Reagan's Evil Empire. The Bushites believe or appear to believe that America is a cause not a nation, with a mission to convert the rest of the world to the American dream and to rid the world of terrorists and tyrants. For them, sovereignty is conditional for other states, but unconditional for the United States, because the United States represents 'good'. Hence the United States can act unilaterally; it can reject treaties like the Climate Change Protocol, the Land Mines Convention, the Biological Weapons Convention and, above all, the International Criminal Court, because America is right; but others do not have the same option. This view was expressed by Assistant Secretary of State, Richard Haas:

> What you are seeing in this administration is the emergence of a new principle or body of ideas . . . about what you might call the limits of sovereignty. Sovereignty entails obligations. One is not to massacre your own people. Another is not to support terrorism in any way. If a government fails to meet these obligations, then it forfeits some of the advantages of sovereignty, including the right to be left alone inside your own territory. Other governments, including the United States, gain the right to intervene. In the case of terrorism, this can even lead to a right of preventive . . . self-defense. You essentially can act in anticipation, if you have grounds to think it's a question of when, and not if, you're going to be attacked.[29]

This dual approach to sovereignty is well expressed in Bush's new security strategy, which argues that it is America's duty to protect freedom 'across the globe'. 'Some worry', says Bush, 'that it is somehow undiplomatic or impolite to speak the language of right and wrong. I disagree. Different circumstances require different methods, but not different moralities.'[30] What is alarming about the new security strategy is that through the use of new concepts, the administration has claimed an extraordinarily wide mandate for military action. First of all, the enemy is no longer defined. The enemy is anyone who might be a terrorist and who might acquire weapons of mass destruction (WMD). During the 1990s, great efforts were expended in 'imagining' new 'worst-case scenarios' and new post-Soviet threats. With the collapse of the Soviet military-industrial complex, US strategists came up with all sorts of inventive new ways in which America might be attacked, through spreading viruses, poisoning water systems, causing the collapse of the banking system, or disrupting air traffic control or power transmission. Of particular importance was the idea of state-sponsored terrorism and the notion of 'rogue states' that sponsor terrorism and acquire long-range missiles, as well as weapons of mass destruction. These new threats emanating from a collapsing Russia or from Islamic fundamentalism were known as 'asymmetric' threats, as weaker states or groups develop weapons of mass destruction or other horrific techniques to attack US vulnerabilities to compensate for conventional inferiority. Since September 11, these ideas appear to have been substantiated and the notion of the 'enemy' extended even further to those we don't necessarily know; hence the shift from a 'threat-based approach' to a 'capabilities-based' approach. According to Rumsfeld: 'There are things we know that we know. There are known unknowns. That is to say, there are things we know that we don't know. But there are also unknown unknowns. There are things we don't know we don't know . . . Each year, we discover a few more of these unknown unknowns.'[31]

Secondly, against these new unknown enemies, the US has developed new doctrines of 'pre-emption' in place of deterrence, and 'proactive counter-proliferation' instead of nonproliferation. According to Bush, deterrence no longer works; that was the lesson of September 11. 'Traditional concepts of deterrence will not work against a terrorist enemy whose avowed tactics are wanton destruction and the targeting of innocents; whose so-called soldiers seek martyrdom in death and whose most potent protection is statelessness.'[32] Hence, the United States reserves the right to act pre-emptively, using the tools of 'spectacle war' against those states who are believed to harbour terrorists or possess weapons of mass destruction. Interestingly, the rhetoric seems to switch between states that pose a threat to their own people (tyrants) and those that pose a threat to the United States (through the possession of WMD or through sponsoring terrorists).

This expanded mandate for military action amounts to an agenda for a permanent war much like the Cold War, in which periodic victories sustain public support and the rightness of the cause stifles dissent. The National Military Strategic Plan for the War on Terror (NMSP-WOT) reads rather like the manner of the Iraqi Minister of Information during the Iraq war. The introductions by Donald Rumsfeld and Peter Pace, the chairman of the Joint Chiefs of Staff, are strikingly reminiscent of the language of the Second World War. 'Our Nation', writes Peter Pace, 'is entering the fifth year of sustained combat operations. Our successes thus far in the war are clearly due to the dedicated and courageous service of our Nation's Soldiers, Sailors, Airmen and Marines and Coast Guardsmen who are serving within our borders and around the globe . . . They are truly our Nation's most precious and important assets.'[33]

Yet if it is the case that military compellance is much more difficult than the Bushites claim, then 'spectacle war' cannot be expected to defeat terrorism. On the contrary, it may stimulate the spread of terrorism because the strategy itself discredits the claim to political legitimacy. This is for three reasons. First, the crusade, the 'war on terrorism', raises the profile of the terrorists and dignifies them as enemies rather than criminals. The moment that Bush chose to describe what happened on September 11 as an attack on the United States rather than a 'crime against humanity', he firmly placed the event in a traditional war paradigm. By using the term 'war', Bush constructed a language of polarization, accentuated by his famous sentence 'you are either with us or against us'.[34] Moreover, the language of 'war on terrorism' has spread throughout the world, legitimizing a range of local 'wars on terrorism' (Chechnya, Palestine, Kashmir, Karabakh, to name but a few).

Secondly, the US administration put together a global coalition to fight terrorism, but it is an alliance on the Cold War model where the criterion for membership is support for the United States not adherence to international principles as would be the case for a truly multilateral arrangement. The inclusion of undemocratic states like Saudi Arabia, Pakistan or Uzbekistan and states responsible for massive human rights violations like Israel or Russia undermines the claim to be pursuing a just cause. Moreover, this is compounded by the use of the term 'war on terrorism' to justify increased surveillance and curtailment of rights.[35] Pressure on states to agree to exemptions for the United States in relation to the International Criminal Court, as in the case of the so-called 'New Europeans', actually undermines multilateral arrangements.

Thirdly, because 'spectacle war' does not risk casualties, it undermines any claims for legitimacy in the struggle to defeat terrorism. US attacks are accurate but nevertheless they cannot avoid 'collateral damage' or 'mistakes', nor can they prevent humanitarian catastrophes as a result of war. In the war in Afghanistan, there were around 1,000–1,300 civilian casualties from 'collateral damage', but thousands more died as a consequence of the worsening humanitarian crisis, and some 500,000 people fled from their homes; in addition some thousands of Taliban and Al Qaeda troops were killed.[36] There have been 655,000 extra Iraqi deaths since the beginning of the invasion in March 2003 up to July 2006; of these, 600,000 were a direct result of violence, and some 25 per cent were due to Coalition attacks.[37] Most Iraqi deaths were of civilians. By contrast, some 3,316 American soldiers and 144 British soldiers were killed up to April 2007.[38]

In addition, the treatment of prisoners in Guantanamo or Abu Graib, the restrictions on civil liberties in many Western countries, and heightened security and immigration controls all contribute to the perception of double standards and the loss of faith in the superiority of Western democracy.

In the combination of violence and morality, there is a parallel with Al Qaeda and other religious fundamentalists. I do not want to suggest symmetry. But nevertheless, the parallel is significant because it allows for a process of mutual reinforcement. Religion provides a justification for violence that excludes compromise and that overrides rules and procedures. The spectacular nature of attacks like those on September 11 or in Bali are not intended to defeat an enemy, or to be victorious. Rather, they are proof of a struggle between good and evil, ways of mobilizing supporters. It is the struggle itself that matters, the sense of participating in a sacred battle, not victory or defeat. 'What the perpetrators of such acts of terror expect – and indeed welcome', writes Mark Juergensmeyer, 'is a response as vicious as the acts themselves. By goading secular authorities into responding to terror with terror, they hope to accomplish two things. First, they want tangible evidence for their claim that the secular enemy is a monster. Second, they hope to bring to the surface the great war – a war that they have told their potential supporters was hidden, but real.'[39]

For Donald Rumsfeld and George W. Bush, the war against the 'unknowables' has something of the same character. 'Spectacle war' seems to confirm the conceptions of cosmic war promoted by Al Qaeda and others and to justify further acts of terrorism. By the same token, their response sustains a permanent crusading war mentality in the United States, drawn from the experience of the Cold War, which in turn underpins the position of the Republican right and justifies further increases in the defence budget.

Neo-realists and anti-imperialists

There has always been a tension in American foreign policy-making between idealists and realists, between those who believe in the American mission to spread the American way, and those who argue that America is a great power like any other and must pursue a strategy of survival. For the former, the Cold War was a struggle between good and evil, between democracy and totalitarianism; for the latter the Cold War was the inevitable consequence of bipolarity – a strategic order that some described as the 'long peace'.[40]

I have used the term 'neo-realist' to describe that strand of opinion that favours the hardheaded pursuit of national interest, in which humanitarian concerns are largely irrelevant. They are unilateralist because they believe in the use of force by the United States, whether or not it is sanctioned by international rules, and, like the Bushites, they act on the assumption that compellance is still possible. The neo-realists became prominent in the 1970s and 1980s when they argued that the relationship between the United States and the Soviet Union could be better managed. Famously, when Nixon and Kissinger went to Moscow in 1992 to negotiate the first SALT treaty, they ignored the Jewish refuseniks demonstrating at the Kremlin gates.

The neo-realists are critical of the Bush strategy because they do not think it is in the US national interest. Many of them opposed the Iraq war because, although Saddam Hussein was a tyrant, he did not currently pose a direct threat to the United States. Moreover, a war in Iraq would divert resources from the main threat from Al Qaeda. Thirty-four international scholars, including such luminaries as Kenneth Walz, often considered the father of neo-realism, Thomas Schelling, the inventor of 'compellance', and John Mearsheimer of the 'Long Peace', placed an advertisement in the *New York Times* opposing the war in Iraq.[41]

Of course, there is a range of views among the neo-realists. Some, like Henry Kissinger, did favour war with Iraq on geopolitical grounds. Others, while reserving the right to use military power unilaterally, considered that military power was less important nowadays. Joseph Nye, a former Assistant Secretary of Defense, draws a threefold classification of power – military, economic, and what he calls 'soft' power. Nowadays, power resources have shifted away from military power towards economic and 'soft' power. Whereas military power is unipolar, dominated by the United States, economic power is multipolar, and 'soft' power is 'the realm of transnational relations that cross borders outside of government control . . . [Soft] power is widely dispersed and it makes no sense to speak of unipolarity, multipolarity or hegemony'.[42] For Nye, values are part of the national interest. Nevertheless, he considers that what he calls C list priorities – wars in places like Bosnia and Rwanda which do not threaten US interests – are less important than A or B list priorities, direct threats to the US from a 'peer competitor', or threats to strategic US interests in places like the Persian Gulf or the Korean peninsular. For this reason the US has to be able to act unilaterally and cannot accept constraints like the International Criminal Court, which might lead to 'unjustified charges of war crimes' by US troops.[43]

The anti-imperialist left are the inverse of the neo-realists. They see the United States as a great power, an empire, pursuing geopolitical interests such as oil, and they consider that the idealism of the Bush administration (and indeed of earlier administrations) is merely a cover or legitimation for more hard-headed self-interest. They assume that military compellance still works. Hence they view with great suspicion, in Peter Gowan's words,

> Washington's central strategic initiative of the past decade – not the winding down of Nato after the end of the Cold War ... but its first deployment in action in the Balkans, and then expansion full-steam ahead to the frontiers of Russia itself. Since September 11, of course, the 'revolution in military affairs' has carried the American war machine still further, into hitherto unimagined terrain, with bases in five or six Central Asian states, and forward posts in the Caucasus, to add to the eighty countries in Eurasia, Africa and Oceania already in its keep. The staggering scale of this armed girdling of the planet tells its own story.[44]

The positions of the neo-realists and the anti-imperialists are well illustrated by the new interest in resource wars (primarily oil). Both the neo-realists and anti-imperialists often argue that underlying the 'war on terrorism' is a strategic interest in controlling the sources of oil and oil transportation routes. In support of this argument, the Cheney report on energy is often cited. The report advocates seeking new sources of oil apart from the Persian Gulf (Alaska or the Caspian Sea) to ensure cheap oil supplies to the United States for the foreseeable future.[45]

It was always the case that, in the wars of the twentieth century, control over oil supplies was a central part of strategy. Oil was the key factor of production and of warfare in the

Fordist era, and, in a global conflict, the various sides sought ways to cut their enemies off from the supply of this vital commodity. The Second World War, in particular, depended on the mass mobilization of tanks, aircraft and ships fuelled by oil. Both Germany and Japan were obsessed by the need to seek autonomous sources of oil. Nowadays, however, the world has changed. The market for oil is much more globalized and war is much more localized. There are threats to oil supplies but they derive much more from instability and conflict, 'new wars', than from the risk of hostile control of oil. Indeed, it can be argued, especially, for example, in the southern Caucasus, that geopolitical interests actually stimulate local conflicts and make oil supplies less not more secure. There may, of course, be a private greed element, in that the oil companies have a powerful influence on the Bush administration and they see the acquisition of bases as a way of exerting influence to win contracts. But that is the same as a national or geopolitical interest. Some argue that oil is the main reason for going to war with Iraq. But if this were case, are there not easier ways, short of war, to secure the oil?

Indeed, it can be argued that, by stressing the importance of oil, the anti-imperialists endorse the realist justification for unilateral action. In the 1991 Gulf War, George Bush Sr was able to make much of the possibility that Saddam Hussein could strangle Western oil supplies.

Like the Bushites, the neo-realists and the anti-imperialists have an old-fashioned view of military power, drawn from earlier wars. They are perhaps more prudent than the Bushites. Unlike the Bushites, they also have an old-fashioned view of sovereignty. For the anti-imperialists, this tends to mean that they do not take human rights violations or terrorist attacks sufficiently seriously – regarding these concerns merely as justifications for imperialism. For the neo-realists, terrorist threats to the United States are important, but not human rights violations or terrorist threats in other countries.

One difference between the neo-realists and the anti-imperialists is in the economic field. Neo-realists tend to support a liberal world economy. Anti-imperialists are often protectionist, believing that sovereignty is the best way to defend against imperialist exploitation.

Cooperative security

European leaders often deplore the unilateralism of the United States. One strand of European multilateralism continues to be realist. That is to say, the European realists have a vision of the world composed of sovereign states, but based on a set of rules and norms. Underpinning this vision is the philosophy of the so-called English School – people like Hedley Bull or Martin Wight – who trace their thinking to early international legalists like Grotius. According to the English School, there is no single world power but there is, nevertheless, world society, because even in an anarchical context, states operate according to certain principles – the most important of which is non-intervention.

It was assumptions of this kind that underpinned the détente policies during the 1970s and 1980s pioneered by European Social Democrats, who were deeply distrustful of American idealism. They strongly favoured disarmament and arms control, as well as openings to the East, but opposed the muscular language of human rights. I remember Dennis Healey, former Labour Foreign Secretary, saying in the early 1980s when the Polish solidarity movement was at its height: 'I prefer stability to solidarity.'

International lawyers in the United States also make this argument in opposition to the war in Iraq and to the Bush administration's doctrine of pre-emption. Douglas Cassel of Northwestern University argued, for example, that a 'preemptive strike in these circumstances would rupture the framework of international law built since World War II and provide a precedent for future aggression by powerful states whose agendas might be quite different from the United States'.[46] Possible examples are a Chinese attack on Taiwan, India or Pakistan attacking each other, or Russia invading Georgia.

Robert Kagan has criticized the multilateralist view on the grounds that it reflects Europe's weakness. He argues that the multilateralist view is only possible because Europeans can rely on American military force.[47] Of course, Kagan assumes that compellance works and that American military force does preserve stability. But he has a point about Europe's weakness.

Can non-intervention nowadays be sustained in the face of crimes against humanity, genocide or massive violations of human rights? Iraqis were just as distrustful of the countries that opposed the war – Russia, France and Germany – as of those who participated, because they believed that those countries were tacitly upholding Saddam Hussein's regime. And should we not be concerned about Nye's C list threats, since they can impinge on the rest of the world? 'New wars' do, after all, create the black holes that generate criminals, refugees and terrorists. Spectacle war is not the answer. But are there alternative means?

Cosmopolitanism

At the heart of the cosmopolitan position is the notion that a new form of political legitimacy needs to be constructed which offers an alternative to various forms of fundamentalism and exclusivism. The cosmopolitan position is idealist and multilateralist. It draws its inspiration from Immanuel Kant's perpetual peace project published in 1795. Kant argued that perpetual peace could be achieved in a world of states, based on republican (democratic) constitutions, where these states sign a permanent peace treaty with each other (the principle of non-intervention) but where cosmopolitan right (human rights) overrides sovereignty. He argued that cosmopolitan right need only be confined to the right of hospitality, that is, that strangers should be tolerated and respected. It was Kant who pointed out that the global community had shrunk to the point where 'a right violated anywhere could be felt everywhere'.[48]

Thus the cosmopolitan ideal combines a commitment to humanist principles and norms, an assumption of human equality, with a recognition of difference, and indeed a celebration of diversity.[49] To be idealist does not mean to be unrealistic. In a world where compellance no longer works, the only alternative is containment. And this has to be done through political and legal means. Politically, the cosmopolitan ideal has to offer an alternative that can undercut support for extremists. Religious fundamentalism and ultra-nationalism are rarely popular; their support depends on the weakness of alternatives. These exclusive ideologies are bred primarily but not only in 'weak' or 'failing' states, out of the despair of the excluded. In legal terms, the cosmopolitan ideal has to be situated within a multilateralist set of rules and procedures that apply equally to all individuals and can be seen to be fair.

There is a role for military means in this vision, but as containment not spectacle war. A cosmopolitan global community cannot stand aside when genocide is committed, as in Rwanda, for example. But military tasks should be confined to the protection of civilians and the arrest of war criminals, and should be authorized through the appropriate multilateral procedures. Normally, this means UN Security Council authorization, but there could be a set of principles in exceptional cases; if such principles were violated, then there would have to be procedures for appeal. The task of military containment may well include air power, but it would have to be viewed as tactical power in support of protection forces. Hence there is an argument for defence transformation to develop military forces that are not trained either for spectacle war or for classic peacekeeping, but this is a transformation of roles and tactics rather than technology. Military containment needs to be conceived as international law enforcement not as war-fighting.

The cosmopolitans thus share the Bushite assumption that sovereignty is conditional. But conditionality applies to all states and, moreover, the conditions cannot be determined unilaterally but only through a set of multilateral agreed procedures. The cosmopolitans are, for example, deeply critical of the current American attempts to undermine the International Criminal Court by reaching bilateral agreements which would exempt Americans from criminal charges. The United States cannot be exempted from the ICC because this implies that Americans are exceptionally privileged – a position which directly challenges the fundamental assumption of human equality.

Cosmopolitanism has to be able to offer an alternative reality. Paradoxically, it is the current American administration and its enemies who get away with an unreal vision of the world, as illustrated by the NMSP-WOT. War, for them, is a form of escapism, which diverts attention from everyday life. Especially for the religious fundamentalists and ultra-nationalists, war is a way of reminding people of a purer, less difficult past, a form of nostalgia, where spiritual values are more important than the material present. They are often master manipulators of the new media, using television, video-cassettes and radio to convey their message.

This is another reason why cosmopolitans also need to have an economic programme, a multilateralist commitment not just to a liberal world economy but also to global social justice. The commitment to an international rule of law and to global security, based on cosmopolitan principles, is the precondition for improving everyday life. But human rights do also include economic and social rights.

Many European social democrats stress this aspect of multilateralism, as do some parts of the anti-imperialist camp. This argument acquired increased momentum in the aftermath of September 11. Tony Blair, for example, made a strong appeal for a new global justice agenda. 'One illusion has been shattered on 11 September,' he said on a trip to the United States, 'that we can have the good life of the West irrespective of the state of the rest of the world . . . the dragon's teeth are planted in the fertile soil of wrongs unrighted, of disputes left to fester for years, of failed states, of poverty and deprivation.'[50] Or as George Soros put it: 'The terrorist attacks on September 11 have brought home to us in a tragic fashion how interdependent the world has become and how important it is for our internal security what internal conditions prevail in other countries'.[51] The French government proposed a Tobin tax on cross-border currency transactions, with the yield to go to global public goods, and the British and Scandinavian governments have been pushing for a big increase in and untying of development aid, as well as debt relief. The New Partnership for Africa (NEPAD) is also part of the concern for global justice, as are the commitments to debt relief and increased aid agreed at the 2005 Gleneagles G8 Summit. Nevertheless these efforts are so far modest and, despite some nods in this direction, have drawn little serious response from the Bush administration. Moreover, especially in the European case, the commitment to a liberal world economy still does not extend to the free movement of people.

Conclusion

The war on terrorism is not working. At the time of writing, Iraq seems to becoming a safe haven for all kinds of Islamic jihadists who have made common cause with the remnants of the Iraqi regime, turning Bush's assertions about the links between Saddam Hussein and Al Qaeda into a self-fulfilling prophecy.[52] Much the same seems to be happening in Afghanistan, where NATO forces are confronted with a resurgent Taliban allied to Al Qaeda. In May 2003, bombings in Casablanca and Riyadh led to over seventy deaths. There have also been 'raids' in Pakistan, Yemen and Kenya, not to mention the bombing of the Sari nightclub in Bali or the Chechen threat to hold hostage a theatre in Moscow. The bombings in Madrid on 11 March 2004 (two and a half years after September 11) and in London on 7 July 2005 have compounded the sense of insecurity. The FBI has frozen millions of dollars in assets; thousands of known or suspected operatives have been arrested, and perhaps a third of the leadership has been killed.[53] Attacks on aircraft are said to have been thwarted. Nevertheless, by all accounts the network known as Al Qaeda continues to grow. What is important is the ability to recruit young men to the cause; that is what makes possible the multiplication of cells. As Jason Burke has put it: 'Al Qaeda can only be understood as an ideology, an agenda, a way of seeing the world that is shared by an increasing number of young predominantly male Muslims.'[54]

I have argued that only a cosmopolitan vision can at least contain the new sources of violence. We live in a world where privileging groups of people is counter-productive because it is no longer impossible to insulate territory. We also live in a world where the utility of military force is much more limited than formerly. A political, legal and social approach is much more important as a way of dealing with terrorism. American power, despite its wealth and huge military forces, can only be effective within a cosmopolitan framework. This is why we need Americans to be what Richard Falk calls 'cosmopolitan patriots'.[55]

It is sometimes argued that the war on terrorism will be good for the global economy and help to prevent a recession in the United States. Expenditure on the war has permitted deficit financing, and overspending may help to stimulate global growth. Unlike at the beginning of the Cold War, however, the United States no longer enjoys an external surplus. At that time, the world was desperate for dollars, and overseas military spending helped to stimulate both domestic growth in other countries and increases in US exports. Today the US has a substantial current account deficit and is heavily indebted. Some argue that this does not matter because foreign investors are attracted by high American productivity growth. But increased overseas spending, especially going to states with weak rule of law and inadequate governance, could merely end up increasing the deficit. For a new 'golden age', the US needs global growth stimulated through a multilateral programme of assistance that offers the possibility of reconstructing legitimate authority.

Are there any prospects for reorienting American power, for dismantling the straitjacket of the Cold War heritage and harnessing American power to a set of cosmopolitan goals? In the immediate aftermath of September 11, when even *Le Monde* proclaimed that we are all Americans, many people hoped that such a reorientation might happen because the threat was real. Wars often bring about dramatic restructuring, although not immediately. If terrorism continues to spread, if the wars in Iraq and Afghanistan continue to deteriorate, if the economy fails to pick up, and if, above all, American democracy still has some life in it, then change is possible. On the one hand, wars of the new type tend to be polarizing, entrenching extremists on all sides; this is the experience of the Balkans or the Middle East. On the other hand, the global protests against the war in Iraq were unprecedented. Some 15 million people demonstrated worldwide, including in the United States.[56] American war weariness is growing and new connections are being made among generals, who understand the limitations of war, global companies, whose profits depend on global stability, and immigrant groups, especially the Muslim community.

I conclude, therefore, that the Asian human rights activist I quoted at the beginning is wrong. If the American political system continues to be distorted by the manipulation of public opinion through spectacle war, then it no longer represents the ideal of democratic deliberation propounded by the founding fathers, which has been such an inspiration to the rest of the world. The current strategy of 'spectacle war' may have the effect of repressing democracy. But if America is to remain a truly open reasoning society, then it needs democracy in the rest of the world. There is no such thing as democracy in one country any longer.

3

Nationalism and Globalization

Eric Hobsbawm argues that the current wave of nationalism will be short-lived. Nationalism, he suggests, is an anachronism best suited to an earlier historical period dominated by industrialization and print technology. In a much quoted passage, he wrote: 'The owl of Minerva, which brings wisdom, says Hegel, flies out at dusk. It is a good sign that it is now circling round nations and nationalism.'[1]

Anthony Smith takes the opposite view. He does not think that nations have been transcended in the global era. On the contrary, the current wave of nationalism to be observed in various parts of the world testifies to the enduring nature of the national idea, the way in which it responds to some deep-felt human need.

> It would be folly to predict an early supersession of nationalism and an imminent transcendence of the nation. Both remain indispensable elements of an interdependent world and a mass-communications culture. For a global culture seems unable to offer the qualities of collective faith, dignity, and hope that only a 'religious surrogate', with its promise of a territorial culture-community across the generations, can provide. Over and beyond any political and economic benefits that ethnic nationalism can confer, it is the promise of collective and territorial immortality, outfacing death and oblivion, that has helped to sustain so many nations and nation-states in an era of unprecedented social change and to renew so many ethnic minorities

that seemed to be doomed in an era of technological uniformity and corporate efficiency.[2]

In addressing this debate, I want to emphasize the political character of nationalism. I do not agree that nationalism necessarily possesses the kind of transcendent character attributed to it by Anthony Smith. Like Renan, I consider nationalism to be a political process, a 'daily plebiscite', a subjective affirmation and reaffirmation; nationalism will only persist to the extent that individuals, movements and groups choose to be nationalists. On the other hand, I do not think that nationalism will necessarily go away in an era of globalization. We are in the midst of a period of political experimentation, as earlier political ideas and institutions have been eroded by dramatic socioeconomic and cultural change. Various political ideologies are currently in competition, including market fundamentalism, Global Islamism, cosmopolitanism, Europeanism, and, of course, nationalism. Some of these ideologies are forward-looking or reformist, that is to say, they offer a policy prescription for coming to terms with underlying structural change, ways in which individuals are expected to be able to benefit from globalization. Others are backward-looking or regressive, appealing to an imagined past, and proposing to reverse at least some aspects of the current changes. Future developments will be determined by the outcome of this competition; unfortunately, there is no a priori reason to suggest that the more forward-looking ideologies will triumph over the backward-looking ideologies.

One of these ideologies is nationalism. What I call the 'new nationalism' is both shaped by and shapes the various phenomena we bunch together under the rubric of globalization. I would argue that the 'new nationalism' is regressive, and, in so far as it persists, will contribute to a wild, anarchic form of globalization, characterized by violence and inequality. Certain types of political religious movements such as Global Islamism, Hindu nationalism or Zionism can also be included under the rubric of the 'new nationalism'. In putting forward this analysis of the 'new nationalism' as regressive, I do not exclude the possibility of forward-looking small nationalisms, as suggested by Guibernau, but I would argue that they have to be situated within a broader cosmopolitan perspective.

In developing this argument, I start with some preliminary remarks about the theoretical debate on nationalism and how the changing global context alters the parameters of this debate. I then describe some of the key features of the 'new nationalism', with particular attention to Global Islamism, which is a new phenomenon, sharing some but not all of the characteristics of the new nationalism. Finally, I discuss the potential for cosmopolitan and/or European ideologies. In conclusion, I sketch out the possible scenarios that might follow from different ideological combinations.

In Defence of the Modernist Paradigm

What Smith has dubbed the modernist paradigm argues that nationalism is a modern phenomenon, inextricably linked to the rise of the modern state and to industrialization. Perennialists, primordialists and ethno-symbolists criticize the modernist paradigm on several grounds.[3]

First, they argue that the modernists, and in particular the work of Ernest Gellner, are too functionalist. Gellner suggests that the modern state and modern industry require what he calls 'modular man'. The term 'modular' is taken from the idea of modular furniture in which components can be fitted together in different ways, while maintaining a harmonious whole. Modular man has certain basic skills, including a shared language, and can adapt himself to a variety of positions in modern society. Modular man is 'capable of performing highly diverse tasks in the same general cultural idiom, if necessary reading up manuals of specific jobs in the general standard style of the culture in question'.[4] Nationalism, the principle that the cultural and political unit is congruent, is a collective ideology, ideally suited to the construction of modular man, making possible a political authority that creates the conditions for everyday encounters with the state and modern industry.

Gellner contrasts the vertical, territorially based national cultures typical of modernity with the more differentiated cultures of traditional societies. Before the invention of printing and the spread of writing in vernacular languages, it was possible to distinguish between horizontal, that is, non-territorial, 'high cultures' generally based on religion and a scholarly written language, such as Latin, Persian or Sanskrit, and a variety of local vertical low cultures.[5] The emergence of national cultures is associated with the rise of the modern state and the spread of primary education. One of the many local cultures is elevated through printing and education and spread within a territorial area bounded by the state.

The functionalist critique, in my view, fails to take into account the complex relationship between agency and structure. Structural arguments, which are typical of the modernist paradigm, are not necessarily determinist arguments. Rather they point to the importance of structural change and the ways in which different political initiatives or ideologies are helped or hindered by structural conditions. Politics is always about experiment; some policies succeed in the sense of increasing the legitimacy of political institutions, and others fail. Success, at least to some extent, depends on underlying structural conditions. The validity of the modernist argument does not derive from a linear relationship between nationalism and industrialization or the rise of the modern state. The modernist argument, for example, does not need to hold that nationalism arose in order to create the conditions for industrialization, nor that nationalism is an inevitable outcome of industrialization, although I do think that one aspect of industrialization, namely print technology, is a critical component in the rise of nationalism. The rise of the national idea may come about autonomously as a consequence of a variety of factors; the point is rather that as an ideology it fits the modern state and industrialization. Nationalism, industrialization and the modern state reinforce each other, although not always harmoniously.

A second related argument is that the modernist paradigm is too instrumentalist. Modernists, like Gellner or Hobsbawm, suggest that nationalism is inculcated from above through the state's control of culture, particularly language policies and education. Hobsbawm talks about 'social engineering' and 'invention'. Even the variant of modernism put forward by Anderson that the nation is 'imagined' through the spread of secular literature in the vernacular, like the newspaper or the novel, is criticized on the grounds of artificiality.[6] Although they admit certain important elements of mobilization from above, the critics would argue that nationalism only succeeds where it has some popular resonance, appealing to 'authentic' sentiments among ordinary people that derive from folk memories, traditions and customs. I share the view that the populist appeal of nationalism has to reflect populist sentiment. But that sentiment is not necessarily cultural or ethnic; indeed the view that ordinary people need ethnic or cultural symbols seems to me to be overly paternalistic. Popular sentiment can also be based on political demands – for democracy, for example, or anti-colonialism. This difference between the political and cultural basis of nationalism mirrors the distinction between civic or ethnic nationalism or between Western and Eastern nationalism. According to Hans Kohn, the Western

> nations emerged as voluntary unions of citizens. Individuals expressed their will in contracts, covenants and plebiscites. Integration was achieved around a political idea and special emphasis was laid on the universal similarities of nations. In the non-Western world, the nation was regarded as a political unit centering around the irrational pre-civilized folk concept. Nationalism found its rallying point in the folk community, elevating it to the dignity of an ideal or a mystery. Here emphasis was placed on the diversity or self-sufficiency of nations.[7]

Anthony Smith argues that this distinction is overdrawn and that in both variants of nationalism, both political and cultural elements are to be found. This is probably true, but I would argue the more open and democratic a society, the more likely it is that nationalism is a forward-looking political project, and the more authoritarian and closed the society, the more likely it is that cultural and religious traditions will be reinvented from above as a tool of popular mobilization.

Related to the instrumentalist criticism is the charge of 'blocking presentism'; that is to say, the critics accuse the modernists of focusing exclusively on the present generation. Those who argue that nationalism has to have some ethnic popular resonance insist that the nation has to have some prehistory. Nationalism, they say, is not invented or engineered; rather it is reconstructed and reinvented out of the past. Smith strongly disagrees with Gellner that any old 'cultural shred or patch' will serve the nationalists' purpose.[8] He says:

> We need to understand nationalism as a type of collective conduct, based on the collective will of a moral community and

the shared emotions of a putatively ancestral community and
this means that we need to grasp the nation as a political form
of the sacred community of citizens.[9]

But I am concerned about 'blocking past-ism'. The focus on
the history or prehistory of the nation often obscures the
everyday experiences and concerns of present generations; why,
for example, people who have lived together for centuries, as
is the case in many less modernized and therefore culturally
rich societies, should come into conflict with each other. It
also carries with it a sort of determinism that can be very
oppressive, the notion that people cannot escape from their
ethnic pasts.

A third and related argument is about passion. The modernists, says Smith, cannot account for the passion of nationalism.
They cannot answer the question: why die for the nation? For
Smith, the answer lies in the 'sacred community' of shared
memories and ancestry. I would suggest another answer, and
that is war. Passion and, indeed, religious feelings are closely
connected with death, as Smith himself argues. Indeed, I would
invert the argument and suggest that war constructs nationalism rather than the other way round. That is why military
heroes and battles are such an important part of the nationalist
narrative. Nationalism has to be understood, I would argue, as
a nodal point in the intimate relation between the modern state
and war. This is an argument made by both Charles Tilly and
Michael Mann. In the eighteenth and nineteenth centuries, the
state's monopoly of violence was established through war,
which led to increases in taxation, conscription, war loans and
the increased reach and efficiency of public administration, as
well as the consolidation of the idea of the 'nation'. This idea
was reproduced through conscription and military drill in an
imagined war. Both the idea of the 'nation' and the idea of the
'other' were given substance in war. Earlier wars were about
religion or about a variety of overlapping and competing
sovereignties (fiefdoms, city states, princely states, etc.), and
created similarly differentiated loyalties. In the eighteenth and
nineteenth centuries, national wars between states became,
in Europe, the predominant form of warfare. Clausewitz
expounded well the extremist logic that followed from popular
mobilization for war.

The sharp distinction between the internal and external functions of the state dates from this period. The internal functions had to do with the preservation of the rule of law, public services, cultural and socioeconomic policies, and, at least in the West, respect for individual rights and citizenship. The external function of the state was defence of the nation as a whole.

The link between nationalism and war was well understood by contemporary thinkers. One of the earliest theorists of nationalism, Heinrich von Trietschke, argued: 'It is only in the common performance of heroic deeds for the sake of the fatherland that a nation becomes truly and spiritually united.' Echoing Hegel, he insisted on the role of war and bravery in upholding the collective idea: 'The individual must forget his own ego and feel himself a member of the whole; he must recognize what a nothing his life is in comparison with the general welfare . . . The individual must sacrifice himself for a higher community of which he is a member; but the state is itself the highest in the external community of men.'[10]

Of course, there were liberal nationalist thinkers like Mill, Hugo or Mazzini, who conceived of nationalism as a democratic project and who thought that the spread of nationalism would end wars. But these were modernist thinkers. For them, nationalism was about reason not passion, and they entertained the possibility of the nation as a temporary historical phenomenon.

The argument of Hobsbawm and others that nationalism is a passing phenomenon no longer suited to current structural conditions is sometimes used by critics of the modernist paradigm as evidence for the weakness of the paradigm. Guibernau, for example, suggests that Gellner's argument about the way in which industrialism's demands for homogeneity leads to 'culturally unalloyed nations' is much too simple 'when applied to a world in which globalization processes favour constant cultural interconnectedness. If Gellner is right, we should be witnessing a tendency towards a single uniform world nationalism. But in fact, the effect is exactly the opposite.'[11] But this is an overly simple description of globalization. The modernist paradigm is about the construction of ideology in the context of structural change. Globalization processes do not only favour cultural interconnectedness, they favour cultural disconnectedness as well. Globalization breaks down the homogeneity of the nation-state. Globalization involves diversity as well as uniformity, the local as well as the global. I would like to point to three changes, in particular, that have implications for the future of nationalism.

First of all, the rise of the information-based economy reduces the importance of territorially based industrial production. The global economy is both more transnational and more local. Growing sectors of the economy such as finance and research and development are increasingly global. At the same time, markets are increasingly specialized and local as profits are increasingly derived from catering to a differentiated market (economies of scope) rather than from low-cost mass production (economies of scale). What we are witnessing is a profound change in the division of labour. On the one hand, there is a growing class of what Robert Reich calls 'symbolic analysts', people who work with abstract symbols in finance, technology, education or welfare. These are the graduates of the explosion in tertiary education, who communicate across borders and generally speak a global language, usually English. On the other hand, there is a growing underclass of people who service the new symbolic analysts, who work in the informal sector and who trade in cultural diversity through a variety of menial tasks. The classic industrial worker who formed the backbone of the nationalist ideology is increasingly marginalized.

Secondly, the shift from print technology to electronic communications has momentous implications, which it is probably much too soon to describe. On the one hand, as many analysts of globalization point out, internet, satellite television, faxes and air travel make possible new global virtual communities.[12] On the other hand, radio and television reach out to local communities who do not have the reading habit and make possible much more rapid and dramatic political mobilization.

Thirdly, a crucial change is in the nature of war. War between states, as in the eighteenth, nineteenth and early twentieth century, is becoming increasingly rare. I agree with Anthony Smith when he says that globalization does not mean a decline in the nation-state but rather a change in its functions. 'What we have been witnessing is a shift in state functions and powers from the economic and the military to the social and cultural spheres, and from external sovereignty to internal domestic control.'[13] But I believe he underestimates the extent to which the loss of external sovereignty and the decline of the military function weakens the potential for reproducing the national idea. Instead of war, we are experiencing new kinds of political violence that are both local and transnational – terrorism, 'new wars' and American high-tech wars. And these new forms of violence are constructing new ideologies, as I discuss below.

One of the developments often neglected by theorists of nationalism is blocism, which, for fifty years, supplanted nationalism, at least in Europe. Writing in 1945, E. H. Carr wrote that nationalism is under attack.

> On the plane of morality, it is under attack from those who denounce its inherently totalitarian nature and proclaim that any international authority worth the name must interest itself in the rights and well-being not of nations but of men and women. On the plane of power, it is being sapped by modern technological developments, which have made the nation obsolescent as the unit of military and economic organisation and are rapidly concentrating effective decision and control in the hands of great multi-national units.[14]

These 'great multi-national units' were held together through new non-nationalist ideologies constructed out of a great imaginary war far surpassing anything nations had ever achieved. The West was bound together in an imagined struggle of democracy against totalitarianism, while the Eastern bloc cast the struggle as one between socialism and capitalism.[15] Blocism, I would argue, was a transitional phenomenon, combining both the new 'postmodern' elements of horizontal transnational association with a traditional emphasis on territory. Blocism was ideally suited to the Fordist large-scale model of mass production. Blocism failed, I would argue, both because new communications made it impossible to sustain ideologies within closed territorial units, and because it was not possible to sustain the imminent idea of war. The collapse of blocism created an ideological vacuum into which rushed a range of new ideologies, including the revival of nationalism.

Contemporary Nationalisms

A friend from Nagorno Karabakh was visiting England at the time of the Jubilee celebrations. He had been one of the founders of the Karabakh Committee, established in the last years of Soviet rule, to demand that Karabakh, a predominantly Armenian enclave inside Azerbaijan, should become part of Armenia. A bloody war followed after the break-up of the Soviet Union – some 15,000–20,000 people were killed and over a million people were forced to flee their homes, from Armenia and Azerbaijan as well as Nagorno Karabakh. My friend joined the crowds in the Mall, waving flags as the Queen and the royal family passed by. 'So what do you think of British nationalism?' I asked him afterwards. 'That's not nationalism', he replied, 'that was a Soviet crowd. Nationalism is about passion.'

The Jubilee celebrations, like the May Day parades in the Soviet Union or the images of Bush on an aircraft carrier at the moment of supposed victory in Iraq, are one form of contemporary nationalism, what could be called 'spectacle nationalism'. Spectacle nationalism is an evolution from the more militant nationalism of the first half of the twentieth century. It is official ideology, that is to say, the ideology that serves to legitimize existing states. It requires passive participation, watching television or joining a crowd, but its capacity to mobilize active participation such as paying taxes or risking one's life in wars is greatly weakened. It has something in common with 'banal nationalism' although it involves consciously mediated construction, spectacular events like the Jubilee celebrations.

What I call the new nationalism is to be found in places like Nagorno Karabakh or Bosnia-Herzegovina and is bred in conditions of insecurity and violence. The new nationalism is exclusive, that is to say, it excludes others of a different nationality, and has much in common with religious fundamentalism, the insistence that religious doctrines be followed rigidly and imposed on others. Indeed, there is a considerable overlap between militant nationalist and religious political movements.[16] This is not only because of the religious character of nationalism but also because many nations are defined in religious terms – Bosnian Muslims, for example, or Hindu nationalists – and many religions are described in national terms – Judaism, for example, or Islam.

In the last two decades, we have seen an increased political presence of these groups, both in electoral terms[17] and through their involvement in violent episodes, both terrorism and war. These movements have to be understood, not as throwbacks to the past, but as phenomena closely connected to contemporary structural conditions. Just as earlier nationalisms have to be explained in terms of the first phase of modernity, so the new nationalism is both shaped by and shapes what is variously described as globalization, postmodernity or late modernity. It is often claimed that the new nationalism was repressed or frozen during the Cold War years, only to burst forth when the Cold War was over. I would argue that, on the contrary, the new nationalism has been constructed or invented in the post-Cold War period. Both the electronic media and new forms of violence have been important tools of construction.

Like earlier nationalisms, the new militancy was constructed both 'from above' and 'from below'. Political leaders have tended to use nationalist and religious appeals when other tools of political mobilization have failed. Often it was secular leaders who opened the space for these ideologies. Thus the Congress Party in India began to use Hindu rhetoric long before the rise of the BJP. In the former Yugoslavia and Soviet Union, nationalism grew within the administrative confines of the centrally planned system because other forms of ideological competition were excluded. In Africa, patrimonial leaders used tribal networks as a way of rationing out scarce governmental resources. And in the Middle East, the failures of Arab nationalism led many leaders to emphasize a religious identity and the conflict with Israel.

Anthony Smith would argue that these efforts at political mobilization only succeed if they appeal to some popular sentiments derived from memory and tradition. It is undoubtedly true that memories of violence, especially not too long ago, facilitate mobilization. Today's Hindu–Muslim clashes reproduce the clashes of previous generations, while in former Yugoslavia living memories of atrocities during the Second World War provide a fertile source for contemporary nationalism. All the same, it is insecurity and frustration resulting from dramatic structural change that provide a more convincing explanation for why today's generation, often brought up in multicultural environments, are so vulnerable to exclusive ideologies. The last two decades have witnessed, in many regions, substantial decline in state provision and public employment, rapid urbanization, the growth of an informal criminalized economy and large-scale migration from countryside to town and from poor countries to the industrialized West. Typical recruits to these movements are the restless young men, often educated for roles that no longer exist because of the decline of the state or of the industrial sector, often unable to marry because they lack income, and sometimes needing to legitimate semi-criminal activities in which they can find their only source of income. Membership in nationalist or religious groups offers meaning, a sense of historical relevance, and also adventure.

Related to the sense of insecurity is the encounter with globalization and the sense of impotence that arises when crucial decisions that affect everyday life are taken further and further away. The young men who committed suicide on September 11 were all educated in the West. This is typical of many nationalist and religious militants. Seselj, the leader of the extreme nationalist Serb party, had spent time at the University of Michigan. Many of those who are mobilized are migrants, either from countryside to town or from South to West, who have experienced the loss of ties to their places of origin and yet do not feel integrated in their new homes.

The ideologies of these movements can be described as both modern and anti-modern. Most new nationalists believe in territorially based sovereignty and their goal is to control existing states or to create new states, in the name of the nation or the religion. But their ideology is anti-modern in its rejection of the doubt and questioning that characterize modern society; in its vision of a pure and unpolluted past, its nostalgia for a golden age when the aspirations of the nation or religion were fulfilled; and, above all, in the idea of a cosmic struggle between good and evil that is the most common shared characteristic of these movements. These ideologies are backward-looking in that they want to revert to a modern, that is, pre-globalization, conception of the nation-state.

The organization and strategies of these movements, on the other hand, are typical of 'late modernity' and make use of the various phenomena that are known as globalization. In organizational terms, the new nationalism tends to be transnational. Although the goals are often local, the organization depends on the construction of a horizontal network of supporters, involving migrant communities in other countries – diasporas often play a critical role. In many cases, these movements create parallel structures – religious schools, for example, or humanitarian NGOs – that fill the vacuum left by the decline in state provision. Funding comes from wealthy supporters in the diaspora, or else through a range of criminal and informal activities.

All of these groups make use of the 'new media' – television, internet, video-cassettes – both for linking the network and for political mobilization. Many groups have their own TV or radio channels. Hindu nationalists benefit from the new satellite channel, Star TV. Serbian television played a critical role in the years leading up to the Yugoslav wars in promoting nationalist propaganda, interchanging contemporary events with the Second World War and the 1389 Battle of Kosovo. Bin Laden's speeches are circulated through video-cassettes worldwide. In Africa, the radio is literally magic, and it was Milles Collines Hate Radio that incited the genocide in Rwanda.

For many of these movements, violence is a central strategy for political mobilization. In earlier wars or guerrilla struggles, violence was directed against strategic targets, such as the capture of territory or attacks on radio stations or important officials, as part of a clear strategy; political mobilization was needed to implement the strategy. Nowadays, violence is directed against symbolic targets and against civilians. Symbolic violence is a form of message, a way of making a statement. Terrorist attacks against civilians are typical of 'symbolic violence'. Violence is 'deliberately exaggerated' and often macabre. The Lord's Resistance Army in Uganda cuts off ears and lips. Hamas suicide bombers put nails in their bombs so as to kill as many people as possible. Juergensmeyer likens 'symbolic violence' to theatre – these are what he calls 'performance acts' – 'stunning, abnormal and outrageous murders carried out in a way that graphically displays the power of violence – set within grand scenarios of conflict and proclamation'.[18] The targets of such attacks are often important symbols – the World Trade Center, the federal building in Oklahoma that symbolized welfare and gun control, the mosque in Ayodha. These 'rituals of violence' carry with them an other-worldly significance and produce the sense of struggle, of Armageddon or Jihad, or of cosmic war.

The theatrical character of much violence is illustrated by the way many of the perpetrators dress up for killing as though it is not they themselves who perform the acts. The notorious Frenki's Boys, who were responsible for atrocities in Bosnia and Kosovo, wore cowboy hats over ski masks and painted Indian stripes on their faces. Their trademark was the sign of the Serbian Chetniks and a silhouette of a destroyed city with the words 'City Breakers' in English. Joseph Kony, the leader of the Lord's Resistance Army, wears aviator sunglasses and dresses his hair in beaded braids hanging to his neck; sometimes he wears women's clothes.

But violence is not merely symbolic, not just 'letters to Israel' as one Hamas activist described the suicide bombers. In many of the recent armed conflicts, the aim has been deliberate elimination or indeed extermination of the 'other'. The Hutus in Rwanda wanted to get rid of the Tutsis, just as Hitler wanted to get rid of the Jews. The goal of the wars in the former Yugoslavia or the South Caucasus was to create ethnically pure territories. In these cases, exaggerated violence was aimed at making people hate their homes. Systematic rape, for example, was widespread in the former Yugoslavia. This was rape, not as a side-effect of war, but as a deliberate weapon of war with the aim of making women, particularly Muslim women, feel ashamed and defiled so that they would not want to return to their homes. Likewise, violence against symbolic targets was aimed at removing any trace of the culture of the 'other'. In Banja Luka, during the Bosnian war, two unique sixteenth-century Ottoman mosques were razed to the ground. They were blown up on a Friday, and on Monday the bulldozers came and grassed over the site so that you would never know they ever existed.

These new forms of violence can be understood as the way the extremist groups succeed in mobilizing extremist sentiment. It is in situations of pervasive insecurity that fear and hatred, passion and prejudice are more likely to come to dominate political choices. For example, it is difficult to explain the suicide bombers in Palestine as a way of achieving a Palestinian state, just as it is difficult to explain the brutal Israeli responses as a way of improving security. But if the goal is to strengthen extremist sentiment – support for Hamas or the extreme Zionist groups – what is happening is much easier to explain.

In the former Yugoslavia, the killings and displacement in the various conflicts generated the very ideologies that were supposed to have been the cause of the conflict. They left a legacy of fear and hatred, of memories of lost relatives, which provide the fuel for a grass-roots nationalist passion that is much more pervasive than before the wars. Indeed this may have been the point of the violence. Something similar happened in Nagorno Karabakh. The idea that political control depends on the expulsion of those with a different nationality, says one commentator, 'spread as the scale and intensity of the conflict increased' and was 'converted into a deadly ideology by fears of pre-emption and memories of past blood shed'.[19]

In the late 1990s, a new variant of the new nationalism emerged, with wholly novel features. This was the ideology of Global Islamism promulgated by Osama Bin Laden and Al Qaeda. Of course, this is a religious movement but the ideologists of the movement talk about the 'Islamic nation', and the basic idea of uniting around a common culture, Islam, is a nationalist idea. It has more to do with the political rights of Muslims, based on the argument that Muslims are singled out as victims in many 'new wars' – Bosnia, Palestine, Chechnya, Kashmir. It is a network typical of the global era. It is built up through new forms of communication (internet, the circulation of video-cassettes, the use of satellite television, such as Al Jazeera, as well as air travel) and new forms of violent struggle.

The ideology seems to have emerged some time in the mid-1990s, when Bin Laden spent time in Sudan and made contacts with a range of Islamist groups, including those who had fought in South East Asia and in Bosnia and Chechnya. The elements that mark out this ideology as a new phenomenon are:

- First, the global character of the discourse. There are huge differences among Islamic groups both in doctrine and in goals; most political groups are oriented towards local institutions. Bin Laden's hero was Saladin, the Kurdish commander who united Islamic groups against the Crusaders in the twelfth century. Bin Laden's aim was to copy Saladin and to unite these disparate Islamic groups in a global struggle. In August 1996, he issued his 'World Declaration against the Americans occupying the lands of the two holy places', which was the first time the focus of political Islam had been directed towards the

United States as opposed to individual states in the Islamic world. 'It should not be hidden from you', says the Declaration, 'that the people of Islam have suffered from aggression, iniquity, and injustice imposed on them by the Zionist-Crusaders Alliance and their collaborators . . . [Muslim] blood was spilled in Palestine and Iraq. The horrifying pictures of the massacre of Qana in Lebanon are still fresh in our memory. Massacres in Tadjikistan, Burma, Kashmir, Azzam, the Philippines . . . Ogaden, Somalia, Eritrea, Chechnya, and Bosnia-Herzegovina . . . send shivers in the body and shake the conscience.'[20]

- A second novel element is the focus on spectacular violence, using 'martyrs' (suicide bombers) in 'raids'.[21] The targets are no longer local but global, and the 'raid' is designed for maximum media impact – hence both the symbolic character of the targets and the high level of civilian casualties. The raids are viewed as 'jihad as testament', demonstrating to spectators an incredible self-sacrifice for the faith or the nation.

- Thirdly, Global Islamism is much more 'anti-political' than earlier variants of political Islam, which were directed at winning power in local contexts. In part, the rise of Al Qaeda reflects the marginalization of political Islam – many commentators have argued that political Islam had passed its peak by the late 1980s. The current version of Global Islam is much more preoccupied with political mobilization than with specific goals. Of course, Bin Laden and others do express specific demands – for the withdrawal of Americans from Saudi Arabia, or for a Muslim caliphate in the Middle East. But as Bin Laden put it in 1999: 'We seek to instigate the [Islamic] nation to get up and liberate its land.'[22] The attack on the World Trade Center towers succeeded, probably beyond the wildest dreams of the perpetrators, in publicizing the Global Islamic idea. In December 2001, in a videotaped message to Al Jazeera, he said: 'Regardless if Osama is killed or survives, the awakening has started, praise be to God.'[23] A parallel can be drawn with revolutionary terror. The discourse legitimizes nihilistic acts of anger and frustration. And where the idea is millenarian, that is, conceived around some future utopia of liberation, what matters is mobilization, not the achievement of specific goals.

Al Qaeda as an organization had its heyday in the period 1996–2001, when its infrastructure in Afghanistan was able to provide a focal point for training, funding and expert advice on what appear to have been relatively autonomous operations by different local groups.[24] This infrastructure was destroyed in 2001. Nevertheless, the ideology appears to be more powerful than ever. The American 'war on terror' has fed the idea of cosmic struggle and elevated the movement to a worthy enemy of America. The apparent swarming of Islamic militants into Iraq bears testimony to its continuing appeal. As Burke puts it:

> The legitimising discourse, the critical element that converts an angry young man into a human bomb, is now everywhere. You will hear it in a mosque, on the Internet, from friends, in a newspaper. You do not have to travel to Afghanistan to complete the radicalising process; you can do it in your front room, in an Islamic centre, in a park.[25]

Cosmopolitan or European Politics

There is, of course, another type of contemporary nationalism and this is the small nationalism of ethnic minorities who survive in states where national homogenization was incomplete; unlike the new nationalism described above, this small nationalism is non-violent, open and inclusive. I am thinking of Scotland, Catalonia or Transylvania. Some would say that the distinction between these nationalisms and the new nationalism is artificial, just as Kohn's distinction between Eastern and Western nationalism is overdrawn. But the distinction is important because it is about cultural diversity as opposed to cultural homogeneity. The new nationalism favours cultural homogeneity both large (Hindu nationalism or Global Islamism or anti-immigrationism in Europe) and small (Croats, Abkhazians, Chechens) and is therefore closed and exclusive. But small nationalism can also be about enhancing democracy at local levels and the defence of cultural diversity. There are, of course, both camps in places like Scotland or Transylvania, though in these two cases, the democratic process has tended to override ethnic division.[26] It is important to stress the distinction between the two types because it illustrates what is meant by cosmopolitanism.

Critics of the modernist paradigm also tend to be critics of the cosmopolitan idea. This is because modernists argue that the nation is a temporary phenomenon. 'The Nations are not something eternal. They had their beginnings and they will end.'[27] Modernists, therefore, tend to favour what they see as more forward-looking ideologies better suited to the structural conditions associated with globalization.

Two kinds of criticism are levelled by the critics of the modernist paradigm against the cosmopolitan and, by implication, European idea. One is that there is no such thing as a global culture, or if there were, it would be a grey, technological uniform culture, incapable of generating passionate loyalties. This is a misunderstanding of the meaning of the term 'cosmopolitanism'. Culturally, cosmopolitanism means openness to different cultures. According to Urry, cosmopolitanism is 'a cultural disposition involving an intellectual and aesthetic stance of "openness" towards peoples, places and experiences from different cultures, especially those from different "nations". Cosmopolitanism should involve the search for, and delight in, the contrasts between societies rather than a longing for superiority or for uniformity.'[28] Politically, cosmopolitanism must be distinguished from humanism. Humanism is about universal human values, what we now call human rights. Cosmopolitanism combines humanism with a celebration of human diversity. In *Perpetual Peace*, from which the political meaning is derived, Kant describes a world of nation-states in which cosmopolitan right overrides sovereignty. Kant says that the condition for perpetual peace is that cosmopolitan right be confined to the right of hospitality. What he means by this is treating strangers with dignity. Kant, writing at the end of the eighteenth century, was opposed to colonialism but he also criticized those natives who maltreated their European visitors. The right of hospitality means both respect for human rights and respect for difference.

A similar point is made by Kwame Anthony Appiah in his article on 'Cosmopolitan Patriots'.[29] Appiah talks about the importance of the notion of a 'rooted cosmopolitan, someone who loves his or her homeland and culture and feels a responsibility towards making that homeland a better place'. But a cosmopolitan is also free to choose the place where he or she lives and the practices in which they take part; you can migrate out of choice not through pressure, and choose to respect some traditions and not others. Patriotism can mean freedom not exclusion. A cosmopolitan would be one who insisted both on global guarantees for human rights and on a global strategy for promoting the survival of cultures. What makes Sarajevo, for example, such a vibrant place is precisely the fact that different cultures have survived side by side for so long – the mosque, the Orthodox church, the Catholic church and the synagogue are all within a few hundred yards of each other. A cosmopolitan is proud of such diversity. A cosmopolitan respects these different practices and rejoices at the fact that they can coexist.

The second criticism is that a cosmopolitan or European culture has no memory. According to Smith:

> [A] timeless global culture answers no living needs and conjures no memories. If memory is central to identity, we can discern no global identity in the making, nor aspirations for one, nor any collective amnesia to replace existing 'deep' cultures with a cosmopolitan 'flat' culture. The latter remains a dream confined to some intellectuals. It strikes no chord among the vast masses of people divided into their habitual communities of class, gender, region, religion and culture.[30]

Indeed, Smith goes even further and suggests that a European culture would need to forget all the bad things that have happened – wars, imperialism and the Holocaust. This astonishing claim illustrates the way in which the critics of modernism tend to neglect the political character of ideology. Just as national ideologies in Western Europe arose out of demands for democracy, so a European ideology is being built out of demands for human rights and an end to wars. The two main waves of Europeanism were after 1945, when the European movement was founded in The Hague in reaction to the horror of war, and, after 1989 and the end of the Cold War, with the coming together of peace and human rights movements.

Far from forgetting the horrible experiences of European history, these form the basis of a new cosmopolitan memory.

Both Robertson and Shaw argue that the Holocaust and Hiroshima have become global memories that underpin our conception of ourselves as part of a global community.[31] Levy and Sznaider show how memories of the Holocaust are being reproduced through museums, education and scholarly conferences, and the ways in which this memory construction influenced the humanitarian thinking that led to interventions in Bosnia and Kosovo.[32]

People in the West are no longer willing to die for the spectacle brand of nationalism. Despite Smith's assertions, I see no reason why people should not be willing to risk their life for human rights, as human rights activists and humanitarian agencies already do. The police and fire-fighters, after all, risk their lives to save other people, whatever their nationality. Defending human rights is, of course, different from national wars in which people are willing not only to risk their lives but to kill for their nations and to destroy their enemies. Surely, we are better off without that kind of passion.

Conclusion

I have defended the modernist argument that nationalism is a constructed or imagined idea, and that its success is derived from the fact that the idea suited the structural conditions associated with modernity. It provided the glue that made possible the modern state and modern industry. I have also argued that the strength of the idea depends on politics as well as culture, and that politics is more important than culture in open democratic societies. I explain the passion associated with nationalism not in terms of the strength of culture but as a consequence of war and the role of war in constructing nationalism.

The structural conditions that gave rise to modern nationalism have changed. The information economy is supplanting industrialism and requires a much more differentiated workforce. Electronic communications are now much more important than print technology, making possible new horizontal or transborder cultural communities. Wars between states are becoming an anachronism, and new forms of violence are constructing new militant nationalist and religious ideologies.

The vertical homogeneous cultures of the nation-state survive as a sort of spectacle. This form of nationalism is supplemented by new horizontal ideologies. On the one hand, we are witnessing new exclusive and fundamentalist political networks, including nationalism (nowadays both local and global because of diasporas) and Global Islamism. On the other hand, cosmopolitan and European ideologies are being mobilized that include small open nationalisms; they are being mobilized not only from above but also from below by human rights and peace movements.

So will nationalism be transcended? This is a political question. A world in which spectacle nationalism, as in the United States, depends on the idea of a struggle against new nationalism or Global Islamism is at odds with underlying socioeconomic developments. This is why they are backward-looking. It is extremely difficult to sustain closed national societies in a global era and this can only be done through violence and terror. But if spectacle and small nationalisms could be harnessed to a cosmopolitan politics that reflected the complexity of contemporary conditions, then this would allow for global standards combined with cultural and democratic devolution. A cosmopolitan world would prioritize reason and deliberation as opposed to passion. Violence unfortunately squeezes the space for reason and deliberation. The fact that a good case can be made as to why cosmopolitanism is more likely to contribute to progress does not mean that such a world will come about.

The choice between these two ideal-type worlds depends on the actions of individuals, groups and movements. It depends on debates like this one. I do not agree with the critics of the modernist paradigm, which I believe does explain earlier nationalisms, but, as a late or reflexive modernist, I am much more doubtful about the future than some of the earlier proponents of the modernist paradigm.

4

Intervention in the Balkans: An Unfinished Learning Process

The wars in the western Balkans could be considered a laboratory for post-Cold War intervention. There have been five conflicts over the last decade: Slovenia 1991; Croatia 1991–2; Bosnia-Herzegovina 1992–5; Kosovo 1999; and Macedonia 2001. As a consequence of global media attention and civil society pressure, outside powers have been learning to adapt the forms of intervention to an interconnected globalized world.

Broadly speaking, it is possible to distinguish between two types of security philosophy that have guided interventions in the Balkans. One has been the traditional geopolitical approach, in which security is understood as the defence of territory. The geopolitical approach tends to be top-down, using diplomatic, economic and military pressure to influence political leaders and warring parties. The other approach is cosmopolitan, in which security is understood as the defence of individual human beings. This approach is bottom-up; the emphasis is on respect for human rights, support for civil society, economic assistance and regional cooperation. Top-down approaches, of course, remain important, but they are shaped by bottom-up priorities.

My argument is that, in the context of globalization, geopolitical approaches to security have perverse effects – they lead to fragmentation and instability. Indeed, it is the attachment to territory and borders that explains the disintegrative process in former Yugoslavia. By and large, the United States has tended to pursue geopolitical forms of intervention, while the European Union has tended to apply both geopolitical and cosmopolitan approaches, although, over time, as a result of its experiences in the Balkans, the cosmopolitan approaches have become more salient.

It can be argued that the EU itself is a form of experimentation. While most commentators agree that the EU is neither a new European nation-state in the making nor a traditional intergovernmental regime, there is no clear consensus on the nature of this new type of polity. Is it something in between? Is it a new 'network state'?[1] In Europe, nation-states were constructed through war. It was through war that states consolidated their hold on territory, eliminated domestic private competitors and protected borders from external competitors.[2] The EU, by contrast, was established in reaction to war; its founders believed that the gradual integration of economies, societies and, eventually, polities could prevent war in Europe. How the EU relates to areas beyond the member states will influence its own development. Will it apply traditional geopolitical approaches to treat it own borders as nation-state borders? Or will it apply the methods that were adopted in its own internal development? What happens in the Balkans, thus, will have profound effects on the character of the EU itself. Indeed, the future of the EU may well depend on its readiness to apply seriously a cosmopolitan approach to the Balkans.

In this chapter, I develop this argument, first by describing the character of the wars in the Balkans and how they can be understood as a response to globalization. Then I analyse the geopolitical and cosmopolitan approaches to the wars before, finally, drawing some conclusions about future directions.

The New Nationalism in the Balkans

Geopolitical approaches to security in the Balkans have been based, to a large extent, on interpretations of the Balkan wars that derive from statist preoccupations. One dominant interpretation, especially in Europe, has been the notion that the wars can be explained in terms of 'ancient rivalries'; that they were primordial competitions for state power among competing ethnic groups, whose origins are lost in the mists of history. The very term 'Balkans', which seemed to have lost its salience in the Cold War period, conjures up an image of violence and instability, as well as colourful and exotic behaviour.[3] 'Violence was all I knew in the Balkans,' wrote Rebecca West in her book about travelling through what was then Yugoslavia, 'all I knew of the South Slavs.'[4] And this stereotypical view of the Balkans was echoed by contemporary leaders, especially in Britain, up to 1997, and France.

Yet, as most scholars of the Balkans have pointed out, the region was no more violent than the rest of Europe up to the nineteenth century.[5] It was the encounter with modernity, the romantic idea of nationalism and the quest for state power that led to the Balkan wars of the nineteenth and twentieth centuries and the first bouts of 'ethnic cleansing'. 'The introduction of the Western formula [the principle of nationalism] among these people', wrote Arnold Toynbee in 1922, 'has resulted in massacre . . . Such massacres are only the extreme form of national struggle between mutually indispensable neighbours, instigated by this fatal Western idea.'[6] Moreover, in the period 1945–90, the western Balkans enjoyed peace and stability. The proponents of the 'ancient rivalries' thesis argue that Tito's Yugoslavia suppressed but did not eliminate these tendencies; hence once the 'lid' was taken off the 'boiling pot' – a favourite metaphor – these animosities burst forth. But why then have animosities between England and France, or Britain and Germany (equally virulent in their times) gone away? And why, for example, have not animosities between Germany and the Czech Republic burst forth, since the Czechoslovak regime was much more repressive than Tito's Yugoslavia?

Another interpretation, favoured by the United States and Germany in the early stages of the war, was the notion that the conflicts were a struggle between democracy and totalitarianism. Milosevic was seen as the last remnant of communism, and the demand for self-determination by the leaders of Slovenia, Croatia and later Bosnia-Herzegovina was seen as a quest for democracy in the face of Serbian domination. The problem with this argument is that it fails to take into account, on the one hand, the 'new' character of the Milosevic regime and, on the other, the authoritarian exclusivist character of the regimes that were supposed to be democratic, especially Croatia under Tudjman. Milosevic came to power in a sort of coup in 1987, making use of an entirely new form of virulent nationalism, at that time, directed against the demands of the Kosovo Albanians, and it was on the same platform that he secured victory in the post-communist Serbian elections of 1991. Even though Tudjman did not inherit the Communist Party machine, his brand of exclusivist authoritarian nationalism was very similar. Indeed, most of the successor states of Yugoslavia (as in those of the former Soviet Union) exhibit post-totalitarian authoritarian tendencies.

Both the 'ancient rivalries' and the 'democracy versus totalitarian' interpretations derive from a collectivist view of social relations. In the first, the wars were perceived as being between communities competing for state power; in the second, as being between states representing different ideologies. In the one case, the five wars were treated as a single 'civil war'; in the other, as five sequential 'international wars'. Yet, neither interpretation takes into account the particularities of the contemporary context and, in particular, the impact of globalization on formerly authoritarian states. Yugoslavia opened its borders long before other communist states. Its citizens were allowed to travel, and under the framework of 'structural adjustment' various liberalization measures were introduced some ten years earlier than in other communist countries.[7] In other words, it had effectively already experienced some of the consequences of transition.

I prefer to use the term 'new nationalism' to explain the character of the wars in the Balkans. The 'new nationalism' makes use of nineteenth-century romantic nationalism, with new nationalist politicians reviving memories of the first Balkan wars (1912–13) and the Second World War to legitimize their claims to power, just as earlier nationalists 'invented' a history of ancient rivalries. But the roots of the 'new nationalism' lie less in the distant past than in the immediate history of communism and the impact of globalization. The new nationalism does involve a conflict between totalitarianism and democracy, but not between states – rather within states – as it reproduces the totalitarian tendencies of the previous regime in a nationalist guise. A new ideology of the 'other' replaces the discredited ideology of the past and justifies control over the inherited state apparatus. The new nationalist parties are created in the model of the former Communist Party, as a mechanism to control society.

In the former Yugoslavia, as in the Soviet Union, national differences were 'constitutionally enshrined'.[8] The administrative division into republics and provinces was based on nationality. In planned systems, competition exists but it is bureaucratic competition rather than market competition. After 1974, these administrative units received much more autonomy, and nationality became a way to bid for resources in a context where free public debate was disallowed. Yugoslavia was held together by the Communist Party and the JNA (Yugoslav National Army). When these began to disintegrate after 1989, nationalism provided a mechanism for former communist leaders to retain their hold on power.

The impact of globalization is partly to be explained in economic terms. The shrinking of the budget under the impact of IMF policies, the lowering of tax revenues and the liberalization of trade led to inequalities both between town and country and among different regions; tensions were exacerbated between villages, which retained their separate national identities, and secular multicultural towns, and regional claims to resources intensified.[9] The emergence of a parallel market was associated with an increase in criminality and corruption; many of the new nationalists were engaged in shadow activities and sought a way to legitimize their activities. Finally, high levels of unemployment, unprecedented in the communist world, led to a sense of ontological insecurity, which was assuaged by the simplicities of the nationalist rhetoric.

But globalization, in the sense of interconnectedness, also affected the character of the new nationalism. It was Milosevic who was the first to make use of the electronic media as a way of propagating the new nationalism. Serbs were fed an electronic diet of 'genocide' in Kosovo, first by the Turks in 1389 and more recently by the Albanians, and of holocaust in Croatia and Bosnia-Herzegovina, with clips of the Second World War interspersed with recent developments.[10] In effect, the Serbian public experienced a virtual war long before the real war began – a virtual war that made it difficult to distinguish truth from fiction, so that war became a continuum in which the 1389 Battle of Kosovo, the Second World War and the contemporary wars in Yugoslavia all became part of the same phenomenon. The Serbs, like European politicians, were drilled with the 'ancient rivalries' thesis.

In Croatia, Tudjman made use of the global Croat diaspora and his party, the HDZ (Croatian Democratic Union), established branches throughout North America. The diaspora was to provide funds, techniques and ideas. In effect, the diaspora introduced another form of virtuality; through their disproportionate influence, Croatian people abroad tried to impose on Croatia an ideal image which dated from their own departure and not current realities. Likewise, the 'weekend fighters' who came from Germany or Switzerland to fight in Bosnia or Kosovo experienced war as a manufactured adventure, a form of war tourism, and not as an everyday reality.

On this interpretation, the 'new nationalist' war can be understood as a form of political mobilization. In classic wars between nation-states, the aim was, to quote Clausewitz, 'to compel an opponent to fulfil our will'. In general, this was achieved through the military capture of territory and victory in battle. People were mobilized to participate in the war effort – to join the army or to produce weapons and uniforms. In the Yugoslav wars, mobilizing people was the aim of the war effort. The violence was not so much directed against the enemy; rather the aim was to entrench the politics of the new nationalism. The goal was to control territory through political means, with military means being used to kill, expel or silence those who might challenge this control. The wars were fought by a combination of regular forces – the remnants of the JNA and the newly created national armies in Croatia and Bosnia-Herzegovina; paramilitary forces like Arkan's Tigers, Frenki's Boys (notorious in Kosovo) or the Croatian 'wolves'; foreign mercenaries like the Mujahideen or the various British, French or Russian soldiers looking for new sources of income in the context of post-Cold War military redundancies; or self-defence forces, as in the case of volunteers in Tuzla or Zenica who created units to defend their homes. Likewise the KLA in Kosovo and the NLA in Macedonia were a mixture of different types of forces – classic left guerrilla groups, paramilitary groups and self-defence forces. Battles between the warring parties were rare. Rather control of territory was achieved through population displacement – ethnic cleansing. Techniques of terror, ranging from massacres and various atrocities, including systematic rape, to the destruction of historic buildings were deliberate war strategies, at least on the part of the Serbs and the Croatians. The strategy was to gain political power through sowing fear and hatred, to create a climate of terror, to eliminate moderate voices and to defeat tolerance.

Thus the political ideologies of exclusive nationalism were generated through violence. Rather than ancient rivalries being a cause of war, they were constructed through the experience of war. 'The war had to be so bloody', Bosnians will tell you, 'because we did not hate each other; we had to be taught to hate each other.' Violations of humanitarian and human rights law were not a side-effect of war but the central methodology of the wars in the Balkans. And this is why over 90 per cent of the casualties were civilian and why the numbers of refugees and displaced persons were so high. The classic exponents of this strategy were the Serbs and the Croatians. The Bosniac (Bosnian Muslim) strategy was more defensive, although they also committed war crimes. The KLA and the NLA tended to try to gain political control through support of the local population – hence they tended to target soldiers and police, although they were involved in ethnic cleansing as well.

The wars in the Balkans exacerbated the economic tendencies towards criminality and informality. They involved very high levels of physical destruction and a disruption of trade. GDP fell dramatically, as did levels of taxation. Hence the warring parties had to seek alternative methods of finance. Alongside remittances from the diaspora, these included loot and plunder, smuggling drugs, illegal immigrants, cigarettes and alcohol, and the 'taxation' of humanitarian assistance. All of these types of economic activity are predatory and depend on an atmosphere of insecurity. Indeed, the wars in Yugoslavia speeded up the insertion of the Balkans into a globalized informal economy – the transnational criminal and semi-legal economy that represents the underside of globalization and a further source of recruitment for the new nationalists.

For these reasons, each bout of war in the former Yugoslavia strengthened the position of the new nationalists, both in political and economic terms. The trauma of the wars left a trail of fear and insecurity, guilt and mistrust – emotions that cannot be easily allayed but which seek reassurance in the apparent certainties of ethnic identification. The ex-Yugoslav economy was destroyed as a consequence of the disintegration of Yugoslavia and the war. GDP fell dramatically and unemployment rose to unprecedented levels – in many areas it is as high as 40–50 per cent. An illegal informal economy linked to criminal networks and paramilitary groups across the region was established and many people remain dependent on its activities, which, up to now, have received 'protection' from the nationalist parties. And, finally, civil society and non-nationalist political forces were weakened by war. A form of democratic politics was beginning to develop in Yugoslavia during the period of 1990–2, especially in towns. However, it was the urban, educated, secular people – the bedrock of potential democratic politics – who left, or in some cases were killed; this was especially true in Bosnia-Herzegovina, Croatia and Serbia.

The wars in Kosovo and Macedonia, and the smaller conflict in the Presevo valley in southern Serbia, all have to be understood in terms of the legacy of earlier wars. In the case of Kosovo, it can be argued that the tactics of the KLA in 1996–7, in reversing the non-violent strategy of the Kosovo Albanians, precipitated the war. Nevertheless, the extent to which the vested political and economic interests of the new nationalists around Milosevic needed a new bout of violence to confront the growing democratic opposition in Serbia and to find new sources of revenue has been widely ignored in explanations of the war. Likewise, the extent to which the Macedonian conflict has to be understood as a spillover from the war in Kosovo precipitated by veterans of the KLA intent on exposing the fact that the 'Albanian question' was far from solved also seems to have been relatively neglected.

Thus, according to my interpretation, the wars in the former Yugoslavia are wars which spread a new phenomenon – exclusive nationalism, allied to a criminalized informal economy. On this interpretation, intervention from above, unless it is accompanied by intervention from below, will end up strengthening the 'new nationalism'.

The Role of Outside Intervention

The dominant form of outside intervention up to 1999 was geopolitical. Those who interpreted the conflicts as wars of 'ancient rivalries' tended to favour the diplomatic approach – talks among the warring parties. Those who perceived the wars as a conflict between democracy and totalitarianism, with Serbia cast in the latter category, tended to favour economic sanctions and air strikes – ways of putting pressure on Serbia and taking sides with the so-called democrats without risking Western casualties. In practice, both approaches ended up reinforcing the new nationalism.

The talks tended to legitimize the warring parties, transforming war criminals into negotiating partners. In so far as agreements were reached, they rationalized positions on the ground and represented unrealistic fragile compromises among exclusivist demands – the most obvious compromise being ethnic segregation or partition. Thus Dayton effectively divided Bosnia-Herzegovina into three ethnic parts; UN Security Council Resolution 1244 recognized the Kosovars' right to self-government and, at the same time, the sovereignty of Yugoslavia; and the Ohrid Framework Agreement signed in Macedonia in August 2001 gave Albanians more representation in the state apparatus, but at the same time allowed for an autonomous Albanian region.

Sanctions and air strikes did not change the situation on the ground – they were forms of long-distance outside intervention. But they did contribute to the nationalist mindset; in particular, they strengthened the Serbian conviction of victimhood, of being singled out for punishment in a war for which, in their view, the Croats and Muslims were equally responsible. By destroying physical and economic infrastructure, sanctions and air strikes also contributed to the growth of the parallel economy.[11] The Americans claim that it was air strikes that eventually ended the long Bosnian war and that it was the combination of air strikes and sanctions that finally led to the demise of Milosevic. In the case of Bosnia, air strikes may have provided the additional impetus to bring Serbs to the negotiating table, but what really mattered was the rationalization on the ground; ethnic cleansing was virtually complete. The Dayton Agreement was needed by all the warring parties, but especially the Serbs and Croats, to legitimize the status quo. As for the Kosovo war and its aftermath, it is true that Milosevic was defeated, but not because of his responsibility for the wars and the terrible events of the 1990s but because he failed to live up to the promises of Greater Serbia. It was the workers carrying Serbian flags and symbols who defeated Milosevic but this did not mean the defeat of nationalist sentiment, even though the post-Milosevic regime is more democratically minded.

An alternative cosmopolitan approach to security began to be developed during the Bosnian war under pressure from the international media and from civil society both within Bosnia-Herzegovina and in the rest of Europe. A series of significant innovations were introduced which offered the possibility of a new approach centred on human rights. These included human-itarian corridors, safe areas, the no-fly zone, the setting up of an International Criminal Tribunal for the Former Yugoslavia and the notion of international administrations or protector-ates. All of these approaches were aimed at the protection of civilians in a war where they were the primary targets. Prob-lems arose, on the one hand, due to a lack of commitment in implementing these innovations and, on the other, due to the contradictions between this new cosmopolitan approach and the simultaneously unfolding geopolitical approach from above. It is sometimes argued that there were insufficient troops to carry out the various tasks required, such as establishing safe areas. This may be true, but more important was the lack of political will, and a constrained mandate, which limited the degree to which soldiers were allowed to act 'robustly', as the jargon puts it. Moreover, talks going on at a diplomatic level did not deal with the day-to-day operation of the war but rather with finding the final settlement; the very people who were attacking civilians were, at one and the same time, respectable negotiating partners. In some cases, the talks even exacerbated developments on the ground, as the warring parties struggled to take control of particular areas, so as to improve their bar-gaining positions. The nadir was the fall of Srebrenica in July 1995, when Dutch peacekeepers handed over some 8000 men and boys to Serb forces and they were all killed.

The tension between cosmopolitanism and the geopolitical approach persisted after the Dayton Agreement. On the one hand, the Dayton Agreement divided Bosnia into two entities – one Serb and the other Croat and Muslim – and entrenched the position of the nationalist parties, who were responsible together with the international community for implementa-tion. On the other, the agreement contained commitments to human rights, freedom of movement and the integration of the country. In 1997, after the election of a Labour government in

Britain and the Sintra Peace Implementation Council Meeting, greater emphasis was placed on a cosmopolitan approach, in particular the capture of war criminals and support for non-nationalist politicians. This strategy was consolidated after the war in Kosovo, when a new regional approach was initiated with the Stability Pact Initiative, the Stabilization and Association Agreements and a host of other devices designed to foster cooperation and bring the region within the orbit of the EU.

What has been the balance sheet of all these efforts? First, most importantly, the wars have ended. But the various settlements that led to ceasefires (Dayton, 1244, or Ohrid) incorporated exclusive nationalist interests and, hence, contain within them the possibility of renewed conflict. In particular, both Dayton and 1244 are unworkable as long-term solutions without a sizeable international presence. The same may be true of Ohrid.

Second, the most extreme nationalists have been, for the most part, removed from power. Milosevic and Tudjman have gone, although Seselj remains an important political actor in Serbia. A coalition of Social Democrats and moderate nationalists came to power briefly in Bosnia-Herzegovina and may be re-elected. A moderate coalition also holds power in Kosovo. But grass-roots nationalism persists and is much stronger than before the war. Ethnic discrimination is widespread, as are popular expressions of extremist sentiment, such as the demonstrations in Serbia and Croatia against cooperation with the war crimes tribunal, or in the Serbian entity of Bosnia against the rebuilding of mosques, or in the support for the NLA within the Albanian community in Macedonia. Moreover, extreme nationalists are likely to regain power in elections, as they did in Bosnia-Herzegovina.

Third, there has been some progress in reconstruction, economic cooperation and market reforms – the euro, or its exact equivalent, is the official currency in Montenegro, Bosnia-Herzegovina and Kosovo. But there are still widespread restrictions on the movement of people, not only within the region but also with the rest of Europe. Unemployment remains unacceptably high throughout the region, and corruption/criminality is widespread. The rule of law still does not function, neither in an international sense, because the final status of borders is not yet determined, nor domestically. Throughout the region, civil society is much weaker than before the war.

The weaknesses in the Balkans reflect weaknesses in Europe as a whole. Within the region, the EU, by putting the emphasis on economic and social integration, support for civil society and education, has made efforts to replicate its own internal policies. These 'bottom-up' policies do represent important elements of a cosmopolitan approach, but the EU has never succeeded in articulating a distinctive cosmopolitan politics which might challenge the dominant geopolitical approach 'from above'. It has never succeeded in constructing a popular narrative about peace and human rights that could legitimize its own political institutions, and that is why it is so vulnerable to right-wing nationalist tendencies. In the Balkans, there is an important strand of thinking that supports what are known as European civic values. But the EU has never been able to transform this vision into a forward-looking reality that could challenge the backward-looking virtuality of the new nationalist rhetoric. It is partly a matter of resources; actual assistance has never matched the promises. More importantly, however, it is because the EU is afraid to address issues that might unravel the painful geopolitical compromises that sustain the current uneasy peace.

So there is still a lot to learn. Some kind of cosmopolitan political settlement for the whole region needs to be worked out now to complement the efforts from below – a settlement aimed at making easier the lives of individuals not collectivities, of breaking down the gap between everyday life and formal politics, of ending the partitions and mini-partitions that currently characterize so much of the Balkans. The purpose of such a settlement is to improve the lot of the people who live in the region, but it would also help to strengthen the European idea.

5

The Idea of Global Civil Society

The term global civil society only really began to be used in the last ten years – although Kant had referred to the possibility of a universal civil society. It is inextricably linked to the growing interconnectedness of states, the emergence of a system of global governance, and the explosion of movements, groups, networks and organizations that engage in a global or trans-national public debate. These developments do not mean the demise of states. On the contrary, states will continue to be the juridical repository of sovereignty, although sovereignty is likely to be much more conditional than before – more and more dependent on both domestic consent and international respect. Rather it means that the global system (and I use the term global system rather than international relations) is increasingly composed of layers of political institutions, individuals, groups and even companies, as well as states and international institutions.

In this chapter, I explore the evolution of the idea of global civil society and how it challenges classic concepts of international relations as primarily relations between states. I start with a thumbnail sketch of the changing meaning of civil society. I describe the reinvention of civil society simultaneously in Latin America and Eastern Europe, and how it differed from earlier meanings. I then want to say something about how the idea has changed again in the 1990s and the competing versions of the idea, as well as the growing criticisms of the concept. And finally, I ask whether September 11 was a defeat for the idea – a reversion to international relations.

Changing Meanings of Civil Society

Civil society is a modern concept, although, like all great political ideas, it can be traced back to Aristotle. For early modern thinkers, there was no distinction between civil society and the state. Civil society was a type of state characterized by a social contract. Civil society was a society governed by laws, based on the principle of equality before the law, in which everyone, including the ruler (at least in the Lockean conception), was subject to the law, that is, a social contract agreed among the individual members of society. It was not until the nineteenth century that civil society became understood as something distinct from the state. It was Hegel who defined civil society as the intermediate realm between the family and the state, where the individual becomes a public person and through membership in various institutions is able to reconcile the particular and the universal. For Hegel, civil society was 'the achievement of the modern world – the territory of mediation where there is free play for every idiosyncrasy, every talent, every accident of birth and fortune and where waves of passion gust forth, regulated only by reason glinting through them'.[1] Thus Hegel's definition of civil society included the economy, and was to be taken up by Marx and Engels, who saw civil society as the 'theatre of history'.

The definition narrowed again in the twentieth century, when civil society came to be understood as the realm not only between the state and the family but between the market, state and family – in other words, the realm of culture, ideology and political debate. The Italian Marxist Antonio Gramsci is the thinker most associated with this definition. He was preoccupied with the question of why it was so much easier to have a communist revolution in Russia than in Italy. His answer was civil society. In Italy, and I quote, 'there was a proper relation between state and society and, when the state trembled, a sturdy structure of civil society was at once revealed'.[2] His strategy for the Italian Communist Party, which, in fact, was followed right up until the 1980s, was to gain positions in civil society – in universities, in the media and so on – so as to challenge the hegemony of the bourgeoisie. It was Gramsci who drew the distinction between hegemony, based on consent, and domination, based on coercion.

Despite the changing of the content of the term, I want to suggest that all these different definitions had a common core meaning. They were about a rule-governed society based on the consent of individuals, or, if you like, a society based on a social contract among individuals. The changing definitions of civil society expressed the different ways in which consent was generated in different periods and the different issues that were important. In other words, civil society, according to my definition, is the process through which individuals negotiate, argue, struggle against or agree with each other and with the centres of political and economic authority. Through voluntary associations, movements, parties, unions, the individual is able to act publicly. Thus in the early modern period, the main concern was civil rights – freedom from fear. Hence civil society was a society where laws replace physical coercion, arbitrary arrest, etc. In the nineteenth century, the issue was political rights and the actors in civil society were the emerging bourgeoisie. In the twentieth century, it was the workers' movement that was challenging the state and the issue was economic and social emancipation – hence the further narrowing of the term.

Not only did all these definitions have this common core of meaning, but also they all conceived of civil society as territorially tied. Civil society was inextricably linked up with the territorial state. It was contrasted with other states characterized by coercion – the empires of the East. It was also contrasted with premodern societies, which lacked a state and lacked the concept of individualism – Highlanders or American Indians. And, above all, it was contrasted with international relations, which was equated with the state of nature because of the lack of a single authority. Many civil society theorists believed that civil society at home was linked to war abroad. It was the ability to unite against an external enemy that made civil society possible. Thus Adam Ferguson, the Scottish Enlightenment thinker, whose book *An Essay on the History of Civil Society* is one of the core texts on civil society, was deeply concerned about modern individualism. Like the other Scottish Enlightenment thinkers, he wanted to develop a scientific approach to the study of social phenomena and believed this had to be done through empirical study of other societies. To understand the evolution of society, he studied the Highlanders and American Indians and became convinced that modern society had lost the spirit of community, natural empathy and affection among human beings. He believed, taking the example of Sparta, that patriotism and the martial spirit was one way to overcome the dangers of individualism. An even stronger version of this argument was taken up by Hegel, who believed that war was necessary for the 'ethical health of peoples . . . Just as the movement of the ocean prevents the corruption which would be the result of perpetual calm, so by war people escape the corruption which would be occasioned by a continuous or eternal peace.'[3] Of course, not all civil society theorists took this view – Kant was the most important exception; he believed that the perfect constitution of the state could be achieved only in the context of a universal civil society – but it was the dominant view.

The Reinvention of Civil Society

The revival of the idea of civil society in the 1970s and 1980s, I believe, broke that link with the state. Interestingly, the idea was rediscovered simultaneously in Latin America and Eastern Europe. I was deeply involved in the East European discussions and always thought it was they who reinvented the term. However, subsequently, I discovered that the Latin Americans had used the term earlier. Cardoso (the former President of Brazil) was one of the key people to use the term. Indeed, it is a fascinating task in the history of the ideas to explore the way in which this concept proved useful in two different continents at the same time, with as far as I know no communication between them – on the contrary, there seems to have been widespread mistrust, since by and large the Latin Americans were Marxists and the East Europeans were anti-Marxists.

In both cases, the term 'civil society' proved a useful concept in opposing militarized regimes. Latin Americans were opposing military dictatorships; East Europeans were opposing totalitarianism – a sort of war society. Both came to the conclusion that overthrow of their regimes 'from above' was not feasible;

rather it was necessary to change society. Michnik, in his classic article 'The New Evolutionism', first published in 1978, argued that attempts to bring change from above (Hungary 1956 or Czechoslovakia 1968) had failed and that the only possible strategy was through change from below, by changing the relationship between state and society.[4] What he meant by civil society was autonomy and self-organization. Thus the emphasis, and this was shared by the Latin Americans, was on withdrawal from the state – creating islands of civic engagement – a concept shared by both East Europeans and Latin Americans. East Europeans also used terms like 'anti-politics', 'living in truth' – the notion of refusing the lies of the regime or 'parallel polis' – the idea of creating their own Aristotelian community based on the 'good', that is, moral, life. (Forced into inactivity, the East European dissidents, especially in Czechoslovakia where they had to become stokers and window cleaners, spent their time reading classical political thinking and discussing them, which is why, I think, they were able to articulate the ideas of a generation. I remember a friend saying when I visited Prague in the early 1990s in the throes of revolutionary fervour: 'What I really miss are those evenings where understanding a passage from Plato's *Republic* seemed the most important thing in the world.')

As well as the emphasis on autonomy and civil organization, civil society also acquired a global meaning. This was a period of growing interconnectedness, increased travel and communication, even before the advent of the internet. The emergence of 'islands of civic engagement' was made possible by two things:

1 Links with like-minded groups in other countries. The Latin Americans were supported by North American human rights groups. The East Europeans made links with West European peace and human rights groups, who supported them materially and publicized their cases, and put pressure on governments and institutions.

2 The existence of international human rights legislation to which their governments subscribed and which could be used as a form of pressure. For Latin America, it was the human rights legislation that was important. For East Europe, the Helsinki Agreement of 1975 in which East

European governments signed up to human rights provided a platform for new groups like Charter 77 or KOR (Workers' Defence Committee).

In other words, through international links and appeals to international authorities, these groups were able to create political space. Keck and Sikkink, in their book on transnational activism, talk about the 'boomerang effect' whereby, instead of directly addressing your government, appeals to the international community bounce back, as it were, and put pressure on governments to tolerate certain activities.[5]

This transnational or global aspect of the new understanding of civil society has been widely neglected by Western commentaries on the period, perhaps because they understood civil society within their own traditions of thought. Yet it was stressed by the new thinkers themselves, certainly in East Europe. George Konrad, the Hungarian writer, and my favourite of these thinkers, used the word 'globalization' in his book *Anti-Politics* written in 1982. Vaclav Havel talked about the 'global technological civilization':

The post-totalitarian system is only one aspect – a particularly drastic aspect and thus all the more revealing of its real origins – of the general inability of modern humanity to be master of its own situation. The automatism of the post-totalitarian system is merely an extreme version of the global automatism of technological civilisation. The human failure that it mirrors is only one variant of the general failure of humanity. . . . It would appear that the traditional parliamentary democracies can offer no fundamental opposition to the automatism of technological civilisation and the industrial-consumer society, for they, too, are being dragged helplessly along. People are manipulated in ways that are infinitely more subtle and refined than the brutal methods used in post-totalitarian societies. . . . In a democracy, human beings may enjoy personal freedoms and securities that are unknown to us, but in the end they do them no good, for they too are ultimately victims of the same automatism, and are incapable of defending their concerns about their own identity of preventing their superficialisation or transcending concerns about their own personal survival to become proud and responsible members of the polis, making a genuine contribution to the creation of its destiny.[6]

Thus the new understanding of civil society represented both a withdrawal from the state and a move towards global rules and institutions. The group who pioneered these ideas were central to the pressures for democratization in Latin America and the 1989 revolutions. It is sometimes said that there were no new ideas in the 1989 revolutions – that they just wanted to be like the West. But I think this new understanding of civil society was the big new idea, an idea that was to contribute a new set of global arrangements in the 1990s.

Global Civil Society in the 1990s

In the aftermath of 1989, the concept of civil society changed its meaning and was understood in very different ways. Broadly speaking, one can distinguish three main meanings – paradigms, if you like.

(1) First of all, the term was taken up all over the world by the so-called 'new social movements' – the movements that developed after 1968 concerned with new issues, like peace, women, human rights, the environment, and with new forms of protest. The language of civil society seemed to express very well their brand of non-party politics. Ideas about the public sphere or the notion of communicative action, pioneered by Jürgen Habermas, seemed to resonate well with the concept of civil society; indeed in his most recent writing Habermas identifies the public sphere with civil society:

> The expression 'civil society' has in the meantime taken on a meaning different from that of the 'bourgeois society' of the liberal tradition, which Hegel conceptualised as the 'system of needs', that is, as a market system involving social labour and commodity exchange. What is meant by 'civil society' today, in contrast to its usage in the Marxist tradition, no longer includes the economy as constituted by private law and steered through markets in labour, capital and commodities. Rather, its institutional core comprises those non-governmental and non-economic connections and voluntary associations that anchor the communication structures of the public sphere in the society component of the life-world. Civil society is composed of those

more or less spontaneously emergent associations, organisations, and movements that, attuned to how societal problems resonate in private life spheres, distil and transmit such reactions to the public sphere. The core of civil society comprises a network of associations that institutionalises problem-solving discourses of general interest inside the framework of organised public spheres. These 'discursive designs' have an egalitarian, open form of organisation that mirrors essential features of the kind of communication around which they crystallise and to which they lend continuity and permanence.[7]

The term 'civil society' provided a platform for the new social movements, a legitimization of their activities. The concept was enthusiastically taken up in South Asia, Africa, especially South Africa, and Western Europe. Because of the context in which these movements operated, they addressed not just the state – indeed they often felt blocked at state levels because of the dominance of political parties – but layers of institutions (local, national and global). A new phenomenon of great importance during this period was the emergence of transnational networks of activists who came together on particular issues – land mines, human rights, climate change, dams, AIDS/HIV, or corporate responsibility. I believe they had a significant impact on strengthening processes of global governance, especially in the humanitarian field. As I argued in chapter 1, notions of humanitarian norms that override sovereignty, the establishment of the International Criminal Court and the strengthening of human rights awareness were very important in the construction of a new set of multilateral rules – what we might call a humanitarian regime. Towards the end of the 1990s, the emergence of a so-called anti-globalization movement – concerned with global social justice – used the concept of civil society in the same way. I call this understanding the 'activist version'.

(2) Secondly, the term was taken up by the global institutions and by Western governments. It became part of the so-called New Policy Agenda. Civil society was understood as what the West has; it is seen as a mechanism for facilitating market reform and the introduction of parliamentary democracy. I call this the 'neoliberal version'. In contrast to Habermas and the public sphere, this understanding built on American ideas about the 'third sector' (Salamon and Anheier), communitarianism

(Etzioni) or social capital (Robert Putnam).[8] In particular, Robert Putnam's work seemed to demonstrate that thick associational activity, ranging from bowling clubs and picnics to churches and trade unions, is conducive to democracy and economic development. This understanding of civil society is much less political and more passive than the concept of the public sphere. Civil society is primarily about self-organization rather than communication; it offers a substitute for the state, an alternative to excessive state interference, rather than a way of influencing the state. These thinkers trace their ideas back to De Tocqueville and his insight that 'if men are to remain civilised or to become so, the art of associating together must grow and improve in the same ratio as the equality of conditions is increased.'[9]

The key agents of this version of civil society are not social movements but NGOs. I regard NGOs as 'tamed' social movements. Social movements always rise and fall. And as they fall, they are either 'tamed' – institutionalized and professionalized – or they become marginal and disappear or turn to violence. Being 'tamed' means that you become the respectable opposition – the partner in negotiations. Historically, social movements were tamed within a national framework. Campaigners for the suffrage or for anti-slavery in the nineteenth century became absorbed into liberal parties. Labour movements were originally universalist and internationalist but became transformed into official trade unions and Labour and Social Democratic parties. Anti-colonial movements transformed themselves into political parties.

What was significant in the 1990s was that the new social movements became tamed within a global framework. There have always been international NGOs like the Anti-Slavery Society or the International Committee of the Red Cross, but these increased dramatically in the 1990s, often as a result of official funding. (For numbers, see the data we have collected in the yearbooks we publish at LSE.[10]) Indeed NGOs increasingly look both like quasi-governmental institutions because of the way they substitute for state functions and, at the same time, like a market, because of the way they compete with each other. The dominance of NGOs has led some activists to become disillusioned with the concept of civil society. Thus Neera Chandhoke, a civil society theorist from Delhi University, says civil society has become a 'hurrah word' and 'flattened out'. 'Witness the tragedy that has visited proponents of the concept: people struggling against authoritarian regimes demanded civil society, what they got were NGOs. . . . If everyone from trade unions, social movements, the UN, the IMF, lending agencies, to states both chauvinistic and democratic hail civil society as the most recent elixir to the ills of the contemporary world, there must be something wrong.'[11] And Mahmoud Mamdami, the African political scientist, says 'NGOs are killing civil society.'[12]

(3) Yet a third concept of global civil society is what I call the postmodern version. Social anthropologists criticize the concept of society as euro-centric, something borne of the Western cultural context (according to this argument, Latin America and Eastern Europe are culturally part of Europe). They suggest that non-Western societies experience or have the potential to experience something similar to civil society but not necessarily based on individualism. It is certainly true that all cultures have traditions of human dignity, tolerance and the use of reason and public deliberation. In his autobiography, Nelson Mandela tells how his understanding of democracy derived from the debates in his village as a child.[13] Likewise, much of the thinking of classical Islam in the medieval period – the heyday of Islam – anticipates the ideas of civil society in the Western Enlightenment. Thus classical Islamic thought distinguished between the realm of Islam, *dar al-Islam*, and the realm of war, *dar al-harb*. The realm of Islam was a community characterized by a political authority, whose authority derived from the rule of law, *Shari'a*, and a social contract, *Bay'a*. Islam was a system of values contained in the Qu'ran and the Hadith (the sayings and practices of Prophet Mohammed) and interpreted by scholars, *Ulama*, who were independently financed through the *bazaar* and religious foundations (*waqf*). It was based on a notion of human reason, later taken up in Enlightenment thought, which was derived from individual knowledge or awareness of God's will imprinted on human consciousness. This distinction between the realm of Islam and the realm of war paralleled the distinction between civil society and the state of nature in Enlightenment thought. Indeed, the Arabic term for civil society, *Almujtamaa Almadani*, derives both from

the word for city and from Medina, the city where Mohammed first established his Islamic society/city-state. The writing of the famous historian Ibn Khaldun at the end of the fourteenth century reads like a forerunner of Adam Ferguson. Khaldun's central argument is about the establishment of cities and the need for a new form of social solidarity among strangers to replace tribal solidarity. The values of Islam provide a basis for this solidarity.[14]

It is sometimes argued that civil society is different from this concept of Islamic society because it is a secular notion that can apply to all human beings. But Islam was also a universal creed that claimed global relevance to any human community. In practice, however, both were bounded concepts. Civil society was bounded by territory, and Islamic society was bounded by belief and by territory, even if it adopted some measures of religious pluralism. Within these communities, there was a presumption of non-violence, a notion of peace with justice, and this was contrasted with the external world of violence.

Thus postmodernists argue that it was Western dominance that often suppressed more enlightened traditions in the rest of the world. Mamdani and Chatterjee, for example, argue that contractual notions of civil society characterized the colonial elite in cities, and that elsewhere repressive systems of governance were imposed, based on rigidifying Western notions of tradition.[15] They reject the term 'civil society' and argue for the use of the term 'political society'. Others suggest that global civil society must engage with other traditions and recapture notions of civility that can enrich the secular, modernist, individualistic notion of civil society.[16] Thus for postmodernists, new religious and ethnic movements that have also grown dramatically over the last decade are a significant component of global civil society, including the extremist variants, which need to be involved in dialogue. Global civil society can't be just the 'nice, good Northern movements'.

Civil society has always had both a normative and descriptive content. The definition that I gave at the beginning was a normative definition. I said that civil society is the process through which consent is generated, the arena where the individual negotiates, struggles against or debates with the centres of political and economic authority. Today, those centres include global institutions, both international institutions and companies. I think that all three versions have to be included in the concept. It could be argued that state-funded NGOs should be excluded since they are not autonomous from the state. It can also be argued that compulsory communalist groups, which may be the case for religious and nationalist movements, should be excluded because central to the concept of civil society is individual emancipation, and that groups that advocate violence should be excluded. But this would mean confining the definition to the activist version and only including autonomous, non-violent, voluntary and politically engaged groups – in other words a narrowly activist version. If the term global civil society is to have any purchase on global developments, it needs the neoliberal and postmodernist versions. The neoliberal version makes the term respectable, providing a platform for more radical groups to be able to gain access to power (both 'insiders' like NGOs and 'outsiders' like social movements). The postmodernist version offers a basis for many of the most excluded people in the world. In practice, moreover, in actually existing civil society, it is almost impossible to draw boundaries between who is included and who is excluded.

What has happened in the 1990s, I would argue, is the emergence of a system of global governance which involves both states and international institutions. It is not a single world state but a system in which states are increasingly hemmed in by a set of agreements, treaties and rules of a transnational character. Moreover, these rules are based not just on agreement between states but on public support, generated through global civil society. Of particular importance, I think, is a growing body of cosmopolitan law, by which I mean the combination of humanitarian law (laws of war) and human rights law.[17] Cosmopolitan law is international law that applies not just to states but to individuals – something earlier international relations theorists considered to be impossibly utopian. This broadening and strengthening of cosmopolitan law, both immediately after the Second World War and in the 1990s, it can be argued, was largely a consequence of global civil society pressure.

In other words, global civil society is a platform inhabited by activists (or post-Marxists), NGOs, neoliberals, as well as national and religious groups, where they argue about, campaign for (or against), negotiate about, or lobby for the arrangements that shape global developments. There is not one global civil society but many, affecting a range of issues – human rights, the environment, and so on. It is not democratic – there are no processes of election, nor could there be, I think, at a global level since that would require a world state. And such a state, even if democratically elected, would be totalitarian. It is also uneven and dominated by the North. Nevertheless, the emergence of this phenomenon does offer a potential for individuals – a potential for emancipation. It opens up closed societies, as happened in Eastern Europe and Latin America, and it offers the chance to participate in debates about global issues. It is the emergence of this phenomenon – this new global system – that makes the term 'international relations' much less appropriate.

Critics of Global Civil Society

The idea of global civil society has generated a considerable critical literature. The literature focuses on two main lines of criticism. One concerns the demise of states, and the other the normative content of the term 'global civil society'.

The starting point for most of the critics is the intrinsic relationship between civil society and the state. Civil society cannot be separated from the notion of a constitutional order, where the state provides security so that people can engage in politics freely and without fear, and, in turn, civil society provides a check on the authoritarian tendencies of the state. How can there be, therefore, a global civil society in the absence of a world state? This is fundamentally the argument of Chris Brown, who concedes that it might be possible to talk about a Euro-Atlantic civil society since this is a peaceful region.[18] A similar argument is made by David Chandler, who says that there is no such thing as world citizenship because citizenship rights imply the existence of institutions with duties, and only states are those kinds of institutions. Some argue that human rights constitute world citizenship rights, but Chandler insists this is not the case because there is no enforcement mechanism.[19] It also appears that Chandler opposes such an enforcement mechanism since he is a fierce critic of the notion of humanitarian intervention.

A related point has to do with the absence of democracy at a world level. Chandler wants to restore democracy at a national level and argues that this is the level at which activism should be focused. Likewise, Ken Anderson and David Rieff criticize the hubris of any notion of global politics. They argue that the idea of global civil society is a dangerous fallacy, given the absence of representative institutions at a global level. They suggest that the various groups and organizations that call themselves 'global civil society' claim to represent world opinion and to substitute for the functioning of representative democracy at national levels, and that this claim is profoundly anti-democratic. In particular, they suggest that global civil society gets to be equated with a particular group of what might be described as cosmopolitan universalists, standard-bearers of 'environmentalism, feminism, human rights, economic regulation, sustainable development.'[20] These 'social movement missionaries' have arrogated to themselves a supposed legitimacy that does not and cannot reflect the aspirations of individuals worldwide.

In addition to concerns about peace and democracy, some critics also see global civil society as a way of legitimizing the global market. Ronnie Lipschutz uses the Foucauldian term 'govermentality' to describe the activities of global NGOs who ineffectively try to regulate the global market through campaigns about labour standards or environmental standards in the absence of state regulation.[21] They end up becoming part of the texture of globalization, the way of thinking that allows for tacit acceptance of current global arrangements – they generate the 'mentality' of governance that underlies the exercise of power at a global level. They do not challenge the constitution of global power, only the way that power is distributed. Underlying this argument is the notion that globalization is about the demise of state power and the dominance of the market.

All of these arguments seem to reflect a nostalgia for the primacy of the state. Yet the era of state dominance was also an era of terrible wars and totalitarianism, where civil society only really functioned in small privileged parts of the world. Indeed, it could be argued that the existence of bounded civil society depended on a 'state of nature' elsewhere. Even if it were desirable, it is no longer possible to insulate civil society territorially – there are new communities and new loyalties that cross borders, and new levels of authority. Nor can violence be channelled outwards; global terror and organized crime are new types of global risk that break down the spatial boundaries between peace and war.

A useful distinction is made by Iris Marion Young, who points out that the tendency to think of civil society, the state and the market as separate spaces or spheres is misleading. It would be better to think in terms of processes, in which these different terms refer to different ways of coordinating activities, even though they are intermeshed with each other. 'State designates activities of formal and legal regulation backed by legitimate coercive apparatus of enforcement. Economy designates market-oriented activity concerned with the production and distribution of resources, products and wealth, which is constrained by considerations of profit and loss, cost-minimization, and so on. Civil society names activity for self-organization for particular purposes of enhancing social values.'[22] Or in other words, the different forms of coordination are authorized power, money and communicative action.

My point is that the state is not the only form of authorized power, and nor should it be. The development of a system of global governance provides a check on state activities, including the right to make war and to repress citizens. In a world of global risk, civil society can only survive as a global phenomenon. Civil society both depends on the extension of the system of global governance as a basis for its activities and, at the same time, helps to constitute the system; just as in the past the state and bounded civil society were mutually constitutive. It is true that, as yet, enforcement is weak, although communicative action has proved important in opening up closed societies, as in Eastern Europe or Latin America. In practice, enforcement depends both on a coercive apparatus and on the role of civil society as a site for constructing legitimacy. In the global arena, where the coercive apparatus is weak, the role of global civil society is all the more important, both in underpinning regulatory procedures and in pressing for more effective forms of enforcement, for example the extension of cosmopolitan law or the concept of 'responsibility to protect'.

It is also true that it is not possible to imagine a democracy on a world scale, as discussed above, but there are many imaginative proposals for reinforcing democracy through a combination of subsidiarity, issue-based representation and global legal standards in a global era.[23] And although this may not correspond to ideal forms of representative democracy, it is the best hope for substantive or deep democracy, in which citizens are able to influence the decisions that affect their lives; however perfect the democratic constitution at state level, this will not result in substantive democracy if those decisions are taken in other arenas.

Of course, globalization has shifted the balance between state-type activities and market-oriented activities. Many global civil society groups focus on the accountability of multinational corporations. Within the so-called anti-globalization movements, however, there is concern with the constitution of the system of global governance. Some are anti-globalization and favour a return to the primacy of states. Others favour a strengthening of the global capacity to regulate the market. The French talk of *alter mondialisation* – another form of globalization that reflects this possibility.

The other set of criticisms have to do with the normative content of the term 'global civil society'. There is a tendency in much global civil society writing to assume that global civil society plays a positive role. Efforts to give substance to the concept, as is done in the annual global civil society yearbooks, by measuring the participation of international non-governmental organizations (INGOs) in parallel summits or global meetings, or even through a chronology of global civil society events, do tend to give precedence to the 'nice guys' – the new global activists – even though extremist movements, representatives of political establishments and other kinds of civic institutions as well are also described. But the normative content of the concept of global civil society derives not from the participants or the actors of global civil society but rather from the very notion of global public debate or global communicative action. A world where decisions are influenced by such a debate is assumed to be better than a world coordinated through 'blood and iron' – the Bismarckian phrase for realist international relations. Chandler objects that there is no such thing as global communicative space; he claims that it is a 'fiction'.[24] But then what are bloggers, websites, internet fora, parallel summits, satellite television, not to mention local face-to-face debates in the global cities that bring together far-flung communities ranging from globalizing corporate executives to illegal immigrants, or what are Davos and Porto Allegre? Global civil society does, of course, include the critics of the concept, as well as market fanatics and fundamentalists of various hues. The normative thrust of the idea of global civil society is, rather, the belief that a genuinely free conversation, a rational critical dialogue, will favour the spread of a more humane form of global governance. Such debates are never, of course, genuinely free, and the rich and the privileged always dominate them. But the opportunities for inclusion, as Iris Marion Young points out, are greater the more extensive the activities are that can be counted as civil society.

Interestingly enough, this argument is taken for granted within a national context. But perhaps because international relations was always supposed to be about state interest and not norms and reasoned debate, it is considered excessively idealistic in the global context. Yet if we want both to avoid a return to state primacy because of the consequences for war and repression, and, at the same time, to face up to the new global risks, this seems, to me, to be the only realistic approach.

After September 11

Finally, how has the idea of global civil society been affected by September 11? Do terror and war on terror mark a reversal of the developments I describe? Both terror and war on terror are profoundly inimical to global civil society. Terror can be regarded as a direct attack on global civil society, a way of creating fear and insecurity that is the opposite of civil society. Bush's response has been an attempt to reimpose international relations, that is to say, to put the threat of terrorism within a state framework. The US is the only country not hemmed in by globalization, the only state able to continue to act as an autonomous nation-state – a 'global unilateralist', as Javier Solana puts it, or the last nation-state. Bush identified the 'enemy' as states which sponsor terrorism or which possess weapons of mass destruction. But the wars in Iraq and Afghanistan have not reduced terror; on the contrary, the bombings in Madrid, London, the Middle East and Asia seem to suggest that terror and the war on terror feed on each other. Above all, the language of terror, war, and war on terrorism closes down debate, closes the space for different political positions. In 2006, both the Danish cartoon controversy – in which a Danish newspaper published blasphemous cartoons of Mohammed, sparking organized protest throughout the Middle East – and the debate about the Pope's speech – in which he was thought to have much anti-Islamic remarks – illustrated how 'solitarist identities', as Amartya Sen calls them, come to dominate more complex differentiated arguments.[25]

But Bush cannot reverse the process of globalization. The consequences of trying to reimpose international relations are an even more uneven, anarchic, wild globalization. It is a situation in which the 'outside' of international relations, at least in a realist conception, comes 'inside', in which we can no longer insulate civil society from what goes on outside – a perverse boomerang effect. The distinction between war and domestic peace made by the classical theorists of civil society no longer holds. Global civil society offers the promise of bringing the 'inside' outside. Terror and the war on terror offer the opposite.

Is there an alternative? Could we imagine domestic politics on the global scene – something the critics dismiss as impossibly utopian? Yet this is exactly what happened during the decade of the 1990s. And despite terror and the war on terror, global civil society has not gone away. The anti-globalization movement, the peace movement, the various Islamic activists are even more engaged. The war in Iraq seemed to be a defeat for multilateralism, dividing the United Nations and the European Union. Yet both organizations have increasingly been taking alternative positions, in relation, for example, to Iran or Lebanon. Moreover, the failures in Iraq and Afghanistan have provoked a global debate even in the United States.

What happens depends on politics, on the agency of people who make history. The idea of global civil society is an emancipatory idea, allowing every individual the potential to engage in this debate. I do think that we are living through a very dangerous time: the wars in Iraq, Afghanistan and the Middle East are becoming ever more interconnected; there could be a new war in South Asia, including the possible use of nuclear weapons, and we are already witnessing an increase in global terrorism. To what extent can global civil society convince states to adopt an alternative multilateralist framework for dealing with dictators, terrorism and weapons of mass destruction, not to mention poverty, AIDS/HIV, the environment and other desperately important issues?

Many commentators pointed out that the attacks of September 11 should have been dealt with in the framework of international law. They should have seen treated as a crime against humanity; a war crimes tribunal should have been established by the Security Council; and efforts to catch and destroy terrorists, even if they involve the use of military means, should be considered not war but law enforcement.[26] And the same argument can be made about the situation in Iraq. There were ways of dealing with Iraq which might have been gleaned from the experience of Eastern Europe in the 1980s; United Nations Security Council resolutions, especially 687, emphasized human rights and democracy as well as weapons of mass destruction, and could have been used in the same way as the Helsinki Agreement to put pressure on the regime; weapons inspectors could have been accompanied by human rights monitors; and the international community could have made it clear that it would protect Iraqis from Saddam Hussein's forces in the event of an uprising, as it did in northern Iraq in 1991 and failed to do in the case of the Shi'ite uprising.[27]

But this was not done. Is it utopian to suggest that such approaches could be adopted in the future? Is it possible that we are learning from the mistakes of the post-September 11 response, or are we dragged ever deeper into the mire of trying unsuccessfully to recreate state power?

I do not see any other way out of the current dangerous impasse than trying to establish a set of global rules based on consent. We have to find ways to minimize violence at a global level, in the same way that early modern thinkers envisaged civil society as a way of minimizing violence at domestic levels. And this means opening up the conversation about what might be done.

I would like to end with a quotation from George Konrad. He was worried about the threat of nuclear war, the risk of a 'global Auschwitz', as he called it (he himself is a survivor of Auschwitz). That is the 'It' he refers to, although I think it could also apply to terror and the war on terror. Konrad concludes his book by saying: 'Of course, I am small before the great, weak before the powerful, cowardly before the violent, wavering before the aggressive, expendible before It, which is so vast and durable that I sometimes think it is immortal. I don't turn the other cheek to it. I don't shoot with a slingshot; I look, and then I collect my words.'[28]

6

Just War and Just Peace

In one of its modes, just war theory would also abolish war by the (theoretically) simple method of calling unjust wars 'crimes' and just wars 'police actions'. We have here a nice example of what the Chinese call 'the rectification of names', but it presupposes in practice a thoroughgoing transformation of international society.

Michael Walzer, *Just and Unjust Wars*

By just war theory, I mean the type of ethical thinking about war that originated in Christian traditions and became increasingly secularized in the modern period; it also has parallels in other religious traditions, especially Islam. My main argument in this chapter is that just war theory is increasingly stretched and difficult to apply in the context of those changes we lump together under the rubric of globalization. These include growing consciousness of humanity as a single community, the unacceptable destructiveness of war, increased interconnectedness in all fields, the importance of human rights norms and laws, and above all, new forms of overlapping political authority, often described as global governance, involving states and international institutions, as well as civil society and, indeed, individuals. Indeed it can be argued that a thoroughgoing transformation of international society is in fact taking place, even if it does not amount to the establishment of a global state, which is what Walzer implied in the epigraph above. Instead of just war theory, a new ethical approach is needed, grounded in the notion that the rights of individuals supersede the rights of states and that, therefore, international law that applies to individuals overrides the laws of war. In other words, *jus in pace* cannot be suspended in wartime in favour of *jus ad bellum* or *jus in bello*.

There is still a role for legitimate military force, but the way it is used is more akin to domestic law enforcement than war-fighting. I use the term 'human security' to refer to the defence of individuals as opposed to 'state security'. Of course, some of the principles of just war theory are relevant to law enforcement, as is much of the content of humanitarian law, but a change in the language is important. Just war theory does offer a framework for thinking about the justifiable use of force, but that is different from just war. In particular, crucial differences with just war theory include the need to reconceptualize aggression as a gross violation of human rights, to shift the authorization of force from the nation-state to a multilateral set of arrangements, and to reject notions like 'collateral damage', 'double effect' or 'unintentionality'.

In developing this argument, I start by describing some of the key changes that have resulted from the process known as globalization, and then consider the implications for just war theory. I end by setting out the key principles of an alternative approach based on the right of individuals rather than states – a new *jus in pace*.

The Global Context

The term 'globalization' refers to many different phenomena. Nevertheless, its widespread use reflects an awareness of some kind of fundamental change in world order, with specific consequences for the character of state sovereignty. The most common factor that helps to explain these different phenomena is technology, especially but not only the spread of communications and information technology. To say this is not to assert a technologically determinist view of history; rather the emergence and evolution of new technologies can only be understood as the outcome of social interaction. In what follows, I describe various elements of this fundamental change we call globalization, with particular emphasis on the implications for state sovereignty.

Human consciousness, human rights, and democracy

One interpretation of globalization is that we have become conscious of a single human community, as discussed in previous chapters. This is partly the result of global communications, particularly satellite television – we are increasingly aware of human suffering in other parts of the world. Pictures of the earth taken from space or global memories like Hiroshima or the Holocaust contribute to this shared sense of consciousness.

This growing human consciousness is reflected in the growth of human rights and norms in the period since the end of the Second World War. The 1948 Declaration on Human Rights and the various covenants, and most recently, the tribunals for the former Yugoslavia and Rwanda and the establishment of the International Criminal Court, have created a body of international law that applies to individuals and not states. This law has been backed up and strengthened by an emerging human rights lobby, composed of civil society groups and sympathetic governments.

Growing global consciousness means that it is harder and harder to sustain closed authoritarian states. Even in Saddam Hussein's Iraq, there were subversive bloggers and underground opposition groups with links to the outside world. The so-called third wave of democratization in Latin America, Africa, Asia and Eastern Europe was, it can be argued, an outcome of globalization – the links that were made between opposition groups and the outside world and the recourse to international human rights law. Now we seem to be on the brink of a fourth wave, with civil society revolutions of various colours in Serbia, Georgia, Ukraine and Kyrgyzstan, and pressures for democratization elsewhere, especially in the Middle East.

Effectively, these developments imply that state sovereignty is increasingly 'conditional' – dependent both on domestic behaviour and consent of the outside world.

Travel and migration

The last decades of the twentieth century witnessed a new wave of migration. Because of the ease of communication and travel, however, the new migrants, unlike the great waves of migration at the end of the nineteenth century, are able to keep in touch with their homeland. The notion of a diaspora, which earlier applied only to the Jews, has become widespread – these are growing transnational communities based on ethnicities and religion. This also has implications for state sovereignty since the notion of a vertically organized, territorially based community congruent to the state is greatly weakened. It is often argued that the cohesion of states depends on the idea of the 'other' – what Carl Schmitt called the friend–enemy distinction.[1] Yet nowadays, citizens have multiple loyalties, to the state, to their community, which may no longer be congruent with the state, and to humankind. Friend–enemy distinctions, as between Israel and Palestine or Serbia and Croatia, are often reproduced within the global cities of the advanced industrial world.

Interconnectedness

In the social sciences, globalization is often defined as interconnectedness in all fields – economic, political, cultural and social.[2] Effectively, this means that decisions that affect our everyday lives are often taken far away by multinational corporations, international institutions like the IMF, the World Bank or the European Union, or even by powerful foreign states, for example, the United States. Economic policies like 'structural adjustment' or 'convergence criteria', trade and investments agreements, rules about the environment, or even international sporting and cultural events increasingly curtail the autonomy of the state to legislate about developments within its territory. Some authors talk about a 'hollow state' in which civil servants are more often in communication with their counterparts in other countries than their domestic constituencies, and in which the task of political leaders is less to rule than to manage complex relationships with international institutions, other states, international companies and NGOs, as well as domestic interests and the wider public.

In extreme cases, the difficulty of reconciling all these pressures leads to state failure or state collapse, which is the source of many terrible conflicts happening in the world today. Indeed, the risks or threats we face are less likely to come from authoritarian states than from failing states, although the latter are usually a combination of authoritarianism and state failure.

The changing character of warfare

In the twentieth century, military technology became more destructive, more accurate and more widely available. Symmetric war, war between two similarly armed opponents, has simply become too destructive to be fought. The importance of nuclear deterrence in the post-Second World War period can be understood as a metaphor for the destructiveness of war in general. This does not mean that such wars will never again take place. The war between Iraq and Iran in the 1980s was just such a war – millions of young men died in trenches rather similar to those of the First World War and the war ended in a stalemate. (We often forget this trauma and the role of our governments in sustaining that war when we discuss Iraq and Iran today.) There are widespread concerns about the possibility of such wars in East Asia, as a consequence of, say, a Chinese attack on Taiwan or a North Korean attack on Japan.

But what the destructiveness of symmetric war does mean is the growing unacceptability of war in general. This happened after the First World War. The notion that war is a legitimate way for states to pursue their interests that held sway in the post-Westphalian period was rejected in the Charter of the League of Nations, in the Kellogg-Briand pact of 1928 and, above all, in the aftermath of the Second World War when the crime of aggression was enshrined in the Nuremberg trials and in the Charter of the United Nations. As with human rights norms and rules, these prohibitions have been strengthened by civil society pressure, in particular the growth of peace movements, especially in the advanced industrial world.

In other words, the growing destructiveness of war and the growing unacceptability of war mean that states no longer have the option of using war as a policy instrument and therefore have to deal with each other in different ways. Of course, it can be argued that the United States (or China) is an exception to this emerging principle. Clearly, the Bush administration does still regard military power as a policy instrument, as I described in chapter 2. But Iraq may turn out to be the exception that proves the rule. The main lessons from the war in Iraq may well include the difficulty of using the military instrument, the understanding that superiority of military technology does not bring decisive victories and that legitimacy is more important than force.

The destructiveness and unacceptability of wars between states or symmetric warfare does not, of course, mean an end to war. But the new types of war are asymmetric, that is to say violence is primarily directed against unarmed and unprotected civilians rather than against other warring parties; in other words, the increasing use of terror. What I call 'new wars' are wars that have evolved from guerrilla warfare and 'low intensity wars' as ways of getting around concentrations of conventional force; the warring parties try to control territory politically through fear rather than through militarily attacking an enemy. These wars involve a mixture of warfare (political violence), human rights violations and violations of the laws of war (violence against non-combatants, genocide, massacres, torture and atrocities, mass rape) and ordinary crime (loot, pillage, smuggling and other illegal forms of war finance). They involve state and non-state actors and they blur classic distinctions between combatant and non-combatant, competent political authority and lack of authority, international and external – all distinctions that are critical for just war doctrine.[3]

It is sometimes argued that advanced military technology is capable of much greater precision than ever before, so that wars can be more proportionate and discriminate. It is true that contemporary wars fought by the United States make use of precision weapons that greatly reduce collateral damage in comparison with the wars of the twentieth century. Nevertheless, as I shall argue below, such damage is often relatively high in the context of 'new wars' because of the difficulty of distinguishing between combatants and non-combatants.

Global governance

These combined changes can be said to amount to a 'thoroughgoing transformation of international society'. States remain the juridical repository of sovereignty; international institutions derive their legal foundation from treaties agreed among states. But in practice, states are hemmed in by a system of global governance, in which they remain key actors, but along with international institutions, regional organizations like the European Union or the African Union, transnational corporations, NGOs and civil society, and even individuals. Their capacity to act as autonomous agents is greatly circumscribed and, in particular, the recourse to war as an instrument of policy is now prohibited.

A system of global governance is not the same as a 'global state with a monopoly on the legitimate use of force'[4] and, indeed, such a state is probably not desirable since it would have great potential for tyranny. But it is quite different from a world where states act as individuals pursuing their national interests to which just war theory, at least in its post-Westphalian guise, is supposed to apply. Walzer says that the rights of states derive from the social contract within states in which individual rights are transmuted into state rights in exchange for protection against external encroachment and life and liberty at home. The Great Divide, as it is known in the International Relations literature,[5] between the domestic civil society peopled by individuals, norms, law and politics and an external state of nature peopled by states that pursue their self-interest, is an expression of this conception of the rights of states. What is happening today, as I argued in the previous chapter, is that the social contract within states is increasingly being supplemented by a social contract at a global level.[6] Rules and laws that apply to individuals as well as states are being negotiated among the family of individuals, groups and institutions that constitute what we call global governance. This is why it is possible to talk about a blurring of the distinction between inside and outside, domestic and external. The Great Divide has not disappeared but it is no longer so clear-cut. The inside can no longer be insulated from an outside of terror, organized crime or ethnic and religious conflict. The outside is increasingly a world where individual as well as state rights apply, and where states no longer have the same autonomy to pursue their interests. This is the context in which to rethink the applicability of the precepts of just war.

Why the Language of Just War is Awkward

James Der Derian talks about the capacity of 'virtuous war' (the combination of virtual war at long distance and virtue or just war) to 'commute death' not only to keep death out of sight but also to legitimate death.[7] There is a fine line between legitimate killing and murder, between soldiers as criminals and soldiers as heroes. Just war is about managing that fine line. This is why rules of warfare have always been so important. But it also means that just war can be used as easily to legitimate war and evade responsibility as to elucidate what is permissible and what is not, especially in the case of long-distance wars. This argument applies to both parts of just war doctrine – *jus ad bellum* (the right to make war) and *jus in bello* (the right way to make war – restraints and limitations in war).

Jus ad bellum

According to James Turner Johnson, cumulative just war doctrine includes the following elements in *jus ad bellum*: just cause, right authority, right intention, that war do no more harm than good (*ad bellum* proportionality), last resort, and the purpose to achieve peace.[8] In what follows, I focus on just cause and right authority.

Just cause Nowadays, the most common just cause for using military forces is humanitarian intervention, which has been renamed the 'responsibility to protect'.[9] Implementation of such a concept, it can be argued, would be a crucial ingredient of an emerging global social contract whereby the international community takes responsibility for protecting people in the event of genocide, gross violations of human rights or crimes against humanity. The spread of 'new wars', in which violence is directed against civilians, combined with growing human consciousness has greatly increased the pressure not to stand by when terrible tragedies are inflicted on innocent people.

Yet in most accounts of just war theory, humanitarian intervention is an exception, a footnote in discussions of just cause. In the third edition of his seminal work on just war theory, Walzer says that this is the one 'large and momentous shift' that has taken place since he first wrote the book. 'The issues that I discussed under the name "interventions" which were peripheral to the main concerns of the book have moved dramatically to the centre . . . [T]he chief dilemma of international politics is whether people in danger should be rescued by military forces from outside.'[10]

In the twentieth century and in most contemporary accounts of just war doctrine, the main just cause is self-defence in the event of external aggression. This follows from the prohibitions against war introduced as a result of the two world wars. It was not always so. St Augustine, the father of just war theory, was primarily concerned about restoration of the moral order. In Christian teachings on just war, the notion of neighbourly love, the protection of others, was an important element. War was necessary, according to St Augustine, in order to 'curb licentious passions by destroying those vices which should have been rooted out and suppressed by the rightful government'.[11] According to John Langan, this 'punitive' concept of war overrides self-defence. For St Augustine, war can only be authorized by a public authority for public purposes – it is about the protection of others. Thus obedience to a rightful authority is central to his thinking, and individuals, even if they reject temporal rulings, have no right to resist. A just war also excludes passion and revenge. Following St Augustine, medieval scholars, particularly Aquinas, viewed just cause as righting an injury or a fault caused by others. Just war was distinguished from holy war in that it was authorized by secular authorities and recognized certain *in bello* restraints; holy war, by contrast, could be authorized by religious authorities and was waged against non-Christians.

There is an interesting parallel here with classical Islamic thought. Classical Islamic thought distinguished between the realm of peace, *dar-al-Islam*, and the realm of war, *dar-al harb*. The term *jihad* is often translated as 'holy war'. In fact, *jihad* refers to the moral duty to struggle for what is right and is normally peaceful. However, war is only justifiable if it is *jihad*, that is to say, it has a just cause. This is very similar to the Augustinian notion of just cause and is therefore closer to Christian concepts of just war than holy war. Among some branches of Islam, particularly the Shi'a, the only just cause is self-defence. As in Christian theory, war also had to be authorized by a legitimate authority, the Caliph or a political authority, such as the Sultan. But no authority was absolute. God's will was understood to be imprinted upon individual human consciousness and therefore authority depended on interpretation of Islamic law. Most importantly, this implied that all legitimate wars had to be fought justly. Indeed Islamic jurists were much more preoccupied with what in the West is known as *jus in bello*, the means to be employed, than in the issue of legitimate cause (see below).[12] Hence classical Islam had no direct equivalent of the Christian concept of holy war.

In the transition to modernity, scholars like Franciscus de Victoria and Hugo Grotius were, according to Turner Johnson, responsible for the 'dethroning of religion'[13] and the rejection of the notion of holy war. Victoria, in particular made the point that natural law, the law imprinted by God on our consciousness, applies to non-Christians such as American Indians, and Grotius identified just cause with charity, by which he meant something akin to what nowadays we would call humanitarianism – thus echoing classical Islamic thought.

The Western idea that only secular authorities had the right to wage war, and that wars of religion were anachronistic, gradually evolved, after the Treaty of Westphalia, into the notion that wars could be fought for reasons of state. Thus war in Europe came to be regarded in the eighteenth and nineteenth centuries 'as a means – and a highly imperfect one at that – of settling disputes between two sovereigns who recognised no common judge'.[14] The emphasis at that time of just war theory was on restraints and limitations rather than on just cause. The total wars of the twentieth century, however, called into question the legitimacy of reasons of state as well as the possibilities for limiting and restraining wars, giving rise to the current international consensus that only wars of self-defence are legitimate.

So strong is the insistence that self-defence is the only just cause and that the principle of non-intervention should not be violated that many interventions actually undertaken for humanitarian purposes have been forced into the straitjacket of self-defence. In the Indian intervention in Bangladesh in 1971, the Indians justified their use of military forces in terms of the threat of 'refugee aggression', even though as the Indian ambassador to the United Nations pointed out to the Security Council what was happening in East Pakistan at that time was such as to 'shock the conscience of mankind'.[15] In the international intervention in northern Iraq in 1991, where the United Nations established a safe haven for the Kurds, the resolution (Security Council Resolution 688) emphasized the 'threat to international peace and security' posed by refugees.

But in a world where the difference between internal and external and between state and non-state is blurred, what is the difference between aggression and humanitarian catastrophe? In theory, one is an attack by a foreign state and the other is inflicted on a people by their own state or non-state actors. But in new wars, where states are disintegrating and where the warring parties involve paramilitary groups, foreign mercenaries, Mujahideen and the like, this distinction is more difficult to apply than it would seem.

The war in Bosnia-Herzegovina well illustrates these dilemmas. The war was actually fought by a combination of remnants of the Yugoslav army and territorial defence forces and paramilitary groups composed of local and foreign volunteers, both criminal and fanatic. Those who favoured international intervention claimed that this was a war of aggression by Serbia and Croatia against Bosnia-Herzegovina. Those who were against intervention claimed that this was a civil war among Serbs, Croats and Muslims. Yet the case for intervention derived surely from the rights of the victims. This was a war of ethnic cleansing, involving massacres, large-scale population displacement, detention camps and widespread atrocities, including mass rape. Did it matter whether these violations of human rights were inflicted by Serbs from Serbia or Bosnian Serbs, by regular forces or paramilitary groups, or whether Bosnia-Herzegovina was an independent state or part of Yugoslavia?

The problem of how to interpret the attacks of September 11 represents an even more telling case. This was clearly an act that 'shocked the conscience of mankind'. President Bush chose to define it as an act of aggression and drew the parallel with the Japanese attack on Pearl Harbor that brought the United States into the Second World War. By so doing, he was able to use the phrase the 'war on terror' and justify the attacks on Afghanistan and Iraq.

But this was not an attack by a foreign state. It was an attack by a group of individuals. Supposing the attack has been carried out by Christian fundamentalists like Timothy McVeigh who attacked the federal building in Oklahoma, or Muslim fundamentalists who were also American citizens, could President Bush have declared war? As Michael Walzer put it in an op-ed article soon after September 11, the word 'war' is 'unobjectionable as long as those who use it understand what a metaphor is'. But 'there is right now, no enemy state, no battlefield'.[16]

What happened on September 11 was a humanitarian catastrophe. It could be described, and many chose to describe it in these terms, as a 'crime against humanity'. The implication of this description is that the attackers were criminals rather than enemies; they could have been any nationality. In such a horrendous crime, there might well be a case for military action in a foreign country to apprehend the criminals, but the nature of that action would be different from war because the criminals are individuals, not entire states.

Similarly, when Hezbollah killed eight Israeli soldiers and took two soldiers hostage in July 2006, this was clearly a criminal act. Yet Israel chose to interpret this act as foreign aggression by Lebanon and therefore attacked the Lebanese state. Israel was strongly criticized for a disproportionate response; hundreds of Lebanese civilians were killed and huge damage was done to economic and physical infrastructure. But such a response could not even have been contemplated had Hezbollah been, say, a resistance group inside Israel.

Right authority In medieval times, *bellum*, the use of force for public ends, was distinguished from *duellum*, the use of force for private ends. Just war theory spelled out the criteria for justifying the use of force for public ends – the use of force for private ends was considered illegitimate. Only political authorities, who knew no temporal superior, could declare war. The same was true in the Islamic tradition, although religious authorities who were also political authorities (the Caliph) could authorize war.

Nowadays, it is national wars that are becoming illegitimate. National interest can be considered a sort of private interest as opposed to the global public interest. The important distinction, nowadays, is between the use of force for humanitarian ends and the use of force for national ends. Both President Bush and Prime Minister Blair insist that their concern is humanitarian rather than national. But if the concern is humanitarian, it can be argued that it cannot be authorized unilaterally by a government that represents a particular group of citizens; it requires some multilateral authority. According to Article 2.7 of the United Nations Charter, states can unilaterally authorize the use of force in self-defence in the event of foreign aggression. But all other uses of military force, including humanitarian intervention, can only be authorized by the United Nations Security Council under Chapter VII of the Charter. Undoubtedly, this needs to be augmented by a set of rules that allow for situations where the Security Council is blocked, but the principle of multilateral authorization for all uses of military force other than self-defence is critical.

Jus in bello

Just war theory and its codification in international law in the second half of the nineteenth century applied to states. In the Middle Ages, just war was fought among European princes and other political authorities; it did not apply to internal violence or to wars against non-Christians such as the Crusades. James Turner Johnson describes several instances where internal rebellions were put down with great brutality, apparently with the approval of theologians of just war. Thus, for example, Luther approved of the suppression of the German peasant rebellion in the sixteenth century, on the grounds of right authority, even without restraint. Likewise, restraints that were practised in wars within Europe in the nineteenth century did not apply in colonial interventions, which were never described as wars, rather as rebellions, insurrections and so forth. There were attempts by Francis Lieber, who drew up the code of behaviour to be observed by both sides in the American Civil War, to define 'guerrilla parties' and the notion of 'armed conflict', involving volunteer corps or paramilitary groups, which has been incorporated into international law. Nevertheless, George Bush uses the argument that the legal status of such groups is unclear within the framework of the laws of war, to justify the incarceration of what he calls 'illegal combatants' in Guantanamo Bay.

Rebellions against rightful authority were also forbidden in classical Islam. However, in contrast to the Christian tradition, *in bello* restraints were even more stringent in conflicts with dissenting Muslims.

> If Muslims fight one another, the fugitive and the wounded may not be dispatched. Muslim prisoners may not be executed and

women may not be intentionally killed or imprisoned. Imprisoned male Muslims must be released once the fighting, or the danger of continued fighting, ends. Furthermore, the property of Muslims may not be taken as spoils, and any property taken must be returned after the cessation of fighting.[17]

These rules only applied, however, if the rebels were considered to have a plausible reason for fighting based on a valid interpretation of the Islamic sources (*ta'wil*). Thus tribal reasons or greed were not plausible. The rebels also had to be sufficiently powerful (*shawka*). 'As the jurists put it, without the requirement of *shawka*, anarchy and lawlessness will spread . . . They contend that without the requirement of *shawka*, every corrupt person will invent or fabricate a *ta'wil* and claim to be a *baghi* (a legitimate rebel)'.[18]

In the Christian tradition, it was not just in internal conflicts that *jus in bello* did not apply. It also did not apply in holy wars – in these wars the righteousness of the cause was supposed to justify the lack of restraint. Despite the fact that there was no similar concept in the classical Islamic period, contemporary jihadists define their struggle as holy war and make an argument similar to medieval Christian arguments, that the righteousness of the cause justifies lack of restraint. The same argument has been made in ideological wars, for example, in the defeat of Nazism. In the Middle Ages, by and large, just wars applied to wars among Christian European states. Thus the customary rules of war, developed in the Middle Ages, were designed to be applied 'between peoples sharing the same cultural background and worshipping the same Gods'.[19] Thus they were respected, to a greater or lesser degree, in wars within Europe, among warring parties who shared an allegiance to the Christian church, but not beyond. When the Crusaders captured Jerusalem, they had 65,000 'infidels' put to death.

In most wars today, the various warring parties have a nebulous status. They often do not fit the criteria, drawn up by Lieber and others, for being treated as a proto-state, a sort of legitimate authority in waiting. Nor should they. To treat rebels or terrorists like Al Qaeda or the Hutu paramilitaries in Rwanda as potential authorities or as legitimate enemies would raise their status and confer on them an undesirable degree of legitimacy. On the other hand, to act without restraint and to ignore the framework of international law, as the Russians do in Chechnya or as President Bush does in relation to the Guantanamo detainees, can only exacerbate tension and undermine the legitimacy of actual authorities. 'Who will believe your cause when your behaviours are so unjust?' wrote the French Calvinists in relation to the wars of religion.[20]

This is why the language of law enforcement may be more appropriate than the language of just war. Humanitarian intervention usually refers to intervention in a foreign country to protect civilians. Often humanitarian intervention is seen as war because it is the state that is responsible for violations of human rights. But in situations where violations of human rights are inflicted by both state and non-state actors, both domestic and foreign, the term 'war' may not apply and it may be preferable to treat the situation as akin to domestic disorder. Rather than treating this kind of intervention as war or allowing the rules to be lost in the murky environment of peasant rebellions or colonial insurrections, it would be better to extend domestic rules and apply a minimum human rights framework. As Walzer puts it, 'humanitarian intervention comes closer than any other kind of intervention to what we commonly regard, in domestic society, as law enforcement and police work.'[21] The task in all these cases is the protection of civilians and the arrest of criminals rather than the defeat of enemy states. In other words, if humanitarian intervention is viewed as the primary just cause and if humanitarian catastrophes are no longer inflicted only by states, then this has profound implications for the ways in which such interventions are conducted.

The difficulties of applying the principles of *jus in bello* arise from this blurring of the difference between internal and external or friend and enemy, and between state and non-state, combatant and non-combatant. The central assumption underlying the rules in *jus in bello* is the immunity of non-combatants or combatants who are wounded or taken prisoner (what Michael Walzer calls the 'naked soldier'). They should be spared, where possible, the effects of war. They should be 'hors de combat'. The same distinction was made in classical Islamic thought. There were strong codes about the treatment of prisoners and non-combatants in all wars.[22] In a famous quotation, Muslims are instructed by the first Caliph, Abu Bakr:

Do not mutilate; do not kill little children or old men or women; do not cut off the heads of palm trees or burn them; do not cut down the fruit trees; do not slaughter a sheep or a cow or a camel except for food, and if you pass by the monasteries of believers who devoted themselves to worship . . . leave them in peace.

Nowadays, it is often argued that the notion of non-combatant immunity reflects an assumption about the equality of human beings and a notion of respect for enemy populations that earlier only applied within Europe or in conflicts among Muslims.[23] However, the very concept of war implies a friend–enemy distinction in which enemy lives are less valuable than the lives of our own side. This contradiction between the friend–enemy distinction and respect for non-combatant immunity is expressed in different concepts variously known as 'proportionality', 'double effect' and, in contemporary jargon, 'collateral damage'. The idea behind these concepts is that killing or harming enemy civilians can be justifiable if it is a side-effect of an attack on a military target which is necessary in order to win the war, if it is unintentional, and if the harm done is proportional to the harm that might be done if victory was not achieved. Of course, the concepts of 'necessity' and 'proportionality' are notoriously hard to define and allow for considerable leeway.[24] If, as the Americans claim, recent wars in Afghanistan or Iraq are designed to prevent a terrorist from releasing a hideous weapon of mass destruction in a Western city, for instance, surely any amount of destruction would be permissible?

But leaving aside, for the moment, the problem of definition, what these concepts effectively do is to create a hierarchy of lives. Supposing we assume a war between Country X and Country Y, then if you are on X's side, lives are valued in the following order. First come X's civilians, then come X's soldiers, then come Y's civilians, and finally Y's soldiers. Double effect implies that you should minimize all killing, but deliberate killing of Y's soldiers is permissible if it is necessary to achieve victory or to save the lives of X's soldiers and civilians. Unintentional killing of Y's civilians is permissible if it is necessary to achieve victory or to save the lives of X's soldiers and civilians. Actually, not everyone agrees about whether it is permissible to risk the lives of Y's civilians to save the lives of

X's soldiers; during the Second World War, Pierre Mendes France, who flew on Allied bombing missions, deliberately took the risk of flying low so as to be more accurate and save civilian lives. But this view does seem to be accepted within the American military – hence the high flights over Yugoslavia in 1999. As one US soldier put it in Kerbala: 'I think they thought we wouldn't shoot kids. But we showed them that we don't care. We are going to do what we can to stay alive and keep ourselves safe.'[25]

Of course, all of us do have an implicit hierarchy of lives, although this hierarchy is not necessarily defined in territorial terms. Our communities, to whom we feel loyal, may cross borders and be defined in terms of family, ethnicity, religion, class or politics. The British suicide bomber in his suicide video talked about his community as the Muslim Umma rather than his local community in Leeds or the community of British citizens. But this kind of hierarchy, whether national or religious, is increasingly unacceptable as an international principle in the context of growing human rights norms.

There is no question that contemporary armies, American, British or Israeli, try to minimize civilian casualties and indeed claim that, thanks to new technologies, attacks from the air or from the ground are much more accurate and discriminate better than ever before. According to Rumsfeld during the Iraq war: 'We are doing everything humanly possible to avoid collateral damage.'[26] By historical standards, 'collateral damage' in Kosovo, Afghanistan, Iraq or even Lebanon has been relatively low. But what is low by the standards of war is high by the standards of human rights. Thus in the Kosovo war of 1999, some 2,000–3,000 civilians are estimated to have been killed as a consequence of allied bombing; this compares with some 10,000 Albanians killed by Yugoslav forces on the ground. In Afghanistan and Iraq, the number of civilians killed has far exceeded the number killed in the September 11 attacks.

The world is, rightly, horrified by Palestinian suicide bombers' attacks, where Israeli civilians are deliberately targeted. The Palestinian groups – Hamas, Islamic Jihad or the Al Aqsa Brigades – are all included in the US State Department's list of international terrorist groups; since the beginning of the second intifada, they have killed 781 Israelis, according the Israeli newspaper *Haaretz*.[27] On the other hand, the Israeli security forces, who are state actors and are therefore considered legitimate and who are tasked with minimizing civilian casualties, have killed 3,040 Palestinians, mostly civilians, including 606 children. According to the investigations of an Israeli human rights organization, B'Tselem, at least 1,661 of those killed (including 531 children under the age of eighteen) were not involved in hostilities when they were killed.[28] Those Palestinians involved in the second intifada claim that suicide bombing is necessary, and the only means available to them, in order to establish a balance of terror. Or, to take yet another example, in the 2006 war in Lebanon, the Israelis killed some 1,200 Lebanese civilians; estimates of combatants killed vary from 500 (Israeli defence forces estimate) to 74 Hezbollah fighters (Hezbollah estimates) and 46 Lebanese soldiers (Lebanese figures). Some 44 Israeli civilians died and some 119 members of the IDF.[29]

The problem is the changing perception of war. What appears to Americans as relatively low collateral damage in a just war can equally be presented as large-scale human rights violations. From the point of view of the victims, does it make any difference whether they were killed in a war or as a result of repression, or whether the killing was intentional or unintentional? The high civilian casualty figures in recent wars underscore another problem, namely the difficulty nowadays of distinguishing combatants and non-combatants. When insurgents hide in cities, how is it possible to attack them without killing civilians? This is the classic problem of counter-insurgency. Milosevic claimed that attacks by Serbian forces in Kosovo were counter-insurgency not ethnic cleansing; Serb forces were merely trying to root out members of the KLA. In Chechnya, massive population displacement and killing has taken place, dwarfing anything experienced in Kosovo, as a result of Russian attempts to defeat the insurgency. The American attacks on Fallujah resulted in 150,000 displaced persons, as well as large numbers (unknown) of civilian casualties. Likewise, the Israelis counted many civilians in Lebanon as Hezbollah resistance fighters.

The difficulty of distinguishing combatants from non-combatants was the central problem the United States faced in Vietnam. Indeed Walzer makes the case that where it is not possible to distinguish civilians from combatants, *jus in bello* and *jus ad bellum* come together and the war should not even be fought.

> The war cannot be won and it should not be won. It cannot be won because the only available strategy involves a war against civilians, because the degree of civilian support that rules out alternative strategies also makes the guerrillas the legitimate rulers of the country. The struggle against them is an unjust struggle as well as one that can only be carried on unjustly. Fought by foreigners, it is a war of aggression; if by a local regime alone, it is an act of tyranny.[30]

But the difficulty of distinguishing combatants and non-combatants is characteristic of most wars nowadays. Does that not call into question whether we can even continue to talk about just war?

Just Peace

The blurring of the distinction between external and internal, state and non-state, combatant and non-combatant also implies the blurring of the distinction between war and peace. 'New wars' do not have decisive beginnings or endings. Nor are they clearly delineated in geographical space; they spread through refugees and displaced persons, organized crime, diaspora groups and so on. The growing body of human rights law cannot be suspended in wartime in the way that domestic laws, which apply to individual rights, have often been disregarded in the name of national security. That is why it is so important to develop the concept of just peace and its concomitant, the laws of peace, which apply at an international level.[31] Anthony Burke proposes a system of ethical peace that declares the '*illegality* of avoidable harm'.[32]

There is a role in such a framework for the use of military force. But the principles of legitimacy derive from individual rights rather than the rights of states. This is why I favour the term 'human security', which is elaborated in the next chapter.

In a system of just peace, military forces are, of course, under the control of competent authorities, at present states. States remain the only authorities capable of upholding the legitimate use of force, but their use of force is much more circumscribed than earlier by international rules and norms. In other words, the distinctions between inside/outside and between legitimate and illegitimate uses of force do remain, although their meaning has changed; that is why I use the term 'blur' rather than 'supersede' or 'disappear'. Military forces are forces designed for use in external operations but not for war against other states – rather as a contribution to global security and to implementing a global social contract, which enshrines human rights. The legitimate use of military force by states would need to be approved by the United Nations or to conform to a clear set of criteria that are agreed internationally. The adoption of the principle of 'responsibility to protect' by the United Nations General Assembly is an important step in this direction. The Canadian International Commission on Intervention and Sovereignty, which pioneered the 'responsibility to protect', set out criteria drawn from just war approaches covering just cause, in particular the right to intervene in cases of large-scale loss of life and/or large-scale 'ethnic cleansing', and right authority, the importance of multilateral authorization. It also included, in its precautionary and operational principles, the notion that the goal should be the protection of civilians and the means should be 'the minimum necessary to secure the defined human protection objective'. However, there is a need to put more emphasis on the method of implementation and to elaborate the ways in which force should be applied so as to distinguish the methods to be adopted for the protection of individuals from war-fighting methods.

If the main criteria for the use of force were to be those enshrined in the notion of humanitarian intervention, that is, large-scale loss of life or 'ethnic cleansing', then this would actually cover the case of external aggression. Instead of making human rights fit the framework of just war, which they do rather uneasily, still allowing loopholes for 'double effect' and 'collateral damage', aggression can be fitted into the 'responsibility to protect', since aggression is not just against a state but against the individual citizens who compose the state. In other words, states can use military forces under the auspices of the

United Nations, within a multilateral framework and according to criteria that have been agreed. They are to be used for the protection of civilians in conjunction with international police forces and civilian experts.

Using military forces in a human security role is thus quite different from either classic war-fighting or from peacekeeping. Both types of operation are defined in terms of a war between collective enemies. The job of peacekeepers is to separate warring parties, monitor ceasefires or collect weapons; in the past, peacekeepers have often been unable to prevent violations of human rights. The job of war-fighting is about defeating enemies, and even though counter-insurgency operations have sometimes adopted a 'hearts and minds' approach, the task of protecting civilians has been secondary to the task of defeating the enemy. The big gap in all recent operations has been public security. As I describe in chapter 4, the NATO operation in Kosovo failed to prevent ethnic cleansing first of Albanians and then of Serbs, even though it did succeed in liberating Kosovo and enabling the Albanians to return to their homes. Likewise, the Iraq war failed to prevent looting as well as widespread human rights violations in the immediate aftermath of the war. Crime and human rights violations were widespread in Bosnia–Herzegovina as well, even after the Dayton Agreement.

Yet how this is to be achieved has received much less attention than the circumstances in which military means might be used. The methods of civilian protection, the 'how' rather than the 'why' of civilian protection, has been much less debated. It is as though the use of military force were a black box to be applied as a neutral instrument. In what follows, I set out three principles, which demonstrate the difference between an approach based on individual rights and a *jus in bello* approach.

First of all, the primary task of human security operations is the protection of civilians. Killing is never permissible except in self-defence or to save a third party. Thus the killing of an attacker is only permissible if it is necessary to save civilian lives. Of course, it could be argued that this also allows for war-fighting actions that may risk civilian lives. The British forces defending the United Nations safe haven of Goradze in the last stages of the war in Bosnia-Herzegovina did shell Serb forces for several hours in order to prevent the Serbs from overrunning the town and in order to negotiate the safe passage of civilians. This was in contrast to Srebrenica, where Dutch forces failed to prevent the massacre of 8000 men and boys. One of the reasons why mandates were so restricted in Bosnia-Herzegovina was because of fears that active defence of safe havens could slide into war; the term 'crossing the Mogadishu line' was coined by General Rose in reference to the disastrous consequences of a shifting to a war-fighting strategy in Somalia. However, there is a difference between active protection and war-fighting. In 'new wars', the warring parties do try to avoid battle because the growing symmetry of military technology makes the outcome dangerous and uncertain. One should not, of course, dismiss the risk of escalation or of an unconstrained extension of violence; in the confusion and emotion surrounding all wars, warring parties do not behave as expected and an extremist logic often takes over, as Clausewitz argued. But the starting point, in ethical and operational terms, is protection, rather than defeat of an enemy, as opposed to the other way round, which is the characteristic of war.

The second principle, linked to the first, is that protection can be achieved through stabilization rather than victory. Or, as Rupert Smith, the former Commander of UNPROFOR in Bosnia, has put it: 'We do not intervene to take or hold territory . . . Instead we intervene in . . . order to establish a condition in which the political objective can be achieved by other means and in other ways. We seek to create a conceptual space for diplomacy, economic incentives, political pressure and other measures to create a desired political outcome of stability, and, if possible, democracy.'[33]

Stabilization can only be achieved with local support and consent. Of course, it can be argued that military victory is an effective method of stabilization; this is what the Americans claim in Iraq and it is a view that runs deep in military establishments. But in some cases, military victory may simply be beyond reach – every excessive use of force further inflames the situation. In other cases, short-term military victory can be achieved but the cost in terms of both casualties and political legitimacy is too high. Israeli forces, for instance, have succeeded in slowing down the rate of suicide bombing but this has not led to any resolution of the conflict; indeed, it has only inflamed more passion on the Palestinian side. Military victory may mean that stability can only be sustained through massive repression and coercion. In Algeria, the French won militarily but lost politically, and the trauma of that war has left a lasting legacy.

A third principle is that those who violate human rights are individual criminals rather than collective enemies. This means that human security forces have the job of arresting criminals and bringing them to justice. It also delegitimizes the enemy, who are no longer political foes but lawbreakers.[34] Thus British forces operating in Sierra Leone chose to arrest members of the 'West Side Boys' engaged in looting and pillaging a village rather than engaging them in a firefight. This greatly diminished their stature and correspondingly raised the credibility of the British forces. This approach is not, of course, easy; there is often a tension between what counts as political and what counts as criminal. In some cases, it is important to outlaw those who have committed terrible crimes in order to establish a legitimate political process. This is the case in the former Yugoslavia, where, in principle, excluding indicted criminals creates space for more moderate politics. Likewise, the political situation in Iraq would have been greatly improved had there been a legal process, in the initial stages, that led to the indictment of those members of the Ba'ath Party who had committed unspeakable crimes, thus preventing arbitrary revenge attacks, which contributed to the development of sectarian conflict. It would also have meant discriminating between those who committed crimes and those who did not, so that blanket de-Ba'athification could have been avoided. On the other hand, it may also be important to include groups like the IRA or Hamas, who are viewed as legitimate by some parts of the population, in the political process.

The example of the British army in Northern Ireland is instructive in this respect because it is probably closest to the kind of operations I am proposing and it also illustrates some of the difficulties. Northern Ireland was a learning process for the British government because it was effectively a 'new war' on British territory. When British troops were first deployed in Northern Ireland in 1969, the most recent experience of most soldiers was counter-insurgency against anti-colonial insurgents in Aden. As one soldier put it:

> We weren't governed by the same rules that we were in Ireland. The lads over there (Aden) could be a lot rougher, a lot harder because we never had the newspapers there and we never had the Press there or anyone else who could see what we were doing. It made a lot of difference because you were given a freer hand right across the board.[35]

When the army was first deployed in Northern Ireland, the difference between Aden and Northern Ireland or between 'Borneo and Belfast', as another soldier put it, was not sufficiently appreciated. The army relied heavily on the existing civil authority, which was itself a party to the conflict; it failed to protect the nationalist community from house burnings and expulsions, which stimulated the militarization of the IRA; it used interrogation and intelligence techniques developed in colonial wars, later ruled illegitimate by the European Court of Human Rights; and it used excessive force, most notoriously in breaking up IRA-established 'No-Go' areas and on 'Bloody Sunday', 30 January 1972, when the Parachute Regiment fired on a crowd and killed thirteen people.[36] Between 1969 and 1974, some 188 people were killed by security forces and 65 per cent of the deaths were unarmed civilians.[37] This period was the bloodiest period of the whole Northern Ireland conflict, accounting for 90 per cent of all deaths – many more people were killed by Loyalist (Protestant) and Republican (Catholic) paramilitaries.

As a consequence of the failure of the armed forces to maintain peace and security, a new policy was adopted known as 'normalization', 'criminalization' or Ulsterization. The emphasis was placed on police primacy in dealing with insurgents, and captured terrorists were to be treated as criminals rather than enemies. They were to be tried and given the same status in prison as ordinary criminals. The job of the armed forces was to support the police. Army bases were often co-located with police stations, which allowed proper sharing of information and joint tactical planning.[38] This approach lasted until the Good Friday Agreement, in April 1997, which largely ended the violence.

It was an approach that did succeed in containing violence
– over the period as a whole, 1969–97, some 4000 people were
killed, 350 by security forces. But it had its weaknesses. There
was never a clear legal framework, and the procedures used to
deal with captured insurgents represented a considerable modi-
fication of normal law – the notorious 'Diplock' courts did away
with juries and allowed confession-based evidence, which
accounted for the majority of convictions. The IRA always
insisted that they were political and not criminal, and the
hunger strikes in 1981 to achieve political status in prison
mobilized considerable political support for the IRA. The
authorities themselves were often ambiguous, using 'war' arguments when needed to justify certain actions. Moreover, in
the 1980s, undercover operations by the SAS and other
special forces led to the killing (as opposed to arrest), often in
planned ambushes, of many IRA activists. It is sometimes
argued that this strategy of attrition did lead to a situation
where neither side could win and a political agreement was
the only way out. But it is also the case that this behaviour
contributed to the polarization of Northern Irish society so
that the extremist groups on both sides became the dominant
political forces.

What made Northern Ireland different was the fact that the
conflict took place on British territory. Bombing Belfast was not
an option. It could also be argued that the response of
American authorities to the Oklahoma bombing as opposed to
September 11 can be explained partly by the fact that this was
a domestic rather than an international incident. The assumption that underlies a just peace is that it is no longer possible,
or relevant from the point of view of the victims, to distinguish
between foreigners and citizens or between the domestic and
the international. Although the state has primary responsibility
for dealing with domestic violence, there are external situations
– where the local state itself is the cause of violence or where
it is incapable of dealing with violence – where international
forces intervene but through methods that are not so very different from the methods that might be used in a domestic
setting. This reflects both the changed sensibilities of society,
where concerns about people far away have become more
urgent as a result of global communications and transnational

communities, and an emerging global social contract whereby the international community adopts the 'responsibility to protect' and recognizes individual rights and not just state rights.

Of course, elements of these principles can also be found in just war theorizing, particularly in the pre-Westphalian era. Thus the emphasis on the protection of citizens is very much in keeping with notions of charity, humanitarianism and civilization that have run through the just war literature. The need for legitimate political authority and the priority of stabilization or peace rather than victory could be considered an Augustinian principle. The notion that the enemy is an individual was central to the thinking of Victoria. Moreover, any attempt to codify the laws of peace would need to incorporate humanitarian law but alongside human rights law. It is, above all, human rights and the notion of global public authority that marks this approach off from traditional just war approaches.

Conclusion

George Weigel has suggested that the 'new things' in the world today, particularly failing states and rogue states, explain the need for a new kind of just war, in which individual states take responsibility for 'regime change' using new precise and discriminate technology.[39] His argument is reflected in the National Security Strategy, announced by George Bush in 2002. William Wallace describes Europe as a 'zone of peace' that uses 'soft power' – trade, aid, dialogue – in its external relations.[40] I agree with Weigel that in our interconnected world, rogue states and failing states are unacceptable. But I am very sceptical about the use of war-fighting as a way of bringing about 'regime change'. The wars in Iraq and Afghanistan have not created legitimate political authorities – they have speeded up the process of state failure, contributing to an environment in which various armed groups can operate, and have accentuated a friend–enemy distinction that attracts young disaffected people to extremist causes. However discriminate and proportionate these wars appear to be from a Western perspective, the civilian victims, even if not numerous by the traditions of twentieth-century wars, perceive these actions very differently, as do members of linked transnational communities across the world, especially Muslims.

Yet the 'soft power' approach of the European Union is unable to deal with the needs of millions of people in the world who live in conditions of intolerable insecurity. In the new war zones, whose borders are permeable and undefined, in places like the Middle East, the Balkans, West and Central Africa, Central Asia or the Caucasus, individuals and communities live in daily fear of being killed, robbed or kidnapped, of losing their homes, or being tortured or raped. Neither current security arrangements, based on traditional state-based assumptions about the nature of war and the role of military forces, nor the 'soft' approaches of international and regional organizations seem able to address these everyday risks.

I have proposed that those who are wrestling with the problem of what constitutes the legitimate use of military force should adopt a human security approach rather than try to adapt more traditional just war thinking, even though some of the insights drawn from the notion of just war may be relevant. A human security approach is more straight-forwardly applicable to the real security problems we face today.

Human security is sometimes considered a soft security approach, relegated to the aftermath of conflicts when police and development experts are supposed to 'mop up'. What I have argued is that human security should be regarded as a hard security policy aimed at protecting individuals rather than states. As such, a human security operation is actually more risky than current war-fighting operations. The human security officer risks his or her life to save others, rather as police and firefighters are expected to do in domestic situations. But in 'new wars', the risks are likely to be greater. It is often argued that politicians would be unwilling to take such risks and this is why, in many international missions, force protection receives higher priority than the protection of civilians. Western publics, however, may be more willing to take such risks than politicians assume. After all, human rights activists, who volunteer, rou-tinely take such risks. The case of Marla Ruzicka, the young woman recently killed by a suicide bombing attack on a nearby

US convoy in Iraq, and who single-handedly organized the Campaign for Innocent Victims in Conflict, is perhaps emblematic of the kind of courage that a human security officer would be expected to display.

7

Human Security

Human security potentially offers a new approach both to security and to development. Current security policies still tend to focus on threats to states and on traditional military capabilities. Economic aid consists either of humanitarian assistance or of development aid, which tends to be tied to policies of liberalization, privatization and macro-economic performance. Moreover, the issue of security is usually treated quite separately from the issue of development. Not only are current approaches to security and development inappropriate, in some cases they may actually exacerbate insecurity.

Human security is about the security of individuals and communities rather than the security of states, and it combines both human rights and human development. The idea of human security was first promulgated in the 1994 *Human Development Report* by the United Nations Development Programme (UNDP). The report argued that the concept of security has 'for too long been interpreted narrowly: as security of territory from external aggression, or as protection of national interests in foreign policy or as global security from a nuclear holocaust. It has been related more to nation states than to people.'[1] The report identified seven core elements, which together made up the concept of human security – economic security, food security, health security, environmental security, personal security, community security and political security.

Subsequently, the concept of human security seems to have developed in two directions. One was the approach taken by the Canadian government, which adopted the concept and established a network of like-minded states who subscribe to the concept. Their version is reflected in the *Human Security Report*, published in 2005, and has some affinity to the notion of 'responsibility to protect'.[2] They emphasize the security of the individual as opposed to the state, but their primary emphasis is on security in the face political violence. The other approach was the UNDP approach, also reflected in the work of the United Nations High-Level Panel on Threats, Challenges and Change and the Secretary-General's response, *In Larger Freedom*.[3] This approach emphasized the interrelatedness of different types of security and the importance of development, in particular, as a security strategy. In my view, it is important to combine both approaches and to put the emphasis both on the security of individuals and on the interrelated character of security.

Security is often viewed as the absence of physical violence, while development is viewed as material development – improved living standards. But this is a misleading distinction. Both concepts include 'freedom from fear' and 'freedom from want'. Security is about confronting extreme vulnerabilities, not only in wars but in natural and man-made disasters as well – famines, tsunamis, hurricanes. Development should be about more than a decent standard of living. It is also about feeling safe on the streets or being able to influence political decision-making. In contemporary wars, only a minority of deaths are battle deaths. Most people die in wars either because of violence deliberately targeted against civilians as a result of terror, ethnic cleansing or genocide, or because of the indirect effects of war as a result of lack of access to health care and the spread of disease, hunger and homelessness. Perhaps the indicator that comes closest to a measure of human security is displaced persons. Displaced persons are a typical feature of contemporary crises, both natural disasters and wars. There has been a steady increase in the number of displaced persons per conflict over the last three decades. In Lebanon, for example, over 1,000 Lebanese civilians were killed and over 400,000 people were forced to leave their homes. Hundreds of thousands had to leave New Orleans as a result of Hurricane Katrina. Displaced persons are the victims of both physical and material insecurity.

In the report of the Commission on Human Security, Amartya Sen conceptualizes human security as narrower than either human development or human rights. In relation to human development, he focuses on the 'downside risks': 'the insecurities that threaten human survival or the safety of daily life, or imperil the natural dignity of men and women, or expose human beings to the uncertainty of disease and pestilence, or subject vulnerable people to abrupt penury'. In relation to human rights, he sees them as 'a class of human rights' that guarantee 'freedom from basic insecurities – new and old'.[4] Thus human security could be conceptualized as incorporating minimum core aspects of both human development and human rights.

So human security is part of human development, but it is, if you like, at the sharp end of human development. It is about crisis management. It includes both civilian and military elements; it offers a way to act, a set of principles for crisis management. I think how we act in crises becomes a symbol of how an institution is perceived in general. Security is bound up with political legitimacy. We feel safe if we trust our institutions, and we trust our institutions if we see them acting effectively in crises.

This chapter sets out to make the concept of human security concrete especially in relation to conflicts, and establish how it might be put into practice. It sets out five principles for the implementation of human security and then briefly describes policies that are relevant both to security and to development.

The Principles of Human Security

In elaborating the notion of human security, it is possible to identify a set of principles which elucidate the ways in which such an approach differs from conventional approaches to security and development.

These principles cover both ends and means. There is a lot of discussion nowadays about the 'responsibility to protect' and the conditions under which it is right to use military force. But there is much less discussion about how military forces should be used in such a role, and yet this is critical for effective protection. There are also discussions about how civilian elements of crisis management are to be used, with an emphasis on helping to establish a rule of law, but much less about how and when they work together with the military. Thus the principles apply to both 'how' and 'why', both ends and means.

The principles do not only apply to hot conflict situations. A distinction is often drawn between the 'prevention' of crises and post-conflict reconstruction. But it is often difficult to distinguish between different phases of conflict precisely because there are no clear beginnings or endings and because the conditions that cause conflict – fear and hatred, a criminalized economy that profits from violent methods of controlling assets, weak illegitimate states, or the existence of warlords and paramilitary groups – are often exacerbated during and after periods of violence. As Rupert Smith puts it: 'In a world of industrial war, the premise is the sequence peace-crisis-peace, which will result in peace again, with the war, the military action, being the deciding factor. In contrast, the new paradigm . . . is based on the concept of a continuous criss-crossing between confrontation and conflicts.'[5] The principles for a human security policy should therefore apply to a continuum of phases of varying degrees of violence that always involves elements of both prevention and reconstruction.

Principle 1: The primacy of human rights

The primacy of human rights is what distinguishes the human security approach from traditional state-based approaches. Although the principle seems obvious, there are deeply held and entrenched institutional and cultural obstacles that have to be overcome if it is to be realized in practice. Human rights include economic and social rights as well as political and civil rights. This means that human rights such as the right to life, the right to housing, or the right to freedom of opinion are to be respected and protected even in the midst of conflict.

This has profound implications both for security policy and for development. In security terms, the central preoccupation of both practitioners and analysts of foreign policy in recent years has been with the conditions under which human rights concerns should take precedence over sovereignty. This debate often neglects the issue of the means to be adopted in so-called human rights operations. This is especially important where military means are likely to be deployed. It is often assumed that the use of military force is justifiable if there is legal authority to intervene (*jus ad bellum*), and the goals are worthwhile. However, the methods adopted must also be appropriate and, indeed, may affect the ability to achieve the goal specified.

What this principle means is that unless it is absolutely necessary and legal, killing is to be avoided. For the military it means the primary goal is protecting civilians rather than defeating an adversary. Of course, sometimes it is necessary to try to capture or even defeat insurgents but this has to be seen as a means to an end, civilian protection, rather than the other way round. So-called collateral damage is unacceptable. At the same time, the application of this principle to saving life directly under threat from other parties might involve the effective use of force and a much more robust interventionist policy. Human security interventions would aim to prevent a repeat of future Srebrenicas and Rwandas.

In humanitarian operations, protection of civilians is an end in itself. The aim is to prevent attacks on civilians and to uphold human rights, even though the process might also help to separate the population from armed groups or to gain intelligence. Chapter 6 described the British intervention in Northern Ireland as an example of this kind of approach, even though it had its problems. The British developed a response that reflected the fact that the inhabitants of Northern Ireland were British citizens (and voters) and that therefore their protection had to come first. Bombing Belfast was not an option. In effect, this principle implies that everyone is treated as a citizen.

The primacy of human rights also implies that those who commit gross human rights violations are treated as individual criminals rather than collective enemies. Torturing suspects who have been arrested is also illegitimate and illegal.

In economic terms, the primacy of human rights means the primacy of human development as opposed to the growth of national economies. This has profound implications for development policies as well as for more specific issues such as conditionality. In many post-conflict areas, economies have been stabilized and very high rates of growth achieved. Yet individual insecurity as a consequence of joblessness and the high levels of informal economic activity remains a potential contributor to future conflict. Ways have to be found to help the individual even where a country has poor governance or fails to meet various forms of conditionality. Sanctions may therefore be problematic. Different voices within a country should be consulted on the use of conditionality, and means have to be found to assist communities that bypass local authorities.

Principle 2: Legitimate political authority

Human security depends on the existence of legitimate institutions that gain the trust of the population and have some enforcement capacity. Again this applies both to physical security, where the rule of law and a well-functioning system of justice are essential, and to material security, where increasing legitimate employment or providing infrastructure and public services requires state policies. Legitimate political authority does not necessarily need to mean a state; it could consist of local government or regional or international political arrangements like protectorates or transitional administrations. Since state failure is often the primary cause of conflict, the reasons for state failure have to be taken into account in reconstructing legitimate political authority. Measures like justice and security sector reform, DDR, the extension of authority, and public service reform are critical for the establishment of legitimate political authority.[6]

This principle explicitly recognizes the limitations on the use of military force. The aim of any intervention is to stabilize the situation so that a space can be created for a peaceful political process rather than to win through military means alone, as discussed in Chapter 6. Diplomacy, sanctions, the provision of aid, and civil society links are all among the array of instruments available to states and international institutions in aiming to influence political processes in other countries – opening up authoritarian regimes, strengthening legitimate forms of political authority and promoting inclusive political solutions to conflict – as is the capacity to deploy civilian personnel. It is in cases of impending humanitarian catastrophe, a threatened genocide for example, that military forces may need to be used. In such cases, they can only succeed on the basis of local consent and support. The most that can be achieved through the use of military forces is stabilization. Again, this is a difficult cognitive shift for the military, since they tend to see their roles in terms of defeating an enemy.

Actually, in most counter-insurgency operations, victory is very difficult and can only be achieved, if at all, through widespread destruction and repression. This principle explicitly recognizes the impossibility of victory and aims instead to establish safe zones where political solutions can be sought. The military's job is enabling rather than winning. Thus techniques like safe havens, humanitarian corridors or no-fly zones are typical of a human security approach.

This principle also means that politics is in command. Both economic and security policies have to be guided by political considerations and, in operational terms, this means that there needs to be a single commander, political or military, who understands politics and has access to political authority.

Principle 3: Multilateralism

A human security approach has to be global. Hence it can only be implemented through multilateral action. Multilateralism means more than simply 'acting with a group of states'. In that narrow sense, nearly all international initiatives might be considered multilateral. Multilateralism is closely related to legitimacy and is what distinguishes a human security approach from neo-colonialism.

First, multilateralism means a commitment to work with international institutions and through the procedures of international institutions. This means, first and foremost, working within the United Nations framework, but it also entails working with or sharing out tasks among other regional organizations such as the OSCE and NATO in Europe, the AU, SADC and ECOWAS in Africa, or the OAS in the western hemisphere.

Second, multilateralism entails a commitment to creating common rules and norms, solving problems through rules and cooperation and enforcing the rules. Nowadays, legitimate political authority has to be situated within a multilateral framework. Indeed state failure is partly to be explained in terms of the failure of traditionally unilateralist states to adapt to multilateral ways of working.

Third, multilateralism has to include coordination, rather than duplication or rivalry. An effective human security approach requires coordination between intelligence, foreign policy, trade policy, development policy and security policy initiatives, of the member states, the Commission and the Council of the European Union, and of other multilateral actors, including the United Nations, the World Bank, the IMF and regional institutions. Preventive and pro-active policies cannot be effective if they are isolated and even contradictory.

Principle 4: The bottom-up approach

Notions of 'partnership', 'local ownership' and 'participation' are already key concepts in development policy. These concepts should also apply to security policies. Decisions about the kind of security and development policies to be adopted, whether or not to intervene with military forces or through various forms of conditionality – and how – must take account of the most basic needs identified by the people who are affected by violence and insecurity. This is not just a moral issue; it is also a matter of effectiveness. People who live in zones of insecurity are the best source of intelligence. Thus communication, consultation and dialogue are essential tools for both development and security, not simply to win hearts and minds but in order to gain knowledge and understanding. This principle seems obvious but there is often a built-in tendency to think 'we know best'. After all, bottom-up includes criminals, mafia and warlords. The solution is to talk to everyone and it should not be so difficult to identify people of conscience and integrity who could act as local guides.

Particularly important in this respect is the role of women's groups. The importance of gender equality for development, especially the education of girls, has long been recognized. The same may be true when managing conflict. Women play a critical role in contemporary conflicts, both in dealing with the everyday consequences of the conflict and in overcoming divisions in society. Involvement and partnership with women's groups could be a key component of a human security approach.

Principle 5: Regional focus

New wars have no clear boundaries. They tend to spread through refugees and displaced persons, through minorities who live in different states, through criminal and extremist networks. Indeed most situations of severe insecurity are located in regional clusters. The tendency to focus attention on areas that are defined in terms of statehood has often meant that relatively simple ways of preventing the spread of violence are neglected. Time and again, foreign policy analysts have been taken by surprise when, after considerable attention has been given to one conflict, another conflict springs up seemingly out of the blue in a neighbouring state. The war in Sierra Leone could not be solved without addressing the cause of conflict in Liberia, for example. Today's war in Afghanistan can only be contained if the neighbouring states, especially Pakistan, are involved.

By the same token, a regional focus is important in restoring and/or fostering legitimate economic and trade cooperation. The breakdown of transport and trade links, associated with war, is often a primary reason for falls in production and employment that contribute to poverty and insecurity and the spread of an illegal/informal economy.

Implications for Policy

According to the *Human Security Report*, there was a decline in the number of conflicts in the world and the number of people killed in conflicts in the first five years of the twenty-first century. It can be argued that the international community has contributed to the decline in conflicts both through efforts to broker peace agreements and, more importantly, to sustain them through the deployment of troops and the influx of aid.

However, although conflicts may have been stabilized, individuals still experience high levels of physical insecurity as a consequence of high crime rates, high human rights violations and high levels of violence against women. The presence of peacekeeping troops may help to separate warring parties and deter violations of ceasefire agreements, but they are not very effective at providing public security and dealing with illegal armed groups. Moreover, the physical insecurity is linked to material insecurity. New wars involve high levels of population displacement, rapid urbanization, loss of rural livelihoods, destruction of infrastructure and productive assets, and greater vulnerability to natural disasters. Economic assistance tends to focus on meeting humanitarian needs and on macro-economic stabilization. Thus in many post-conflict areas, economic growth is often fairly high and inflation relatively low, but there are very high levels of unemployment. And disgruntled unemployed young men armed with surplus weapons are a reason for a resurgence of conflict. Neither the political/military situation nor the economic situation is sustainable. The apparent calm depends on the international presence, both political and military, and economic stabilization depends on externally generated revenue.

A human security approach would aim both to stabilize conflicts and to address the sources of insecurity. In security terms, the key emphasis has to be on public security – the establishment of a rule of law and the instruments for law enforcement. In effect, it also means development since it involves institution-building, finding alternative legitimate livelihoods to criminal activity, and dealing with illegal armed groups. International law to which states have signed up does provide an instrument for the international community. Multilateral institutions, particularly the European Union and the United Nations, need:

- An *expanded international presence* in areas of insecurity. This is needed as a symbolic form of protection, for early warning and to acquire local knowledge to help guide policy. The problems of long-distance intelligence have been graphically illustrated in Iraq and Afghanistan. Human intelligence based on engagement with local people should increasingly be considered the centrepiece of intelligence. It is possible to envisage new tools, like, for example, the EU monitoring missions. Another proposal is to establish law shops or citizens advice bureaux in areas of actual or potential insecurity where the local population could gain legal advice about their rights and how to defend them. In so far as monitoring missions or advice bureaux are staffed by international personnel, it is also important to create institutions to make their behaviour accountable to a local population.

- New *human security forces* that involve a mixture of military, civilians and police and whose main task is to protect civilians and to provide public security. Specific proposals for a Human Security Response Force for the EU are put forward in the report of the Study Group on Europe's Security Capabilities.[7] A Human Security Response Force would operate in quite different ways from either traditional peacekeeping or traditional armies. Its main job would be to act in support of law enforcement, so it would be more like a police force, although more robust. The principles described above, such as the primacy of human rights, the establishment of legitimate political authority and the bottom-up approach, would all shape the way the force is used. The aim should be to protect people and minimize all casualties. This is more akin to the traditional approach of the police, who risk their lives to save others, even though they are prepared to kill *in extremis*, as human security forces should be. Rather than taking territory or destroying enemy forces, human security forces would develop techniques like safe havens or humanitarian corridors aimed at protecting the civilian population.

- A *legal framework*. The capacity of international institutions, especially the EU, to act as 'norms promoters', operating within international law, furthering international law and using legal instruments to enhance security, is hindered by the absence of a single and coherent body of international law governing foreign deployments. There is a need for a human security legal framework which would tackle these deficits in the international legal system and encourage the development of a multilateral legal context for international human security missions. This framework should clarify the legality of international deployments and the legal regimes that govern deployed personnel, military and civilian, and locals in a conflict area. These would build on the domestic law of the host state, the domestic law of the sending states and the rules of engagement, international criminal law, human rights law and international humanitarian law. Such a legal framework would also need to incorporate existing law dealing with prohibitions on weapons, in particular the Chemical Weapons Convention and the Biological Weapons Convention. WMD should be treated as a humanitarian issue rather than an arms control issue, since the latter is predicated on state security policies and the functioning of deterrence. Any use of WMD would represent a grave violation of human rights; hence the importance of international legal norms.

A human security approach implies *more* not less assistance for development, since human development is a key component of human security. As stated above, a human security approach would also endorse some key principles of development practice such as partnership, local ownership, engagement with civil society and gender sensitivity. At the same time, however, policies needed for conflict prevention and reconstruction require a different hierarchy of priorities from predominantly development concerns. These policies do not apply only to countries already prone to insecurity but may offer an alternative paradigm for development in general. Countries whose population live in precarious economic conditions also tend to be countries vulnerable to conflict. In particular, a human security approach implies that the economic and social well-being of the individual matter more than economic growth and macro-economic stabilization, even though macro-economic stabilization may be a necessary condition for helping individuals.

Key economic and social priorities for conflict prevention and reconstruction include:

- *Combining humanitarian and development assistance.* Humanitarian assistance is often problematic in conflicts because it attracts people away from their sources of livelihood, especially if it is delivered in camps, and it is often 'taxed' by the warring parties. It is important to sustain development assistance through all phases of conflict since development contributes to prevention as well as reconstruction.[8]

- *The creation of legitimate employment and self-sustaining livelihoods.* Many people join paramilitary groups or criminal organizations because they have no alternative source of employment or income. In very poor countries, sustaining primary production is key. In middle income countries (like the Balkans or Iraq) public works and restructuring state enterprises are the main ways to generate employment.[9]
- *Institution-building, including the rule of law.* This would include measures that are already beginning to come under the rubric of development, such as public service reform and measures to build governance capacity and state authority; justice and security sector reform, combined with DDR (cuts in military spending without expenditure on security tasks, conversion or destruction of weapons, and alternative employment for demobilized soldiers can easily increase insecurity as the latter try to generate income by selling their services or weapons), on the model of human security rather than state security; measures to implement the rule of law, including transitional justice; constitution building and democratic procedures, including the establishment of parliaments and municipal authorities.
- *Attention to the importance of infrastructure and public works.* Energy, communications and transport links are essential for maintaining production, especially in middle income countries. Integrated infrastructure, often on a regional basis, is an important way to prevent the separation and division of communities. As in the case of coal and steel in the early days of European integration, expenditure on infrastructure can be viewed both as generating employment and a stimulus to reconciliation.
- *Education and social services.* In many conflict zones, social safety nets and educational opportunities have been greatly weakened or are non-existent. Extremist groups (nationalists or religious fundamentalists) often offer these services and consequently have a profound ideological influence, especially on young people. Education is key to developing new skills, especially for those affected by conflict (displaced persons and demobilized combatants), while social services reduce insecurity. The

importance of education has long been acknowledged in development, but it has yet to be recognized as an instrument of security policy.

*   *Generating tax revenue.* If legitimate political authority is to be restored and sustained, tax revenue is essential. States in conflict typically are dependent on foreign and/ or criminal sources of income. If the relationship between the state and the citizens is to be meaningful, tax revenue is essential. Moreover, structural adjustment needs to be achieved by raising revenue rather than reducing expenditure. The best source of revenue is income tax, since sales taxes tend to encourage smuggling and customs duties, typically the main source of revenue for countries in conflict, pose an obstacle to trade. However, income tax depends on employment – another reason for prioritizing employment.

A key component of both security and development approaches is the engagement of civil society. Legitimacy depends on some sort of social contract between the rulers and the ruled. Civil society is the medium through which such a contract is negotiated, debated and struggled for. There is a tendency on the part of donors to treat civil society as a passive phenomenon to be funded and to be helped in terms of capacity-building. What is really important is access to policy-makers and the creation of spaces for debate and deliberation. After all, democracy is about the peaceful management of conflicts.

Conclusion

The world faces a critical juncture. On the one hand, international efforts to stabilize conflicts since the end of the Cold War have had some limited successes. On the other hand, these achievements risk being undermined both by the failure to deal with the underlying conditions that lead to 'new wars' and which are the sources of human insecurity, and by the spread of terror and the war on terror. Millions of people in the world still live in situations of intolerable insecurity, especially in zones of conflict – West, Central and the Horn of Africa, the Balkans, the Middle East, the Caucasus and Central Asia.

Human security policies are usually considered to complement state security policies, as an add-on to the primary task. Clearly, individual states will maintain a capacity for territorial defence in the event of external aggression. And multilateral institutions, like Nato or the United Nations, will come to the defence of states like Kuwait if they are attacked by other states. However, as the world becomes more interconnected and as states are increasingly integrated into layers of global governance, the need for classic state security policies is likely to come to complement the more urgent human security tasks, rather than the other way round.

Among the development community, there are rightly concerns about the securitization of development. In the past, in theory at least, security issues were seen as the realm of foreign affairs – high politics – while development was viewed as the domestic realm, having to do with the low politics of economy and society. In so far as security did invade the realm of development – and, of course, during the Cold War period, security concerns profoundly affected development policy – it was viewed as a sort of neo-colonialism. Among the humanitarian community, there is concern about the loss of humanitarian space. Preserving the autonomy of humanitarian agencies is considered a precondition for the provision of humanitarian assistance.

Today, however, it is impossible to separate security and development. The distinctions between foreign and domestic policy, or between high and low politics, are breaking down. If we stick to an old-fashioned view of security, this could indeed have a deleterious effect on development. This is because a narrow statist view of European security would do nothing to overcome the insecurity experienced by individuals and communities in large parts of the world, especially the developing world. Indeed, the use of military forces in a war-fighting mode can actually exacerbate insecurity, as in Iraq. Humanitarian space no longer exists in the 'new wars', where there are no clearly demarcated 'innocent' sectors because the sides are no longer distinct and it is difficult to distinguish between combatants and non-combatants. Moreover, insecurity can no longer be contained – violence has a tendency to cross borders not in the form of attacks by foreign enemies but through terrorism, organized crime or extreme ideologies.

A human security approach could benefit development in several ways:

- First, human security is aimed at providing the conditions (physical safety, rule of law and sustainable institutions) that are integral to development.
- Second, a human security approach necessarily involves an emphasis on human development because it is very difficult to disentangle physical and material security. Indeed it is the absence of human development – weak institutions, lack of legitimate livelihoods – that constitute the conditions that can give rise to violence.
- Third, the development aspects of human development put more emphasis on the needs of individuals and communities than on economic performance indicators and thus could help to reorient development strategies.

Likewise, a human security approach would aim to protect humanitarian space rather than to distinguish it from military space.

The adoption of a human security approach by the European Union, in particular, could be an important contribution to global security. The weakness of the United Nations is the consequence of the weakness of its members. European countries currently have some 1.8 million men and women under arms, yet the capacity for deployment of human security missions is extremely small. Polls show that Europeans consistently support the idea of a European foreign policy. A commitment to expand and restructure Europe's capacities to contribute to global security and development would also increase the legitimacy and visibility of the EU itself, both within Europe and in the wider world. And this alone would be a contribution to security.

Notes

Introduction

Chapter epigraph from Rupert Smith, *The Utility of Force: The Art of Making War in the Modern World* (London: Allen Lane, 2006), p. 1.

1 Rupert Smith, *The Utility of Force: The Art of Making War in the Modern World* (London: Allen Lane, 2006); Mary Kaldor, *New and Old Wars: Organized Violence in a Global Era* (Cambridge: Polity, 1999).
2 Charles Tilly, *Coercion, Capital and European States, AD 990–1900* (Oxford: Blackwell, 1990).
3 Ibid., p. 67.
4 Carl Schmitt, *The Concept of the Political* (Chicago: University of Chicago Press, 1990), p. 33; first published in 1932 as *Der Begriff des Politischen.*
5 Ibid., p. 52.
6 Mary Kaldor, *The Imaginary War: Understanding the East–West Conflict* (Oxford: Blackwell, 1990).
7 Isaac Deutscher, *The Great Contest: Russia and the West* (Oxford: Oxford University Press, 1960).
8 Quoted in Kaldor, *The Imaginary War*, pp. 202–3.
9 Michael Howard, *The Invention of Peace: Reflections on War and International Order* (New Haven: Yale University Press, 2000).
10 See Ian Clark, *Globalization and International Relations Theory* (Oxford: Oxford University Press, 1999); Rob Walker. *Inside/Outside: International Relations as Political Theory* (Cambridge: Cambridge University Press, 1992).

11 Michel Foucault, *Discipline and Punish: The Birth of the Prison* (London: Penguin, 1977).

12 I am very grateful to Sabine Selchow for pointing this out.

13 Mary Kaldor, 'A Decade of Humanitarian Intervention: The Role of Global Civil Society', in Helmut Anheier, Marlies Glasius and Mary Kaldor (eds), *Global Civil Society 2001* (Oxford: Oxford University Press, 2001).

14 Mary Kaldor, 'American Power: From "Compellance" to Cosmo-politanism', *International Affairs*, 79, no. 1 (2003): 1–22.

15 Mary Kaldor, 'Nationalism and Globalisation', *Nations and Nationalism* 10, nos 1–2 (2003): 161–77.

16 First published in Peter Siani-Davies (ed.), *International Intervention in the Balkans since 1995* (London: Routledge, 2003).

17 Mary Kaldor, *Global Civil Society: An Answer to War* (Cambridge: Polity, 2003).

18 Mary Kaldor. 'The Idea of Global Civil Society', *International Affairs* 79, no. 3 (May 2003): 583–93.

19 *A Human Security Doctrine for Europe: The Barcelona Report of the Study Group on Europe's Security Capabilities*, presented to EU High Representative for Common Foreign and Security Policy Javier Solana, Barcelona, 15 Sept. 2004, available at www.lse. ac.uk/Depts/global/Publications/HumanSecurityDoctrine.pdf (accessed 23 Dec. 2006); Marlies Glasius and Mary Kaldor (eds), *A Human Security Doctrine for Europe* (London: Routledge, 2005); UN Development Programme, 'Evaluation of UNDP Assistance to Conflict-Affected Countries', 2007, at www.undp.org.

Chapter 1 A Decade of Humanitarian Intervention

This chapter draws on Mary Kaldor 'A Decade of Humanitarian Intervention: The Role of Global Civil Society', in Helmut Anheier, Marlies Glasius and Mary Kaldor (eds), *Global Civil Society 2001* (Oxford: Oxford University Press, 2001).

I should like to thank Mark Bowden, Kayode Fayemi, Yasmin Jusu-Sheriff, and John Hirsch for giving interviews, and Zainab Bangura, Walid Salem, and Abdul Tejan-Cole for responding to my questions via e-mail.

1 Human Rights Watch, *World Report 2000*, New York, at www. hrw.org/reports/2000.

2 T. Allen and D. Styan, 'A Right to Interfere? Bernard Kouchner and the New Humanitarianism', *Journal of International Development* 12, no. 6 (2000): 825.

3   The peak of UN operations was 1993 when some 78,000 military troops were involved. The biggest operations were UNPROFOR in Bosnia-Herzegovina and UNOSOM II in Somalia. The Balkans operations are now undertaken by the European Union.

4   Stockholm International Peace Research Institute, *SIPRI Yearbook 2000: Armaments, Disarmament and International Security* (Oxford: Oxford University Press, 2000); UN Peacekeeping Department, at www.un.org/depts/dpk.

5   See M. Ignatieff, *The Warrior's Honor: Ethnic War and the Modern Conscience* (London: Chatto and Windus, 1998); C. Moorehead, *Dunant's Dreams: War, Switzerland and the History of the Red Cross* (London: HarperCollins, 1998).

6   Local anti-slavery campaigning groups existed long before the founding of the Anti-Slavery Society in places like Manchester and Philadelphia.

7   For all European groups, see the website of the European Platform for Conflict Prevention and Transformation at www.euconflict.org.

8   N. Anjelic, *Bosnia-Herzegovina: The End of a Legacy* (London: Frank Cass, 2003); Independent International Commission on Kosovo, *Kosovo Report: Conflict, International Response, Lessons Learned* (Oxford: Oxford University Press, 2000).

9   See C. Cockburn, 'The Women's Movement: Boundary-Crossing on Terrains of Conflict', in R. Cohen and Shirin M. Rai (eds), *Global Social Movements* (London: Athlone Press, 2000).

10   L. Mahoney and L. E. Eguren, *Unarmed Bodyguards: International Accompaniment for the Protection of Human Rights* (Bloomfield: Kumarian Press, 1997).

11   See Carnegie Commission on Preventing Deadly Conflict, *Preventing Deadly Conflict: Final Report* (Washington, DC: Carnegie Commission on Preventing Deadly Conflict, 1997); Carnegie Endowment for Peace, *Unfinished Peace: Report of the International Commission on the Balkans* (Washington, DC: Carnegie Endowment for Peace, 1996).

12   *Report on the Fall of Srebrenica*, UN Doc. A45/549, 15 Nov. 1999; *Report of the Independent Inquiry into Actions of the United Nations during the 1994 Genocide in Rwanda*, UN Doc. S/1999/1257, 15 Dec. 1999; *Report of the Panel on United Nations Peacekeeping Operations*, UN Doc. A/55/305-S/2000/809, 21 Aug. 2000.

13   *The Responsibility to Protect: Report of the Commission on Intervention and State Sovereignty*, New York, 2001.

14   Quoted in A. de Waal, *Famine Crimes: Politics and the Disaster Relief Industry in Africa* (Oxford and Indiana: James Currey/Indiana University Press, 1997), p. 83.

15 H. Bull (ed.), *Intervention in World Politics* (Oxford: Clarendon Press, 1984), p. 3.
16 Ibid., p. 4.
17 M. Akehurst, 'Humanitarian Intervention', in ibid.
18 In the case of the Indian intervention of 1971, the Indian ambassador to the United Nations Security Council used humanitarian arguments. He claimed that the suffering of the Bangladeshi people was sufficient to 'shock the conscience of the world'. And he asked, 'what has happened to our conventions on genocide, human rights, self-determination and so on? . . . Why [are members of the Security Council] so shy about speaking of human rights? . . . What has happened to the justice part [of the UN Charter]?' Quoted in Nicholas Wheeler, *Saving Strangers: Humanitarian Intervention in International Society* (Oxford: Oxford University Press, 2000), p. 63. But he did not invoke these arguments to justify the intervention; instead he referred to the (outlandish) crime of 'refugee aggression'.
19 Ibid., p. 93.
20 Bull, *Intervention in World Politics*, p. 183.
21 See Kaldor, *New and Old Wars*.
22 Interview with Mark Bowden of Save the Children, 9 Mar. 2001.
23 Allen and Styan, 'A Right to Interfere?', pp. 831–2.
24 See Margaret E. Keck and Kathryn Sikkink, *Activists beyond Borders: Advocacy Networks in International Politics* (Ithaca: Cornell University Press, 1998), ch. 3.
25 *Washington Post*, 25 Apr. 1991.
26 A. Roberts, *Humanitarian Action in War*, Adelphi Paper 305, International Institute of Strategic Studies (Oxford: Oxford University Press, 1996), p. 16.
27 Quoted in O. Ramsbotham and T. Woodhouse, *Humanitarian Intervention in Contemporary Conflict: A Reconceptualization* (Cambridge: Polity, 1996), p. 206.
28 Interpress Service, 12 Aug. 1992.
29 Africa Rights, 'Somalia and Operation Restore Hope: A Preliminary Assessment', London, May 1993.
30 Allen and Styan, 'A Right to Interfere?', p. 838.
31 T. G. Weiss, *Military–Civilian Interactions: Intervening in Humanitarian Crises* (Lanham: Rowman and Littlefield, 1999), p. 90.
32 See Wheeler, *Saving Strangers*, pp. 224–5.
33 *Financial Times*, 3 Dec. 1996.
34 Quoted in Weiss, *Military–Civilian Interactions*, p. 184.
35 See Independent International Commission on Kosovo, *Kosovo Report*.

36   These included cases where NATO forces 'conducted air attacks using cluster bombs near populated areas; attacked targets of questionable military legitimacy including Serb Radio and Television, heating plants and bridges; did not take adequate precautions in warning civilians of attack; took insufficient precautions in identifying the presence of civilians when attacking convoys and mobile targets; and caused excessive civilian casualties by not taking sufficient measures to verify that military targets did not have concentrations of civilians (such as Korisa)'; Human Rights Watch, 'Civilian Deaths in the NATO Air Campaign', New York, Feb. 2000, at www.hrw.org/reports/2000/nato.

37   D. Petrova, 'The Kosovo War and the Human Rights Community', paper presented to London School of Economics seminar, 18 Nov. 2000.

38   Interview with Human Rights Watch, Feb. 2001.

39   Noam Chomsky, *The New Military Humanism: Lessons from Kosovo* (London: Pluto Press, 1999).

40   See Wheeler, *Saving Strangers*; Ramsbotham and Woodhouse, *Humanitarian Intervention in Contemporary Conflict*; Robert Jackson, *The Global Covenant: Human Conduct in a World of States* (Oxford: Oxford University Press, 2000).

41   Quoted in Weiss, *Military–Civilian Interactions*, p. 90.

42   R. J. Goldstone, *For Humanity: Reflections of a War Crimes Investigator* (New Haven and London: Yale University Press, 2000), p. 74.

43   T. Blair, 'Doctrine of the International Community', Chicago, 23 Apr. 1999, at www.primeminister.gov.uk.

44   R. Brauman, *Humanitaire: le dilemme. Conversations pour demain* (Paris: Éditions Textuel, 1996).

45   Allen and Styan, 'A Right to Interfere?', p. 836.

46   Giulio Marcon and Mario Pianta, 'New Wars, New Peace Movements', *Soundings: A Journal of Politics and Culture* 17 (2001): pp. 11–24.

47   A. Tejan-Cole, 'The Legality of NATO and ECOMOG Interventions', MS, 2001.

48   *A Human Security Doctrine for Europe.*

49   J. L. Hirsch, *Sierra Leone: Diamonds and the Struggle for Democracy*, International Peace Academy Occasional Papers (Boulder and London: Lynne Rienner, 2001).

50   Paul Richards, *Fighting for the Rainforest: War, Youth and Resources in Sierra Leone* (Oxford: International African Institute and James Currey, 1996).

51   According to Paul Richards, 'Rebel violence in Sierra Leone is not an instinctive response to population pressure but a mobilization of youth on behalf of a small group of people angry at their exclu-

sion from an opaque patrimonial political system serving mineral extraction interests. In working through their anger some of the cultural scar tissue from the days of the slave trade – a trade active in the forests of eastern Sierra Leone until mid-nineteenth century – is once more exposed. The upper Guinean forests continue to resonate with the seizure of young people and their induction into a world of heightened violence' (ibid.).

52 I. Smillie, L. Gberie and R. Hazleton (eds), *The Heart of the Matter. Sierra Leone: Diamonds and Human Security* (Ottawa: Partnership Africa, 2000), p. 1.

53 *Conciliation Resources*, no. 9 (2000): 13.

54 Hirsch, *Sierra Leone*, p. 80.

55 Interview with Yasmin Jusu-Sheriff, a prominent member of the Sierra Leone women's movement, 27 Mar. 2001.

56 Yasmin Jusu-Sheriff in *Conciliation Resources* (2000): 47–9.

57 O. Oludipe, (ed.), *Sierra Leone: One Year After Lomé*, One-Day Analytical Conference on the Peace Process, London, 15 Sept., CDD Strategy Planning Series no. 5 (London: Centre for Democracy and Development, 2000), p. 88.

58 Interview, Mar 2001.

59 At http://freespace.virgin.net/ambrose.ganda/.

60 'Saturday Debate: Should the UN Get out of Sierra Leone?', *Guardian*, 22 May 2000.

61 Centre for Democracy and Development, *Engaging Sierra Leone*, CDD Strategy Planning Series no. 4 (London: Centre for Democracy and Development, 2000).

62 At www.fosalone.org.

63 Interview, Mar. 2001.

Chapter 2   American Power

This chapter draws on Mary Kaldor. 'American Power: From "Compellance" to Cosmopolitanism', *International Affairs*, 79, no. 1 (2003): 1–22.

1 Jeffrey C. Goldfarb 'America versus Democracy? Losing Young Allies in the War against Terror', *International Herald Tribune*, 21 Aug. 2002.

2 See Walter A. McDougall, *Promised Land, Crusader State: The American Encounter with the World since 1776* (Boston: Houghton Mifflin, 1997).

3 Robert Kagan, 'The Power Divide', *Prospect*, Aug. 2002; Hubert Védrine, with Dominique Moisi, *France in the Age of Globalization* (Washington, DC: Brookings Institution, 2001).

4 Thomas C. Schelling, *Arms and Influence* (New Haven: Yale University Press, 1966).

5 See, for example, Paul Kennedy, *The Rise and Fall of the Great Powers: Economic Change and Military Conflict from 1500–2000* (New York: Random House, 1987); Robert Gilpin, *War and Change in World Politics* (Cambridge: Cambridge University Press, 1981).

6 See, for example, Joshua Goldstein, *Long Cycles: Prosperity and War in the Modern Age* (London and New Haven: Yale University Press, 1988).

7 Charles P. Kindleberger, *The World in Depression, 1929–1939* (London: Penguin, 1987).

8 For a brilliant exposition of this argument, see Carlota Perez, *Technological Revolutions and Financial Capital: The Dynamics of Bubbles and Golden Ages* (Cheltenham: Edward Elgar, 2002).

9 David Held, Anthony McGrew, David Goldblatt, and Jonathan Perraton, *Global Transformations* (Cambridge: Polity, 1999); Anthony Giddens, *Runaway World: How Globalisation is Reshaping our Lives* (London: Profile Books, 1999).

10 Held et al., *Global Transformations*.

11 See David Holloway, *The Soviet Union and the Arms Race* (New Haven: Yale University Press, 1983).

12 For this argument, see James Fallows, 'The Fifty-First State?', *Atlantic Monthly*, Nov. 2002.

13 General Wesley Clark at NATO press conference, 1 Apr. 1999.

14 In the elections of January 2007, the radical nationalist party of Seselj, who had advocated expelling all Kosovars from Kosovo, and even, at one point, infecting them with the AIDS/HIV virus, and who is now on trial in The Hague, became the largest single party, winning 28.7% of the vote.

15 See Michael O'Hanlon, 'A Flawed Masterpiece', *Foreign Affairs*, May–June 2002.

16 Germany's blitzkrieg against France, Netherlands and Belgium in the Second World War cost it 27,000 casualties.

17 The term was first used by Michael Mann in 'The Roots and Contradictions of Modern Militarism', in *States, War and Capitalism* (Oxford: Blackwell, 1988), pp. 166–87. Colin McInnes uses the term 'spectator-sport' warfare.

18 See James Der Derian, *Virtuous War: Mapping the Military-Industrial-Media-Entertainment Network* (Boulder: Westview Press, 2001).

19 James Der Derian '9/11: Before, After and Between', in Craig Calhoun, Paul Price and Ashley Timmer (eds), *Understanding September 11* (New York: New Press, 2002), p. 180.

20 See Kaldor, *The Imaginary War*.
21 Ibid., chs 11 and 12.
22 See Lawrence Freedman, *The Revolution in Strategic Affairs*, Adelphi Paper 318 (London: International Institute of Strategic Affairs, 1998).
23 In the aftermath of September 11, the military recruited the University of Southern California's Institute of Creative Technology to involve Hollywood in imagining terrorist worst-case scenarios. See Der Derian '9/11: Before, After and Between'.
24 According to Max Boot, the *New York Times* report left out the phrase 'a bit', thereby exaggerating American difficulties. See Max Boot 'The New American Way of War', *Foreign Affairs*, July–Aug. 2003.
25 Elliott A. Cohen, 'A Tale of Two Secretaries', *Foreign Affairs*, May–June 2002, p. 39.
26 Donald H. Rumsfeld, 'Transforming the Military', *Foreign Affairs*, May–June 2002, p. 21.
27 Kersti Hakansson has demonstrated this point in a comparison of tactics in Vietnam and Afghanistan. See 'New Wars, Old Warfare? Comparing US Tactics in Afghanistan and Vietnam', in Jan Angstrom and Isabelle Duyvesteyn (eds), *The Nature of Modern War: Clausewitz and his Critics Revisited* (Stockholm: Swedish National Defence College, 2003).
28 See David Gold, 'US Military Expenditure and the 2001 Quadrennial Defense Review', Appendix 6E, in *SIPRI Yearbook 2002: Armaments, Disarmament and International Security* (Oxford: Oxford University Press, 2002).
29 Quoted in G. John Ikenberry, 'America's Imperial Ambition', *Foreign Affairs*, Sept.–Oct. 2002, p. 52.
30 *National Security Strategy of the United States*, at www.nytimes.com/2002/09/20/politics/20STEXT_FULL.html.
31 Quoted in G. John Ikenberry, 'America's Imperial Ambition', p. 50.
32 *National Security Strategy of the United States*.
33 Chairman of the Joint Chiefs of Staff, 'The National Military Strategic Plan for the War on Terrorism', Washington, DC, Feb. 2006.
34 See Michael Howard, 'What's in a Name?', *Foreign Affairs*, Jan.–Feb. 2002.
35 For a partial list of these types of actions, see box 1.3 in Marlies Glasius and Mary Kaldor, 'The State of Global Civil Society before and after September 11', in Marlies Glasius, Mary Kaldor and Helmut Anheier (eds), *Global Civil Society 2002* (Oxford: Oxford University Press, 2002).

36 See Carl Connetta, 'Strange Victory: A Critical Appraisal of Operation Enduring Freedom and the Afghanistan War', Project on Defense Alternatives, Research Monograph no. 6, 30 Jan. 2002. Estimates of Taliban and Al Qaeda troops killed vary from 4,000 to 10,000.

37 This study was based on a sampling of clusters of households and, in the majority of cases, actual death certificates were produced. See Gilbert Burnham, Riyadh Lafta, Shannon Doocy and Les Roberts, 'Mortality after the 2003 Invasion of Iraq: A Cross-Sectional Cluster Sample Survey', *The Lancet*, 11 Oct. 2006.

38 See www.icasualties.org/oif/

39 Mark Juergensmeyer, 'Religious Terror and Global War', in Calhoun, Price and Timmer, *Understanding September 11*, p. 40.

40 John Lewis Gaddis, *The Long Peace: Inquiries into the History of the Cold War* (Oxford: Oxford University Press, 1987). John Mearsheimer,. 'Why We Will Soon Miss the Cold War', *The Atlantic*, Aug. 1990.

41 'War with Iraq is not in America's National Interest', advertisement, *New York Times*, 26 Sept. 2002.

42 Joseph S. Nye, Jr, *The Paradox of American Power* (Oxford: Oxford University Press, 2002), p. 39.

43 Ibid., p. 160.

44 Peter Gowan, 'The Calculus of Power', *New Left Review* (July–Aug. 2002): 63.

45 Michael Klare, 'Global Petro-Politics: The Foreign Policy Implications of the Bush Administration's Energy Plan', *Current History* (Mar. 2002).

46 Quoted in Adele Simmons, 'Iraq: Who's Leading the Protest', *Chicago Sun-Times*, 13 Oct. 2002.

47 Kagan, 'The Power Divide'.

48 Immanuel Kant, 'Perpetual Peace' (1795), in *Kant's Political Writings*, ed. Hans Reiss (Cambridge: Cambridge University Press, 1992).

49 Kwame Anthony Appiah, 'Cosmopolitan Patriots', in Joshua Cohen (ed.), *For Love of Country: Debating the Limits of Patriotism: Martha C. Nussbaum and Respondents* (Cambridge, Mass.: Beacon Press, 1996).

50 Tony Blair, quoted in United Nations Development Programme, *Human Development Report 2002: Deepening Democracy in a Fragmented World* (New York: UNDP and Oxford University Press, 2002), p. 101.

51 George Soros, *George Soros on Globalization* (London: Perseus Books, 2002), p. 17.

52 Interestingly something similar seems to have happened after the 1998 air strikes on Afghanistan in response to the bombings of American embassies in Kenya and Tanzania. Jason Burke shows how the Taliban were initially deeply suspicious of Al Qaeda on doctrinal as well as political grounds despite Osama Bin Laden's offers of financial support. But they were thrown together after the air strikes. See Jason Burke, *Al Qaeda: Casting a Shadow of Terror* (London: I. B. Taurus, 2003).

53 International Institute for Strategic Studies, *Strategic Survey 2003* (London: IISS, 2003).

54 Ibid.

55 Richard Falk 'Testing Patriotism and Citizenship in the Global Terror War', in Ken Booth and Tim Dunne (eds), *Worlds in Collision: Terror and the Future of World Order* (London: Palgrave, 2002).

56 See Mary Kaldor, Helmut Anheier and Marlies Glasius (eds), *Global Civil Society 2003* (Oxford: Oxford University Press, 2003).

Chapter 3 Nationalism and Globalization

This chapter draws on Mary Kaldor, 'Nationalism and Globalisation', *Nations and Nationalism* 10, nos 1–2 (2003): 161–77.

1 Eric J. Hobsbawm, *Nations and Nationalism since 1870: Programme, Myth, Reality* (Cambridge: Cambridge University Press, 1990).

2 Anthony D. Smith, *Nationalism: Theory, Ideology, History* (Cambridge: Polity, 2001), p. 160.

3 See, for example, ibid., and Umut Özkirimli, *Theories of Nationalism: A Critical Introduction* (London: Macmillan, 2000).

4 Ernest Gellner, *Conditions of Liberty: Civil Society and its Rivals* (London: Hamish Hamilton, 1994), p. 102.

5 Ernest Gellner, *Nations and Nationalism* (Oxford: Blackwell, 1983).

6 Benedict Anderson, *Imagined Communities: Reflections on the Origins and Spread of Nationalism* (London: Verso, 1983).

7 Quoted in Özkirimli, *Theories of Nationalism*, p. 42.

8 Quoted in Smith, *Nationalism*, p. 65.

9 Ibid., p. 82.

10   Quoted in Montserrat Guibernau, *Nationalisms: The Nation-State and Nationalism in the Twentieth Century* (Cambridge: Polity, 1995), p. 8.

11   Ibid., p. 78.

12   Joshua Kaldor-Robinson, 'The Virtual and the Imaginary: The Role of Diasphoric New Media in the Construction of a National Identity during the Break-up of Yugoslavia', *Oxford Development Studies* 30, no. 2 (June 2002): 177–87.

13   Smith, *Nationalism*, p. 125.

14   Quoted in Özkirimli, *Theories of Nationalism*, p. 47.

15   Kaldor, *The Imaginary War*.

16   See Mary Kaldor and Diego Muro, 'Religious and Nationalist Militant Networks', in Kaldor, Anheier and Glasius, *Global Civil Society 2003*.

17   Nationalist parties captured power in the Balkans, for example, and in India. Islamic parties are ruling in Iran and Turkey and have done well in elections in Pakistan and Algeria, where electoral victory led to a military coup. In Western Europe, right-wing anti-immigrant parties have increased their share of the vote, and in the United States Christian fundamentalist and Zionist groups are increasingly influential in the Republican Party.

18   Mark Juergensmeyer, *Terror in the Mind of God* (Berkeley: University of California Press, 2000), p. 222.

19   Erik Melander, 'The Nagorno-Karabakh Conflict Revisited: Was the War Inevitable?', *Journal of Cold War Studies* 3, no. 2 (spring 2001): 65.

20   Jason Burke, *Al Qaeda*, p. 147.

21   In the last ten years before his death, the Prophet redefined the notion of a 'raid', which had been characteristic of pre-Islamic nomad groups, as part of Jihad, to mean a raid aimed at the benefit of the whole community and not individual gain. Al Qaeda has resurrected the term and it is used to describe its form of action, for example the attacks on the World Trade Center and other operations. Hassan Mneimneh and Kanan Makiya, 'Manual for a "Raid"', *New York Review of Books*, 17 Jan. 2002.

22   Jason Burke, *Al Qaeda*, p. 35.

23   Ibid., p. 238.

24   Kaldor and Glasius, 'Global Civil Society before and after September 11'.

25   Jason Burke, *Al Qaeda*, p. 248.

26   See Karoly Gruber, 'From the Beginning of Reason to the End of History: The Politics of Postmodernism and Ethno-Nationalist Renaissances of Pre-Postmodern Nations', D.Phil. thesis, University of Sussex, 1999.

27 Ernest Renan, 'What is a Nation?' (1982), in Homi K. Bhabha (ed.), *Nation and Narration* (London: Routledge, 1990), p. 20.
28 John Urry, 'The Global Media and Cosmopolitanism', Department of Sociology, Lancaster University, 2000, at www.comp.lancs.ac.uk/sociology/soc056ju.html.
29 Appiah, 'Cosmopolitan Patriots'.
30 Anthony D. Smith, *Nations and Nationalism in a Global Era* (Cambridge: Polity, 1995), p. 24.
31 Roland Robertson, *Globalisation: Social Theory and Global Culture* (London: Sage, 1992); Martin Shaw, *The Global State* (Cambridge: Cambridge University Press, 2000).
32 Daniel Levy and Natan Sznaider, 'Memory Unbound: The Holocaust and the Formation of Cosmopolitan Memory', *European Journal of Social Theory* 5, no. 1 (2002): 87–106.

Chapter 4   Intervention in the Balkans

This chapter draws on my contribution to Peter Siani-Davies (ed.), *International Intervention in the Balkans since 1995* (London: Routledge, 2003).

1 M. Castells, *End of Millennium*, vol. 3: *The Information Age: Economy, Society and Culture* (Oxford: Blackwell, 1998); M. Leonard, *Network Europe: The New Case for Europe* (London: Foreign Policy Centre, 1999).
2 Tilly, *Coercion, Capital and European States*.
3 M. Todorova, *Imagining the Balkans* (Oxford: Oxford University Press, 1997).
4 R. West, *Black Lamb, Grey Falcon: Record of a Journey through Yugoslavia in 1937* (London: Macmillan, 1942).
5 M. Glenny, *The Balkans 1804–1999: Nationalism, War and the Great Powers* (London: Granta, 1999); M. Mazower, *The Balkans* (London: Phoenix, 2000); Todorova, *Imagining the Balkans*.
6 Quoted in Mazower, *The Balkans*, p. 129.
7 See S. L. Woodward, *Balkan Tragedy: Chaos and Dissolution after the Cold War* (Washington, DC: Brookings Institution, 1995).
8 R. M. Hayden, 'Constitutional Nationalism in the Former Yugoslav Republics', *Slavic Review* 51, no. 4 (1995): 654–73.
9 Woodward, *Balkan Tragedy*.
10 See M. Thompson, *Forging War: The Media in Serbia, Croatia, and Bosnia-Herzegovina* (London: Article XIX, 1994).

11 V. Bojicic and D. Dyker, 'Sanctions on Serbia: Sledgehammer or Scalpel?', SEI Working Paper no.1, Sussex European Institute, University of Sussex, June 1993.

Chapter 5 The Idea of Global Civil Society

This chapter draws on Mary Kaldor, 'The Idea of Global Civil Society', *International Affairs*, 79, no. 3 (May 2003): 583–93.

1 Quoted in John L. Comaroff and Jean Comaroff, *Civil Society and the Political Imagination in Africa: Critical Perspectives* (Chicago: University of Chicago Press, 1999) p. 3.
2 Quoted in John Ehrenberg, *Civil Society: The Critical History of an Idea* (New York: New York University Press, 1999), p. 209.
3 G. W. F. Hegel, *The Philosophy of Right* (1820), trans. S. W. Dyde, originally published in English in 1896 (London: Prometheus Books, 1996), p. 331.
4 Adam Michnik, 'The New Evolutionism', in *Letters from Prison and Other Essays* (Berkeley: California University Press, 1985).
5 Keck and Sikkink, *Activists beyond Borders*.
6 Vaclav Havel, 'The Power of the Powerless', in John Keane (ed.), *The Power of the Powerless: Citizens against the State in Central-Eastern Europe* (London: Hutchinson, 1985), pp. 90–1.
7 Quoted in Ehrenberg, *Civil Society*, pp. 222–3.
8 See Lester M. Salamon and Helmut K. Anheier, *The Emerging Nonprofit Sector: An Overview* (Manchester: Manchester University Press, 1996); Amitai Etzioni, *The Third Way to a Good Society* (London: Demos, 2000); Amitai Etzioni, *The Active Society: A Theory of Societal and Political Processes* (London: Collier-Macmillan, 1968); Amitai Etzioni, *The Spirit of Community: Rights, Responsibilities, and the Communitarian Agenda* (New York: Crown, 1993); Robert D. Putnam with Robert Leonardi and Raffaella Y. Nanetti, *Making Democracy Work: Civic Traditions in Modern Italy* (Princeton: Princeton University Press, 1993), Robert D. Putnam, *Bowling Alone: The Collapse and Revival of American Community* (New York: Simon and Schuster, 2000).
9 Alexis de Tocqueville, *Democracy in America* (first published in 1835) (New York: Vintage, 1945), p. 118.
10 Anheier, Glasius and Kaldor, *Global Civil Society 2001*; Glasius, Kaldor and Anheier, *Global Civil Society 2002*.

11 Neera Chandhoke, 'A Cautionary Note on Civil Society', paper presented at the conference on Civil Society in Different Cultural Contexts, London School of Economics, Sept. 2001.

12 Intervention at Expert Conference for *Human Development Report 2002*, New York, 2002.

13 Amartya Sen, *The Argumentative Indian: Writings on Indian History, Culture and Identity* (London: Penguin, 2006).

14 See Ibn Khaldun, *The Muqaddimah: An Introduction to History*, trans. Franz Rosenthal from the Arabic (London: Routledge and Kegan Paul, 1958).

15 See Mahmood Mamdani, *Citizen and Subject: Contemporary Africa and the Legacy of Late Colonialism* (Princeton: Princeton University Press, 1996); Partha Chatterjee, 'On Civil and Political Society in Postcolonial Democracies', in Sudipta Kaviraj and Sunil Khilnani (eds), *Civil Society: History and Possibilities* (Cambridge: Cambridge University Press, 2001); Partha Chatterjee, *The Nation and its Fragments: Colonial and Postcolonial Histories* (Princeton: Princeton University Press, *c.*1993).

16 Heba Raouf Ezzat, 'Beyond Methodological Modernism: Towards a Multicultural Paradigm Shift in the Social Sciences', in Helmut Anheier, Marlies Glasius and Mary Kaldor (eds), *Global Civil Society 2004/5* (London: Sage, 2004); Abdullahi AnNa'im, 'Religion and Global Civil Society: Inherent Incompatibility or Synergy and Interdependence?', in Glasius, Kaldor and Anheier, *Global Civil Society 2002*.

17 See Geoffrey Best, 'Justice, International Relations and Human Rights', *International Affairs* 71, no. 4 (Oct. 1995).

18 Chris Brown, 'Cosmopolitanism, World Citizenship and Global Civil Society', *Critical Review of International Social and Political Philosophy* 3, no. 1 (Summer 2001): 7–27.

19 David Chandler, *Constructing Global Civil Society: Morality and Power in International Relations* (New York: Palgrave Macmillan, 2004); Gideon Baker and David Chandler (eds), *Global Civil Society: Contested Futures* (London: Routledge, 2005).

20 Kenneth Anderson and David Rieff, 'Global Civil Society: A Sceptical View', in Anheier, Glasius and Kaldor, *Global Civil Society 2004/5*.

21 Ronnie D. Lipschutz, 'Power, Politics and Global Civil Society', *Millennium: Journal of International Studies* 33, no. 3 (2005): 747–69; see also Ronnie D. Lipschutz and James K. Rowe, *Globalization, Governmentality, and Global Politics: Regulation for the Rest of Us?* (New York: Routledge, 2005).

22   Iris Marion Young, *Inclusion and Democracy* (New York: Oxford University Press, 2000), p. 160.

23   Ibid.; David Held, *Democracy and the Global Order: From the Modern State to Cosmopolitan Governance* (Cambridge: Polity, 1995); see also the contributions in Daniele Archibugi and David Held (eds), *Cosmopolitan Democracy: An Agenda for a New World Order* (Cambridge: Polity, 1995).

24   David Chandler, 'Holding a Looking-Glass to the "Movement": A Response to Worth and Abbott', *Globalization* 3, no. 1 (Mar. 2006).

25   Amartya Sen, *Identity and Violence: The Illusion of Destiny* (London: Allen Lane, 2006).

26   See Howard, 'What's in a Name?'.

27   See Mary Kaldor, 'In Place of War: Open Up Iraq', 12 Mar. 2003, at www.opendemocracy.net.

28   George Konrad, *Anti-Politics: An Essay* (written in Hungarian in 1982) (New York: Harcourt, Brace and Janovich, 1984), p. 243.

Chapter 6   Just War and Just Peace

Chapter epigraph from Michael Walzer, *Just and Unjust Wars: A Moral Argument with Historical Illustrations*, 2nd edn (New York: Basic Books, 1992), p. xxii.

1   Schmitt, *The Concept of the Political*, p. 33.

2   Held et al., *Global Transformations*.

3   I have elaborated the character of these wars in Kaldor, *New and Old Wars*.

4   Michael Walzer, *Arguing about War* (New Haven: Yale University Press, 2004), p. xiv.

5   See Clark, *Globalization and International Relations Theory*.

6   See David Held, *The Global Covenant: The Social Democratic Alternative to the Washington Consensus* (Cambridge: Polity, 2004); Kaldor, *Global Civil Society: An Answer to War*.

7   Der Derian, *Virtuous War*; see also Anthony Burke, 'Just War or Ethical Peace? Moral Discourses of Strategic Violence after 9/11', *International Affairs* 80, no. 2 (2004): 239–353.

8   James Turner Johnson, *Just War Tradition and the Restraint of War: A Moral and Historical Enquiry* (Princeton: Princeton University Press, 1981).

9   *A More Secure World: Our Shared Responsibility*, Report of the High-Level Panel on Threats, Challenges, and Change (A/59/56), United Nations, Dec. 2004.

10 Michael Walzer, *Just and Unjust Wars: A Moral Argument with Historical Illustrations*, 3rd edn (New York: Basic Books, 2000), p. xii.

11 Quoted in John Langan, 'The Elements of St Augustine's Just War Theory', *Journal of Religious Ethics* 12 (1984): 19–38.

12 Khaled Abou Al-Fadl,. 'Two Rules of Killing in War: An Enquiry into Classical Sources', *The Muslim World* 89, no. 2 (1999): 144–57.

13 Johnson, *Just War Tradition and the Restraint of War*.

14 François Bugnion, 'Just Wars, Wars of Aggression and International Humanitarian Law', *International Review of the Red Cross* 84, no. 847 (Sept. 2002): 523–46.

15 For a discussion of the debates around humanitarian intervention, see Wheeler, *Saving Strangers*.

16 Michael Walzer, 'First, Define the Battlefield', *New York Times*, 21 Sept. 2001.

17 Al-Fadl, 'Two Rules of Killing in War', pp. 144–5.

18 Ibid., p.148.

19 Bugnion, 'Just Wars, Wars of Aggression and International Humanitarian Law'.

20 Quoted in Johnson, *Just War Tradition and the Restraint of War*, p. 234.

21 Walzer, *Just and Unjust Wars*, p. 106.

22 Al-Fadl, 'Two Rules of Killing in War', p. 156.

23 See Toni Erskine, 'Embedded Cosmopolitanism and the Case of War: Restraint, Discrimination, and Overlapping Communities', paper presented at the British International Studies Association Special Workshop on Cosmopolitanism, Distributive Justice and Violence, 1–3 May 1999.

24 James Turner Johnson distinguishes between *ad bellum* proportionality and *in bello* proportionality. The former refers to the criteria for war itself, that it should do less harm than good; the latter refers to the application of minimal force, no more than is necessary to achieve a particular goal.

25 Quoted in A. Burke, 'Just War or Ethical Peace?'.

26 Quoted in Neta C. Crawford, 'Just War Theory and the US Counterterror War'.

27 Ze'ev Schiff, 'Summit Analysis', *Haaretz*, 5 June 2003.

28 Human Rights Watch, 'Promoting Impunity: The Israeli Military's Failure to Investigate Wrongdoing', New York, 2005, at http://hrw.org/reports/2005/iopt0605/. According to the Palestinian Red Crescent Society, which does not distinguish between combatants and civilians, between 29 Sept. 2000 and 13 May

2005, 3607 Palestinians died and 28,695 were injured; see www.palestinercs.org/the_fourth_year_intifada_statistics.htm.

29 See http://en.wikipedia.org/wiki/Casualties_of_the_2006_Israel-Lebanon_conflicthiff.

30 Walzer, *Just and Unjust Wars*, p. 196.

31 See Christine Chinkin, 'An International Law Framework for a European Security Strategy', in Glasius and Kaldor, *A Human Security Doctrine for Europe*.

32 A. Burke, 'Just War or Ethical Peace?'.

33 Smith, *The Utility of Force*, p. 270.

34 Mary Kaldor and Andrew Salmon, 'Military Force and European Strategy', *Survival* 48, no. 1 (2006).

35 Quoted in Peter Taylor, *The Brits: The War against the IRA* (London: Bloomsbury, 2001).

36 Peter Pringle and Philip Jacobson, *Those are Real Bullets, Aren't They?* (London: Fourth Estate, 2000).

37 Fionnuala Ní Aoláin, *The Politics of Force: Conflict Management and State Violence in Northern Ireland* (Belfast: Blackstaff, 2000).

38 Kaldor and Salmon, 'Principles for the Use of Military Force'.

39 See George Weigel, 'The Development of Just War Thinking in the Post–Cold War World: An American Perspective', in Charles Reed and David Ryan (eds), *The Price of Peace: Just War in the Twenty-First Century* (Oxford: Oxford University Press, 2007).

40 See William Wallace, 'Is There a European. Approach to Peace?', in ibid.

Chapter 7   Human Security

1 United Nations Development Programme, *Human Development Report 1994* (New York: UNDP and Oxford University Press, 1994).

2 *Human Security Report: War and Peace in the 21st Century*, Human Security Centre, University of British Columbia (Oxford: Oxford University Press, 2005); *The Responsibility to Protect*.

3 *In Larger Freedom: Towards Development, Security and Human Rights for All*, Report of the Secretary-General, United Nations, 2005, at www.un.org/largerfreedom/contents.htm.

4 Amartya Sen in Commission on Human Security, *Human Security Now: Protecting and Empowering People* (New York: Commission on Human Security, 2003), pp. 8–9.

5 Smith, *The Utility of Force*, p. 17.

6 See Herbert Wulf, 'The Challenges of Re-establishing a Public Monopoly of Violence', in Glasius and Kaldor, *A Human Security Doctrine for Europe*.

7   *A Human Security Doctrine for Europe: The Barcelona Report.*
8   See F. Stewart and V. Fitzgerald (eds), *War and Underdevelopment*, vol. 1: *The Economic and Social Consequences of Conflict* (Oxford: Oxford University Press, 2001), esp. ch. 9, 'The Costs of War in Poor Countries: Conclusions and Policy Recommendations'.
9   Restructuring state enterprises may or may not require privatization. But unregulated privatization programmes, allowing elites to enrich themselves at the expense of the wider population, have sometimes been a cause of conflict themselves. See David Keen, 'Sierra Leone's War in a Regional Context: Lessons from Interventions', in Glasius and Kaldor, *A Human Security Doctrine for Europe.*

Index

Abacha, General, 69
Abkhazia, 22, 117
Abramowitz, Morton, 25, 27
Abu Bakr, 168–9
Abu Graib, 90
Action Council for Peace in the
    Balkans, 45
Aden, 177
Afghanistan
    Al Qaeda in, 117
    American military power, 80
    casualties, 83, 90
    failure of NATO forces, 99
    humanitarian intervention, 22,
        38
    jus in bello, 169
    new war, 9
    NGOs in, 40
    political failure, 180
    regional approach to
        security, 190
    Soviet war, 8
    US weapons, 87
    war on terror and, 151, 164
Africa Rights, 47
African Union, 22, 160, 188
Aideed, General, 48
Al Qaeda, 80, 90, 91, 92, 99,
    115, 116, 117, 167, 170

Alagiah, George, 36–7
Albright, Madeleine, 51
Algeria, 29, 188
Amnesty International, 29, 69
Anderson, Benedict, 104
Anderson, Ken, 147
Annan, Kofi, 16
anti-globalization movement,
    141, 151
anti-imperialism, 93–5
Anti-Slavery Society, 29, 142
Appiah. Kwame Anthony,
    118–19
Aquinas, Thomas, 162
Aristotle, 135, 138
Arkan's Tigers, 127
arms race, Cold War, 6–7
Augustine, Saint, 162, 179
Auschwitz, 5, 17, 152
Ayodha mosque, 113
Azerbaijan, 110
Azzam, 116

Bali bombings, 91, 99
Balkans
    civil society, 129
    cosmopolitan interventions,
        122–3, 131–2
    earlier wars, 125, 126

economy, 128–9
geopolitical interventions,
    122–3, 129–31
globalization and, 126–7
international criminal tribunal,
    45, 56, 131
intervention approaches,
    122–3, 129–32
intervention debate, 27
learning process, 14
new nationalisms, 111, 114–15,
    123–9
NGOs, 30–4
postwar politics, 132–3
terminology, 123–4
war criminals, 177
wars, 43, 114, 122–4, 164
websites, 37
see also specific states
Band Aid, 27, 40
Bangladesh, 24, 38, 163
Bangura, Zainab, 66, 67
Barre, Mohammed Siad, 47
Benedict XVI, 151
Bettani, Mario, 40
Biafra, 17, 24, 28, 39
Bin Laden, Osama, 80, 113, 115,
    116
Bismarck, Otto von, 149
Blair, Tony, 57, 98, 165
blocism, 109
Bono, 27
Bosnia-Herzegovina
    1992–5 conflict, 122
    anti-war movement, 29
    Banja Luka, 114
    casualties, 5
    civil society, 61, 129, 131
    Croatian militia, 3
    Cuny in, 25
    Dayton Agreement, 46, 50,
        130, 131, 132
    Helsinki Citizen's Assembly,
        31–4
    humanitarian interventions,
        43–6, 56, 58, 120

media role, 36
Muslim victims, 115, 116
neo-realist view, 93
networks, 34
new war, 2, 4
NGOs, 30
paramilitaries, 127
postwar politics, 132
protectorate, 45, 61
safe havens, 61, 82–3, 131,
    175
war actors, 164
Boutros Ghali, Boutros, 43
Bowden, Max, 47, 49
Brandt Commission, 35
Brown, Chris, 146
Brundtland Commission, 35
B'Tselem, 171
Bull, Hedley, 38–9, 95
Burke, Anthony, 172
Burke, Jason, 117
Burma, 116
Burundi, 22
Bush, George H., 46, 47, 94
Bush, George W., 1, 7, 8, 14, 72,
    82, 86–9, 91, 93, 95, 97, 99,
    110, 150–1, 158, 164, 165,
    166, 168, 179

Cambodia, 17, 24, 38
Campaore, Blaise, 67
Canada, 183
Cardoso, President, 137
CARE, 28, 47
Carnegie Endowment, 27, 35
Carr, E. H., 109
Carter Center, 29
Casablanca bombings, 99
Cassel, Douglas, 95
Catalonia, 117
Centre for Democracy and
    Development (CDD), 66,
    67
Chandhoke, Neera, 142–3
Chandler, David, 146–7, 149
Charter 77, 139

Chatterjee, Partha, 144
Chechnya, 26, 50, 80–1, 82, 89,
    99, 115, 116, 117, 168, 171,
    188
Cheney, Dick, 93
Chile, 41
China, Taiwan and, 95, 158
Chomsky, Noam, 52, 57
Churchill, Winston, 11
citizenship, world, 146–7
civil society
    1990s concepts, 140–6
    Balkans, 61, 129, 131
    historical concepts, 135–7
    human security and, 195
    Islam, 143–4
    reinvention, 137–40
    Sierra Leone, 64–6
    see also global civil society
Clapham, Christopher, 68–9
Clark, Wesley, 80
clash of civilizations, 9
Clausewitz, Karl von, 7, 13, 106,
    127, 175
climate change, 87
Clinton, Bill, 48, 49
Cohen, Elliott, 205–25
Cold War, 5–9, 38, 42, 58, 76,
    77, 84, 86–7, 90, 91, 91–2,
    100
colonialism, 118
commissions, 35–6
Commonwealth of Independent
    States, 22, 50
Comoros, 22
Conciliation Resolution, 29
conflict resolution, NGOS, 29
Congo (DRC), 4, 22, 36, 49
cooperative security, 95–6
cosmopolitanism
    American power and, 96–8
    Balkans, 122–3, 131–2
    cosmopolitan law, 145, 148
    European politics, 117–20
Council of Europe, 45
counter-terrorism *see* war on terror

Croatia
    authoritarianism, 124, 125
    civil society, 129
    Dayton Agreement, 130
    diaspora, 127
    nationalism, 117, 127
    war, 43, 122, 164
    war crimes tribunal and, 132
Crusades, 115, 166, 167
Cuny, Fred, 23–6, 47
Czech Republic, 44
Czechoslovakia, 5, 38, 138

Dallaire, Romeo, 48
Dayton Agreement, 46, 50, 130,
    131, 132
De Waal, Alex, 47
defence transformation, 86
democracy
    Balkans, 124
    global civil society and, 147,
    149
    globalization and, 156
    South Africa, 143
    US approach, 73, 100
    war on terror and, 90
Denmark, cartoons, 151
Derian, James Der, 84, 86, 160–1
Deutscher, Isaac, 6
development, 193–4, 196–7
diamonds, 62, 64, 68
diasporas, 127, 157
displaced persons, 183, 191
Djilas, Milovan, 31
Dresden bombing, 5
Dunant, Henri, 28

Eagleburger, Lawrence, 46
East Timor, 52, 58
ECOMOG, 50, 60–1, 63, 67, 69
ECOWAS, 22, 50, 188
education, 29, 194–5
El Salvador, 24
Engels, Friedrich, 135
English School, 95
Enlightenment, 136–7

Eritrea, 116
Ethiopia, 24, 36, 39–40
European Union
  approaches to security, 123,
    133
  cosmopolitanism, 117–20
  distant decision making, 157
  human security and, 189, 191,
    192, 197
  interventions in Balkans, 22
  soft power, 180
  United States and, 151
Eurostep, 47
Evans, Gareth, 36
Executive Outcome, 63, 67

famines, 39–40
Fayeme, Kyode, 67, 69
Ferguson, Adam, 136–7, 144
Fordism, 75, 76, 77, 82, 85, 109
Foucault, Michel, 11, 147
France
  Algerian war, 188
  alter mondialisation, 149
  Bosnian war and, 44, 45
  humanitarian intervention
    debate, 27, 42, 58
  Kouchner politics, 25, 26, 40
  opposition to Iraq War, 96
  religious wars, 168
  Rwandan intervention, 49
  tiermondisme, 41
  Tobin tax, 98
Frenki's Boys, 114, 127
Friends of Sierra Leone, 69
functionalism, 103, 104

Ganda, Ambrose, 68
Gberie, L., 62
Geldof, Bob, 27
Gellner, Ernest, 31, 103, 104,
    105, 107
Genocide Convention, 29
geopolitical approaches to
    security, 122–3, 129–32
Georgia, 82, 95

Geremek, Bronislaw, 31
Germany, 44–5, 59, 94, 96, 124,
    166
global civil society
  1990s concepts, 140–6
  commissions, 35–6
  concept, 14
  critics, 146–50
  debate, 2
  humanitarian interventions and,
    23–37, 59, 61, 70
  media role, 36–7
  networks, 30–4
  new social movements, 140–1
  NGOs, 142–3
  post-9/11, 150–3
  postmodernist version, 143–4
  Sierra Leone, role in, 64–6
  social movements, 29–30
  terminology, 12, 134
  think tanks, 35–6
  websites, 37
  see also NGOs
global governance, 159–60
Global Islamism, 102, 115–17,
    121
Global Witness, 69
globalization
  Balkans, 126–7
  global consciousness, 156
  global culture, 118, 119
  interconnectedness, 157
  just war and, 155–60
  labour standards, 147
  migration, 156–7
  nationalism and, 101–2, 107–8,
    112
  state sovereignty and, 12, 74,
    77–8, 108–9
Goldstone, Richard, 36, 56
Gowan, Peter, 93
Gramsci, Antonio, 135–6
Great Divide, 8, 160
Great Lakes Policy Forum, 34
Grebo, Zdravko, 31, 32
Greece, 37

Grotius, Hugo, 37, 95, 163
Guantanamo Bay, 90, 166, 168
Guibernau, Montserrat, 102, 107
Gulf War (1991), 25, 42, 80, 90
Gurkha Security Group, 63

Haas, Richard, 87
Habermas, Jürgen, 140–1
Haiti, 49–50, 58
Hamas, 113, 114, 170–6, 177
Hamburg bombing, 5
Hannay, David, 42
Havel, Vaclav, 31, 139
Hazleton, R., 62
Healey, Dennis, 95
Heath, Edward, 56
Hegel, Georg, 101, 107, 135, 137
Helsinki Accords, 8, 9, 138–9,
    152
Helsinki Citizens' Assembly,
    30–4, 45, 59
Hezbollah, 81, 165, 171
Highlanders, 136, 137
Hindu nationalism, 102, 110,
    111, 113, 117
Hiroshima, 5
Hirsch, John, 63
Hitler, Adolf, 114
Hobbes, Thomas, 56
Hobsbawm, Eric, 101, 104, 107
Hollywood, 86
Holocaust, 39, 114, 119, 120
Honduras, 24
Howe, Admiral, 48
Hugo, Victor, 107
human rights
    development of movement,
        8–9, 41
    globalization and, 156
    human security and, 185–7
    humanitarian interventions and,
        55, 57, 59–62
    military humanism, 56, 57
    NGOs, 28–9
    overriding norms, 141
    terminology, 29

Human Rights Watch, 16–17, 27,
    29, 47, 51, 52, 63, 69
human security
    approaches, 122, 129–32
    bottom-up approach, 189–90
    civil society, 195
    concept, 182–4
    development and, 193–4,
        196–7
    education, 194–5
    expanded international
        presence, 191–2
    geopolitical approaches, 122–3,
        129–32
    human rights primacy,
        185–7
    infrastructures, 194
    institution building, 194
    legal framework, 192–3
    legitimate political
        authority, 187–8
    multilateralism, 188–9
    policy implications, 190–5
    principles, 172–81, 184–90
    regional focus, 190
    security gap, 10
    socio-economic priorities,
        193–5
    soft security, 179–80
    tax revenue, 195
    terminology, 12, 173
humanism, 118
humanitarian interventions
    chronological list, 18–22
    commissions, 35–6
    debate, 23
    definition, 17
    disappointing results, 22
    evolution, 22–3, 37–53
    global civil society actors,
        23–37
    global public debate, 4, 53–62,
        70–2
    historical memories and, 120
    human rights enforcement, 55,
        59–62, 67, 69–70, 71

humanitarian peace alternative,
55, 58–9, 68–9, 71
individuals, 23–7
just war, 54, 57–8, 67, 70–1,
168
media role, 36–7
networks and, 30–4
NGOs, 27–9
reformists, 59–62
rejectionists, 53–7, 67,
71–2
responsibility to protect, 17,
148, 173–4, 184–5
social movements, 29–30
think tanks, 35–6
Hungary, 5, 138
Huntington, Samuel, 56
Hurricane Katrina, 183

Ibn Khaldun, Abd al-Rahman ibn
Muhammad, 144
ICRC *see* Red Cross
idealism, 11, 83, 84, 87, 96
identities
new wars, 3–4
solitarist identities, 151
IMF, 126, 143, 157, 189
imperialism, 56–8
India, 38, 64, 95, 111, 163
Indonesia, 52
information technology, 1, 76,
85–6, 108
infrastructures, 194
Institute for War and Peace
Reporting, 32, 35
interconnectedness, 157
International Alert, 29
International Criminal Court, 90,
93, 97, 141, 156
international criminal tribunals,
45, 56, 156
International Crisis Group, 35
international humanitarian law
concepts, 3
jus in bello, 163, 166–71
Kosovo campaign and, 51

necessity and proportionality,
169
international law
cooperative security, 95–6
stengthening, 70
see also multilateralism
International Workers' Aid, 44
Intertect Relief and
Reconstruction, 24
IRA, 176–7
Iran, 9, 151, 158
Iraq
bloggers, 156
Kurds, 25, 42–3
safe haven policy, 42–3, 53
war with Iran, 9, 158
Iraq War (2003)
American power and, 81
casualties, 81, 90, 170–1
failure, 98–9, 175, 179
Fallujah, 171
global protests, 100
humanitarian intervention, 22
international law alternative,
152
lessons, 158–9
liberal supporters, 58
Muslim victims, 116
neo-realist view, 92
new war, 8, 9, 81–2
opponents, 96
postwar justice, 176
pre-emptive war, 95
technological war, 1–2
victims' support for
intervention, 58
war on terror and, 151, 164
warfare methods, 169, 170
Islam
civil society, 143–4
conduct of war, 166–7, 168–9
Global Islamism, 102, 115–17,
121
holy war, 162–3
political Islam, 116
Islamic Jihad, 170

Israel
  Hamas terrorism, 114
  Hezbollah attacks, 165
  human rights violations, 90
  Lebanon War (2006), 81, 165,
    170, 171–2
  Middle East nationalism and,
    111
  military power, 81
  Palestinian conflict, 171
  suicide bombers, 176
  violence, 114
Italian Consortium for Solidarity,
  44
Italy, 59, 135–6

Japan, 75–6, 94, 158, 164
Jean, François, 59
Jetley, Vijay, 64
jihad, 162–3
Johnson, James Turner, 161, 163,
  166
Jordan, 64
Jospin, Lionel, 26
Juergensmeyer, Mark, 91, 113
jus ad bellum, 161–6
jus in bello, 163, 166–71
just war
  global context, 155–60
  humanitarian interventions, 54,
    57–8, 67, 70–1, 168
  jus ad bellum, 161–6
  jus in bello, 163, 166–71
  just cause, 161–5
  just peace, 172–8
  right authority, 165–6
  terminology, 154–5, 160–73
  theory, 14–15, 154–5
justice, global social justice, 98

Kabbah, Ahmad Tejan, 63
Kagan, Robert, 73, 95–6
Kant, Immanuel, 96, 118, 134,
  137
Kashmir, 37, 89, 115, 116
Keck, Margaret, 139

Kellog-Briand Pact (1928), 158
Kenya, 99
Khmer Rouge, 38
Kindleberger, Charles, 76
Kissinger, Henry, 11, 92
Kohn, Hans, 105, 117
Konrad, George, 139, 152–3
Kony, Joseph, 114
KOR, 139
Korean War, 8
Koroma, Johnny Paul, 63
Kosovo
  1999 conflict, 122, 171
  American tactics, 170
  Battle of Kosovo (1389), 113,
    126
  casualties, 170
  cosmopolitan approaches, 132
  education programme, 29
  historical legacy, 113, 126, 129
  humanitarian intervention
    debate, 57, 58, 60, 61
  Kouchner in, 26
  military ineffectiveness, 80,
    172–3
  NATO intervention, 17, 22,
    50–2, 53, 120
  postwar politics, 132
  protectorate, 45
  resistance movement, 29–30
  Serb propaganda, 125, 126
  United Nations, 130
  websites, 37
Kosovo Commission, 36
Kosovo Liberation Army, 50,
  127, 128, 129, 171
Kouchner, Bernard, 17, 23–6, 36,
  40, 47, 51, 58, 59
Kovalev, Sergei, 50
Kurds, 25, 42–3, 50, 58, 163
Kuwait, 42, 80, 196

labour standards, 147
Langan, John, 162
Lange, Alexander, 34
League of Nations, 158

Lebanon, 24, 81, 116, 151, 165, 170, 171, 183
Leningrad, Siege of, 158
Leprette, Ambassador, 38
Levy, Bernard Henri, 27
Levy, Daniel, 120
liberal internationalists, 58
liberal nationalists, 107
Liberia, 50, 64, 190
Lieber, Francis, 166, 167
Lipschutz, Ronnie, 147
Locke, John, 135
Lomé Agreement (1999), 63, 66, 68
Lord's Resistance Army, 113, 114
Luther, Martin, 166

Macedonia
  NLA, 127, 128, 132
  Ohrid Framework
    Agreement, 130, 132
  war, 122, 129
Mackenzie, Robert, 63
McVeigh, Timothy, 164
Mamdami, Mahmoud, 143, 144
Mandela, Nelson, 143
Marx, Karl, 135
Mazzini, Giuseppe, 107
Mearsheimer, John, 92
Médecins du Monde, 25
Médecins Sans Frontières, 24, 28, 36, 59
media, 25, 36–7, 113, 126, 131
Memorial, 50
Mendes France, Pierre, 170
Mengistu, Haile Mariam, 40
mercenaries, 127, 164
Michnik, Adam, 31, 138
migration, 156–7
military forces
  changed functions, 10, 78–83
  defence transformation, 86
  Revolution in Military Affairs, 85–6
  see also use of force; wars

Mill, John Stuart, 107
Milles Collines Radio, 48, 113
Milosevic, Slobodan, 50, 51, 80, 124–5, 126, 130–1, 132, 172
modernist paradigm, 103–9, 118, 121
modular man, 103
Montenegro, 132
Mozambique, 29, 40
multilateralism, 83, 84, 95–6, 98, 151, 188–9

Nagasaki, 5
Nagorno-Karabakh, 2, 89, 109–10, 115
Napoleonic wars, 75
National Missile Defence, 7
nationalism
  Balkans, 111, 114–15, 123–9
  cosmopolitan nationalisms, 117–20
  current wave, 101–3
  discourse, 11–12
  European politics, 117–20
  Global Islamism, 102, 115–17, 121
  globalization and, 101–2, 107–8, 112
  liberal nationalism, 107
  media use, 113
  modernist paradigm, 103–9, 118, 121
  modernity and, 112–13
  new nationalisms, 102, 109–17, 123–9
  passion, 106, 110
  political construction, 102, 111, 120, 127
  recruiting grounds, 111–12
  religious character, 110
  spectacle nationalism, 110
  transnational movements, 112–13
  violence, 107, 113–15, 121, 127–8

NATO
  Afghan failure, 99
  interventions in Yugoslavia, 17,
    46
  Kosovo, 17, 50–2, 53, 57,
    173–4
  military humanism, 57
  multilateralism, 188, 196
natural law, 163
Neier, Aryeh, 58
neo-colonialism, 196
neo-realism, 91–5
NEPAD, 98
Netherlands, 44–5
networks, 30–4
New Policy Agenda, 141
new social movements, 140
new wars
  battle avoidance, 175
  competing discourses, 11–12
  displaced persons, 183, 191
  evolution, 158–9
  global new war, 10
  Iraq War (2003), 82
  Muslims as victims, 115
  old wars and, 1–9
  rape, 114
  social relations of warfare, 9
  solutions, 9–10
  spreading, 71, 190
  terminology, 12
  visibility, 42
  war on terror and, 72
NGOs
  conflict resolution, 29
  human rights, 28–9
  humanitarian NGOs, 27–8,
    39–40
  Rwanda, 49
  Somalia, 47
  state-funded, 145
  tamed social movements,
    142–3
Nicaragua, 24
Nigeria, 39, 69
Nixon, Richard, 92

non-intervention principle, 17,
  95, 96, 163
North Korea, 158
Northern Alliance, 80
Northern Ireland, 82, 176–9, 186
nuclear weapons, 7, 79
Nuremberg trials, 158
Nye, Joseph, 92–3

Ogaden, 116
oil wars, 93–4
Omaar, Rakkiya, 47
Open Society Foundation, 27
Organization of American States,
  188
Orwell, George, 5
OSCE, 22, 52, 188
Ottoman Empire, 4, 37
Oxfam, 28, 43, 47

Pace, Peter, 89
Pakistan, 90, 95, 99, 190
Palestine, 81, 114, 115, 116, 170,
  175
Palme Commission, 35
peace
  Cold War, 5–6
  just peace, 172–8
  new peace, 8
  see also human security
Peace Brigades International, 35
Pearl Harbor, 164
Perle, Richard, 7
Peru, 24
Petrova, Dimitrina, 51–2
Philippines, 116
Plato, 138
pre-emptive war, 88–9, 95
Putin, Vladimir, 82
Putnam, Robert, 142

Radio B92, 37
rape, 114
Reagan, Ronald, 7, 87
realism, 56, 83, 84, 95
Red Cross, 24, 28, 39, 40, 47, 49

Reich, Robert, 108
religious fundamentalism, 90, 96,
    97–8
Renan, Ernest, 102
resource wars, 93–4
Revolution in Military Affairs,
    85–6
Revolutionary United Front
    (RUF), 62, 63, 64, 66, 67
Rieff, David, 147
Roberts, Adam, 43
Robertson, Roland, 120
Robinson, Mary, 63
Rocard, Michel, 25
Roosevelt, Eleanor, 29
Roosevelt, Franklin, 11
Rose, General, 175
rule of law, 61, 107
Rumsfeld, Donald, 1, 86, 88, 89,
    91, 170
Russia
    Chechnyan war, 80–1, 82, 168,
        172, 188
    Georgia and, 82, 95
    human rights violations, 90
    interventions, 22, 50
    opposition to Iraq War, 96
Ruzicka, Marla, 180
Rwanda
    failure to intervene, 17, 22,
        48–9, 53, 60
    genocide, 49, 113, 114
    international criminal tribunal,
        45, 56
    neo-realist view, 92
    paramilitaries, 167
    UN report, 36
    victims' support for
        intervention, 58

SADC, 188
Saddam Hussein, 42, 92, 94, 96,
    99, 152, 156
Sahnoun, Mohamed, 36, 47
Saladin, 115
SALT Treaty, 92

San Egidio, 29
Sankoh, Foday Saybana, 62, 66
Saudi Arabia, 90, 99, 116
Save the Children, 28, 40, 47, 49
Schelling, Thomas, 7, 74, 79, 92
Schmitt, Carl, 3, 10, 157
Scotland, 117, 136–7
self-defence, 163–4
Sen, Amartya, 151, 184
September 11 attacks
    Bush discourse, 88–9
    destruction level, 78–9
    global civil society post-9/11,
        150–3
    Global Islam success, 116
    international law and, 152
    interpretation, 164–5
    military budget increase, 86
    multilateral approach, 98, 100
    objectives, 91
    reality shock, 74
    theatricality, 113
    Western-educated attackers,
        112
Serbia
    civil society, 129
    nationalism, 56–7, 80, 130–1
    NATO air strikes, 17
    sovereignty, 30
    television, 113
    totalitarianism, 130
    victimhood, 130
    war crimes tribunal and, 132
    war with Bosnia, 164
    websites, 37
Seselj, Vojislav, 112, 132
Shaw, Martin, 120
Sierra Leone
    amnesty, 63
    civil society role in, 64–6
    humanitarian intervention case
        study, 60–1, 62–70
    intervention debate, 67–70
    Liberia and, 190
    West Side Boys, 64, 176
Sikkink, Kathryn, 139

Slovenia, 31, 43, 122
Smillie, I., 62
Smith, Anthony, 13, 101, 102, 103, 105–6, 108, 111, 119, 120
Smith, Rupert, 1, 2, 175, 185
social capital, 142
social movements
  humanitarian interventions and, 29–30
  new social movements, 140
  taming, 142
Solana, Javier, 150
Soldiers' Mothers, 50
Solferino, battle of, 28
Somalia, 25, 46–8, 53, 56, 83, 116, 175
Soros, George, 25, 26, 27, 98
South Asia Citizens Web, 37
South Ossetia, 22
sovereignty
  anti-imperialist concept, 94
  concepts, 83, 87
  conditional sovereignty, 97
  cosmopolitanism and, 118
  global civil society and, 30, 134
  globalization and, 74, 77–8
  human rights and, 141
  humanitarian interventions and, 53–7, 67, 71–2
  non-intervention principle, 95
  origins, 37–8
  UN principle, 40
Soviet Union, 5
  Cold War framework, 6, 79, 84–5, 91
  collapse, 88
  control of central Europe, 7, 77
  loss of Cold War, 8
  new nationalisms, 111
  see also Russia
Sparta, 137
spectacle war, 84–91, 100
Srebenica, 22, 36, 46, 131, 175, 186
Sri Lanka, 24

Stalin, Joseph, 6, 11
Stalinism, 7
Star Wars, 7
states
  defence function, 3
  disintegration, 3
  functions, 107
  global civil society and, 146–7, 147–8
  global governance and, 159–60
  globalization and, 12, 108–9
  monopoly of violence, 2–3
  sovereignty *see* sovereignty
  war as state-building, 2, 5, 82, 106, 123
  see also nationalism
Strategic Defence Initiative, 7
Sudan, 24, 40
suicide bombers, 113, 114, 116, 170, 176, 180
surveillance, 90
Sweden, 36
symbolic analysts, 108
Sznaider, Natan, 120

Taiwan, 95, 158
Tajikistan, 22, 50, 116
Taliban, 80, 90, 99
Tanzania, 38
Taylor, Charles, 62, 67
think tanks, 35–6
Tilly, Charles, 2, 106
Tito, Marshal, 124
Tobin tax, 98
Tocqueville, Alexis de, 142
Tokyo bombing, 5
Toynbee, Arnold, 124
Transdnestr, 22
Transylvania, 117
Trietschke, Heinrich von, 107
Tudjman, Franjo, 124, 125, 127, 132
Turkey, Kurds in, 50

Uganda, 38, 113
UNAMIR, 48

UNAMSIL, 63–4, 67, 69
UNDP, 182, 183
UNICEF, 40
unilateralism, 83, 84, 87, 95
UNITAF, 48
United Kingdom
  Bosnian war and, 44
  development funding, 98
  nationalism, 110
  Northern Ireland strategy, 82,
    176–8, 186
  postwar, 5
  power, 75
  Sierra Leone intervention, 64,
    67, 82
  war methods, 170
United Nations
  East Timor, 52
  human rights covenants, 29
  human security, 188, 189, 191,
    196
  Iraq War, 151
  Kosovo, 51, 130
  Kurds in Iraq, 42–3, 163
  non-intervention principle, 17,
    38, 163
  peacekeeping operations, 17, 36
  responsibility to protect, 17,
    40, 173–4
  Rwanda, 48
  Security Council legitimacy,
    60, 68
  Sierra Leone, 68–9
  Somalia, 47–8
  use of force, 57, 97, 158,
    165–6, 173
United States
  Balkan wars and, 45, 124, 130
  Cold War framework, 76, 77,
    84, 86–7, 90, 100
  'Crusader State', 73
  Cuny's influence, 25
  democracy and, 73, 100
  European Union and, 151
  geopolitical approaches to
    security, 122–3

Global Islamism and, 116
Gulf War (1991), 42
Haiti, intervention in, 49–50
humanitarian interventions, 52,
  57, 58
Hurricane Katrina, 183
International Criminal Court
  and, 90, 93, 97
Iraq War *see* Iraq War (2003)
Kosovo intervention, 51
Lieber Code, 166
native Americans, 136, 137, 163
9/11 *see* September 11 attacks
Oklahoma bombing, 113, 164
political discourse, 11
power *see* US power
Rwanda and, 49
Somalia and, 48, 56
war on terror *see* war on terror
Universal Declaration of Human
  Rights, 29
UNOSOM II, 48
Urry, John, 118
US power
  alternative visions, 83–98
  anti-imperialist view, 93–5
  changing global context, 75–83
  compellance, 13, 74, 92, 95
  cooperative security, 95–6
  cosmopolitan approach, 96–8
  effectiveness, 74
  Gulf War (1991), 42, 80
  humanitarian interventions, 52,
    57, 58
  imperialism, 58
  military budget, 86, 99–100
  National Security Strategy, 179
  neo-realist view, 91–5
  nuclear arms race, 6–7
  pre-emptive war, 88–9
  spectacle war, 84–91, 100
  unilateralism, 83, 84, 87, 95,
    150
  war methods, 170, 171
  wars, 158–9
  weapons, 79–80

use of force
  just war *see* just war
  self-defence, 163–4
  UN authorization, 173
  UN Charter, 57, 165–6
  see also military forces; wars
Uzbekistan, 90

Vattel, Emerich de, 37
Vedrine, Hubert, 73
Verona Forum, 30
Victoria, Franciscus de, 163, 179
Vietnam, intervention in
    Cambodia, 38
Vietnam War, 8, 24, 85, 172
virtuous war, 84, 160–1

Wallace, General William, 86, 179
Walz, Kenneth, 92
Walzer, Michael, 154, 161,
    164–5, 168, 172
war on terror
  Cold War continuation, 8
  cosmic struggle discourse, 117
  global civil society and, 150–3
  ineffectiveness, 98–9
  labelling, 10
  National Military Strategic Plan,
    89, 97
  new wars and, 72
  support for, 82
  surveillance, 90
  undefined enemy, 88
wars
  Balkans, 122, 123, 126–8
  civil wars, 5, 39, 164
  Cold War *see* Cold War
  old v new wars, 1–9
  old war discourse, 11

privatized wars, 5
religious fundamentalism and,
    97–8
resource wars, 93–4
spectacle war, 84–91
state-building function, 2, 5,
    82, 106, 123
virtuous war, 84, 160–1
  see also new wars
weapons of mass destruction, 88,
    89, 151, 193
websites, 37
Weigel, George, 179–80
West, Rebecca, 124
West Africa peace-building
    network, 34
West Side Boys, 64, 176
Westphalia, Treaty of (1648), 37,
    158, 160, 163
Wheeler, Nicholas, 38
Wight, Martin, 14, 95
Wolff, Christian von, 37
Women in Black, 34
Women's Forum, 65, 66
women's groups, 34, 65, 189–90
Workers' Aid for Tuzla, 44
World Bank, 157, 189
World War I, 4, 5, 79, 158
World War II, 5, 6, 9, 11, 79, 94,
    158

Yemen, 99
Young, Iris Marion, 148, 150
Yugofax, 32
Yugoslavia *see* Balkans

Zaire *see* Congo (DRC)
Zepa, 46
Zionism, 102